Russell T. McCutcheon
On Making a Shift in the Study of Religion and Other Essays

Russell T. McCutcheon

On Making a Shift in the Study of Religion and Other Essays

—

DE GRUYTER

ISBN 978-3-11-099551-0
e-ISBN (PDF) 978-3-11-072171-3
e-ISBN (EPUB) 978-3-11-072186-7

Library of Congress Control Number: 2021931723

Bibliographic information published by the Deutsche Nationalbibliothek
The Deutsche Nationalbibliothek lists this publication in the Deutsche Nationalbibliografie;
detailed bibliographic data are available on the Internet at http://dnb.dnb.de.

© 2022 Walter de Gruyter GmbH, Berlin/Boston
This volume is text- and page-identical with the hardback published in 2021.
Cover: Photograph by Caitlyn Bell; used with permission.
Printing and binding: CPI books GmbH, Leck

www.degruyter.com

―――

"I think a lot of people still believe in the sacred."

– Aaron Hughes, "Reflections on 'Thinking with Jonathan Z. Smith'" (2019)

For the faculty, staff, and students of the Department of Religious Studies at the University of Alabama—past and present

Contents

Preface —— XI

Acknowledgments —— XIII

Sources —— XV

Introduction —— 1

Part I Current State

1   The Enduring Presence of Our Pre-Critical Past —— 11

Part II Critical Shift

2   Classification Matters or, Why You Should Care About Scholarship on the Category Religion —— 63

3   Shifting From Experience to the Discourse on Experience —— 76

4   "There's No Original in This Business" —— 96

5   What Happens After the Deconstruction? —— 111

Part III Institutional Implications

6   Theses on Creating Successful Religion Programs in an Anti-Humanities Age —— 119

7   Growth, Identity, and Branding: An Interview with *Religious Studies News* —— 123

8   Reinventing the Study of Religion in Alabama: An Overview —— 138

9   Learning to Code: Digital Pebbles and Institutional Ripples —— 148

10   On Making a Shift in the Study of Religion —— 167

Afterword: Five Examples —— 189

Index —— 204

Preface

One evening, as I was reading over, for one last time, the revised essays collected together as chapters in this book, I happened across a series of posts on Twitter, begun with someone noting how, given the current prevalence of critiques of the category religion, they almost welcome someone who just goes ahead and uses the term religion, as troublesome as it may be: "Look, it's problematic, but here's what I mean when I say religion ...." What caught my eye more than this initial tweet, as curious as I admit that it was—after all, there's quite a few troublesome things in our scholarly archive, including categories whose continued use (no matter how explicitly or carefully one might be in their redefinition) would likely *not* be greeted by many people's applause ("uncivilized primitives" to name but one obvious one, begging the question as to why a redefined "religion" deserves a continued place—was a response that amounted to criticizing those who inhabit departments of religious studies but who nonetheless say such things as, "Well, actually, religion doesn't exist ...." This struck me as a caricature of the critique of "religion" in which I, among some others, have invested a significant portion of my academic career—so, yes, I intervened with a few tweets of my own, with a worthwhile exchange resulting over the next few hours.

What is particularly intriguing in all this for me is that some of us in the field have addressed just these sorts of concerns quite explicitly, and repeatedly, over the past two decades, though such responses to the critique of "religion" persist, as if no one has addressed why, for instance, it is worth having departments of religious studies if religion turns out to be but a name that some people give to what scholars understand rather differently. In fact, this exchange indicated to me that yet another collection exploring exactly these issues was as relevant as ever, especially given that, as I wrote in one of my responses that evening, "our Dept is doing pretty well while adopting a rather critical approach. After all, we can still have English depts even if we realize 'literature' is a rhetorical term doing socially formative work, no?" Whether others are open to learning something from our example at the University of Alabama and the shifts that we've made, is, of course, up to them—but, given what some have long seen to be the shaky ground inhabited by many programs that call the humanities their home, I'd hope that not just a few readers are willing to experiment with rather different ways of conceptualizing their material, their syllabi, their approaches, the scope of their expertise, and even their *raison d'être* as scholars of religion. For, as I also commented in that thread, "sociology studies how what we commonly call 'society' happens and is seen as real by members despite, to scholars, always being constituted in practice. This makes 'society' all the more interesting to me. Such an approach to our field is just as viable, I'd argue."

After all, scholars of nationalism don't have to take the word of nationalists of any stripe when they set about studying how this thing that we all call the nation-state comes about, is reproduced, and even critiqued. So why should the study of religion be any different?

Acknowledgments

Apart from thanking Sophie Wagenhofer for her interest in having my work appear once again with Walter de Gruyter, as a follow-up to my 2018 collection *Fabricating Religion: A Fanfare for the Common e.g.*, and apart from also expressing my indebtedness to her team as well as friends and colleagues around the world with whom I routinely exchange ideas and draft manuscripts, I'd like to single out the people with whom I work at the University of Alabama: the faculty, staff, and students who, for the past twenty years, have been willing to experiment with what it meant to study and teach about religion in a public university. For much of what follows could be read as an extended report on what we've been up to in Tuscaloosa. Some of the people whom I have in mind were members of the department far longer than others, of course, while some went on to work in other settings, but the personnel in the department, along with the willingness of our students to upend their expectations for what happens in a religious studies classroom, have consistently made it a particularly good place to work and to test a few unorthodox (at least for some) ideas and a few novel practices. So it's to these people that I dedicate this book.

With the University of Alabama in mind, I'd be remiss if I did not mention the then-rookie dean, Robert Olin, who took a chance on me when I interviewed on campus for the position of Department chair back in January 2000; the cost-cutting measures being rolled out on our campus back then might have led others to just close what was then a struggling little department, to save whatever money could be saved. (More on this in a later chapter of this volume.) Lucky for us that our dean at the time did not take that path; instead, he invested in us—so thanks, Bob. I recall being hired in time for my new affiliation to make it onto the back cover of my second book, which was already in production; I'm rather proud to have had my affiliation with the University of Alabama on every book since then.

I'd also like to recognize Julie Ingersoll, with whom I worked for two years, in the late 1990s at what was then called Southwest Missouri State University (now just Missouri State). Back in the fall of 2000, she gave me some pretty good advice when, as a recently promoted but untenured associate professor, I was considering applying for the job of chair of a little department in Alabama (a job that I had seen advertised the previous year but which was re-advertised due to a failed search). As I recall, she said that while such a job would probably diminish some of the writing and editing that I would do, I'd already proven that I could do the research and the publishing so maybe now was a good time to tackle an entirely new challenge, such as helping to reinvent a small department that was then on the ropes—putting my money where my mouth was, as I recall thinking of it, what with my obvious interest in how the study of religion could instead be practiced. It was sage advice, for the past two decades have provided plenty of challenges and enough collective successes to make the failures (and yes, not everything went as planned) fade from view. So thanks to you as well, Julie.

Before closing, I would be remiss not to mention the very helpful copyediting work of Becky Brown, with whom I've also had the pleasure to work in the past (this being our second book for Walter de Gruyter). Note: the terribly long sentences that follow I insisted upon, despite her best efforts to rein them in. With this warning in mind, however, readers do owe her their gratitude for ensuring that they're as few as possible.

Finally, I'd like also to acknowledge the readers who come to this text with questions of their own concerning how to reinvent the study of religion in each of their settings. As I write this, the fallout from COVID-19 has not yet been completely appreciated or even experienced on university campuses (since the fall semester is still just around the corner), so I'm hoping that some of our experiences in Alabama will continue to be useful for readers to think with in the largely unexplored post-COVID-19 world—a world where, as I have written to students in various blog updates on the upcoming fall planning, nimbleness and adaptability will surely be among the key skills if any sort of success is to be had—whether individual or collective. (It's also a world where news of the closure of a department of religious studies, due to what are described as budgetary constraints, is not unfamiliar.) I'd like to think that these are exactly the skills that we have brought to the study of religion, in our corner of central Alabama; so, although we cannot control our circumstances, perhaps we can have a say in how we respond. In fact, just this past week I had a teleconference meeting with a faculty member newly appointed, elsewhere in the country, to head up a unit in which religious studies is one of the programs—"I know you have had great success at Alabama doing that [i.e., building a department]," the email said, "and I was hoping to pick your brain. How did you succeed in Alabama?" As I say later in the book, and as I said in that meeting, there was likely as much luck as there was planning, and while the successes were accompanied by some failures, those successes were always shared by a group who collectively put their heads together to figure out a way forward. I was happy to share some of our strategies and experiences during that meeting and now here in this volume. If nothing else, I hope they inspire some to think up and try out initiatives of their own to meet challenges specific to their situation.

Tuscaloosa, Alabama
August 2, 2020

Sources

1. The Enduring Presence of Our Pre-Critical Past: Written originally as one of the four main papers for the November 2019 annual meeting of the North American Association for the Study of Religion (NAASR); a highly redacted version of that paper is scheduled to appear in James Dennis LoRusso's edited volume, *On the Subject of Religion: Charting the Fault Lines of a Field of Study*. Sheffield: Equinox Publishers, 2022. A different brief portion also appears in the online journal e-Rhizome: *Journal for the Study of Religion, Society, and Cognition* 2/2 (2020).

    2. Classification Matters or, Why You Should Care About Scholarship on the Category Religion: Originally written as a paper for the Interdisciplinary Graduate Religion Seminar series at Oxford University, to be delivered March 13, 2020. My thanks to Professor Anna Sapir Abulafia for the kind invitation to address the series and to Lauren Morry for organizing the visit. It was also to be presented at the Religion and Philosophy Forum at the School of Humanities, University of Southern Mississippi on April 14, 2020; my thanks to Professor Amy Slagle for that equally kind invitation and for arranging my visit. Unfortunately, COVID-19 intervened and, like so many others who had planned on traveling in the spring of 2020, I was unable to keep either of these commitments.

    3. Shifting From Experience to the Discourse on Experience: Originally appeared as the introduction to Craig Martin and Russell T. McCutcheon, eds., *Religious Experience: A Reader*. New York: Routledge, 2014. My thanks to Taylor and Francis for permission to use this material here.

    4. "There's No Original in This Business" A version of this is scheduled to appear as the Afterword to Barbara Krawcowicz's edited collection, from a 2019 conference in Norway on Jonathan Z. Smith's contributions to the field, *Imagining Smith: Mapping Methods in the Study of Religion*. Sheffield, UK: Equinox Publishing, 2022.

    5. What Happens After the Deconstruction: Apart from a light rewrite to transition this text from its original blog post, this is largely the same item posted on September 23, 2016, at https://religion.ua.edu/blog/2016/09/23/what-happens-after-the-deconstruction/. It later appeared in *Implicit Religion* 20/4 (2017):401–6. My thanks to Equinox Publishers for allowing it to be reprinted here.

    6. Creating Successful Religion Programs in an Anti-Humanities Age: Although not presented on that occasion, originally written for a session at the 2019 annual meeting of the American Academy of Religion's Academic Relations Committee. My thanks to Martha Newman for the kind invitation to participate.

    7. Growth, Identity, and Branding: An Interview with *Religious Studies News*: An interview done with *Religious Studies News*, a professional periodical in the

study of religion, now published online by the American Academy of Religion. It was originally posted on March 24, 2016, and can be found at http://rsn.aarweb.org/articles/growth-identity-and-branding-department-religious-studies-university-alabama (accessed December 12, 2019). The text has been updated in this version. My thanks to Sarah Levine, for inviting and organizing it, and to the American Academy of Religion for allowing it to be included here.

8. Reinventing the Study of Religion in Alabama: An Overview: An elaboration of a brief introduction to a set of faculty essays that first appeared in what was then known as the *Bulletin of the Council of Societies for the Study of Religion* 33/2 (2004):27–9; this chapter is an updated version of the introduction to Steven Ramey's edited collection, *Writing Religion: The Case for the Critical Study of Religion*. Tuscaloosa: University of Alabama Press, 2015.

9. Learning to Code: Digital Pebbles and Institutional Ripples: Originally appears as "Learning to Code: Digital Tools and the Reinvention of an Academic Discipline," in Christopher Cantwell and Kristian Petersen, eds., *Introduction to Digital Humanities: Research Methods in the Study of Religion*. Berlin: Walter de Gruyter, 2021. My thanks to de Gruyter for permission to include it here.

10. On Making a Shift in the Study of Religion: First appeared as "Critical Thinking Begins at Home: On Making a Shift in the Study of Religion," *Implicit Religion* 22/2–4 (2020):349–72.

Introduction

On a variety of past occasions I have been accused of not providing alternatives but of merely offering criticisms of how the study of religion is being practiced— that I've built a career by doing nothing other than criticizing the work of others. In response to this representation of my work, I've often suggested that such critics have either not read all that much of what I've written or are willfully misportraying it, for an alternative has always been offered—sometimes implicit, sure, but more often than not quite explicitly and worked out in detail. In fact, I've offered such alternatives, and a rationale for them, from the very start, as evidenced in the first peer review essay that I ever published, back in 1990, not to mention the last chapter to my first book, published in 1997. (Bruce Lincoln, who later turned out to have been the press's peer reviewer for the manuscript that had previously been my dissertation, suggested the manuscript needed just that and so I took that advice and added it.) Even my first major review essay, published in 1998, was a long defense of an alternate way of teaching those still-common courses on myths and rituals.

The problem, of course, is that, at least for some in the field then and now, the alternatives that I've suggested are *not* seen as palatable, presumably because they defy the commonsense views on religion that many scholars were brought up with and, apparently bringing them into the academy, on which they base their careers. So the shift that I've offered—moving from studying religion, faith, experience, etc., to studying the practical conditions and effects of discourses on religion, faith, experience, etc.—is, I gather, not taken seriously; instead, it's dismissed out of hand, resulting in these recommendations being treated as if they were not even there. "All he does is criticize," they just keep saying, "offering nothing constructive in return …."

Although I've previously drawn attention to this tendency to, at least as I see it, mischaracterize my work while I have continued to produce a number of resources that either model a different way of studying religion or that provide instructors with practical resources for both conceptualizing and then teaching a different approach in their classes—a number of which, I'm proud to add, have involved the contributions of early-career scholars, in an effort to assist a new generation to get a leg up in the profession (as was once done for all of us, presumably)—this book is meant to tackle it head-on. It does this in two ways: (1) by chronicling what I read as ongoing and by now familiar problems in the field in detail, despite apparent advances that we are said to have collectively made; and then (2) by reporting on how a specific department where I have worked for the past two decades (and been chair, so far, for sixteen of those years) has done it rather differently. My hope is that fully half a book dedicated to spelling out an alternative approach and its ramifications, as it has been successfully institutionalized in a public university in the U.S that values both undergraduate and graduate education as well as scholarly research, will be just a little more difficult to overlook.

Before readers begin, however, there are a few of things that remain to be said—I'll limit myself to five.

First: yes, my writing is redundant. (And I don't just mean my habit of continually re-using the same twenty-six letters over and over again.) But given the manner in which specialists in other areas spend careers focusing on some topic (thereby gaining a badge of expertise), I will defend the fact that some of my writings do indeed keep returning to a series of related topics by simply referring readers to chapter 1 in this volume. There, I argue that despite the appearance of change, or maybe even what some would portray as progress, over the past few academic generations, long enduring theoretical and methodological problems in the academic study of religion remain as firmly entrenched now as they ever were. To put it another way, despite a series of—at least to my mind—persuasive critiques being offered over the past twenty or thirty years, we still see "the sacred," "the holy," as well as "world religions" and "faith traditions," not to mention "Abrahamic religions" along with an untheorized notion of experience and subjectivity as some sort of dynamic, inner source that is only later expressed outward in action, all terms used by scholars as if they each refer to obvious things in the world with transcendental properties. Here, despite our disagreement on a number of matters related to our profession, I am actually in complete, if somewhat ironic, agreement with Robert Orsi when, in the opening to a chapter entitled "The Problem of the Holy," he claimed that "[m]any (not all) scholars of religion become restive sooner or later with the simple sufficiency of explanations of religious phenomena and experiences in terms of the social and the psychological ... [for] they recognize that such accounts fall short of the realness of the phenomena they purport to describe and explain in people's experience" (2012, 84). Indeed! Many do—and (contrary to what his chapter's title might signify for him) that so many in our field are after the so-called *realness* of the supposed experience is, I would argue, precisely *the problem of the holy* (not to mention the problem of faith, the problem of the sacred, the problem of world religions, etc.). That I count myself among his parenthetical "not all" should therefore be obvious. Given the number of people who contact me privately, whether by email or messages on social media, who share these frustrations—a surprising number of them graduate students at other schools trying to do things a bit differently but meeting resistance—I tend to think that I am hardly alone in that set-aside category.

Second: no, not everything that we did at the University of Alabama will work for others. It's not that we're a unique setting—though, yes indeed, some features of our situation will not be shared by everyone—but that not everything that we did to try to reinvent the department worked for us. And that's just how it goes. As discussed in the second half of this volume, from the start we adopted what once might have been called a shotgun approach to addressing our predicament—we tried (and are still trying) a lot of different things to recruit and retain majors as well as to create conditions conducive for innovative faculty research, not all of which were interconnected and not all of which were successful. But, over time, we found a few things that worked, continually tweaked them a bit (or sometimes a lot) and then tried them a second time and a third, etc., while also trying to figure out how they could pull the same oars as other initiatives that we had also developed, aimed at accomplishing different things. So chronicling these initiatives here, with the background and context that prompted us to be far more intentional in our departmental experiment than some other units might be, is meant to provide one model for making a unit successful in the current higher ed climate. And, I should add, while this notion of success can be opaque or ambiguous, of course, or even a constantly moving target (what with all the different, and sometimes competing, measures that an administration can operationalize to assess a unit's productivity), for us it meant attracting students, gaining the confidence of the administration, and creating an environment in which the members of the department feel that their work is valued and consequential. So, what I'm offering here is just an example of what others might try; I hope some of these suggestions are useful or at least inspiring enough to prompt readers to invent some new things of their own—of which they'll hopefully write in the future. For, sadly, by my estimation, too few of us, especially those in more senior positions in the profession, are now writing about the conditions of the field and how to help it along in trying times.

Third: yes, our experiment has been influential, but in ways that are tough to measure, since I'm not sure how many will openly acknowledge it (given that we've made a shift in how we study religion). Thinking back to 2001, when we began reworking the department (for reasons spelled out later in the book), the landscape of the field was rather different than it is now. For, since then, many departments have also come to understand the importance of a pro-active social media identity, of blogging and publicly promoting their students' work, of making films or podcasts, of identifying the department and then sharing that identity with students who have an affinity (or might be developing one) for what it is that we do in our classes and in our research. (Yes, we have had department mugs for close to twenty years, all bearing the imprint of the department: a stylized image of the late-nineteenth century gothic building in which we're housed.) While there's still plenty of faculty out there who just see their data as self-evidently interesting and important, and thus requiring no particular sort of representation, it's gratifying to see the number who instead now recognize that so-called public scholarship on religion also (and some might say primarily) involves conveying to our students, along with their families, *why* it is that what we do is relevant to them, their interests, and their lives. (Because students, who will one day be graduates of our programs, are also members of the public, no?) That a number of faculty have privately contacted us, over the years, seeking advice, or have even just reported paying attention to our experiment from afar is something that we know and, to whatever extent, we also know that our experiment has helped them to think through how best to respond to the requirements of their own situations, so we're pleased to have helped. That we didn't invent what we're doing *ex nihilo*, as the philosophers of religion might have once phrased it, should be clear to everyone, of course, and so we're breathing the same air as those who separately came to some of the same realizations about how to represent their department to the benefit of its various members. (Several years ago our department, with the dean's assistance, sponsored a weekend event for public university department chairs; several came to Tuscaloosa, representing a real diversity of programs, and I learned much from reports on their local experiments as well.) But, given the number who have been keeping an eye on the Alabama experiment and who are considering a little tweaking of their own, I'm hoping that the second half of this book is handy—even if not everything in the first half is equally persuasive or agreeable to them.

Fourth: yes, there's a number of examples in the following chapters (not to mention the afterword) from the various instances of what I see to be enduring problems in the field to a variety of possible solutions, some deriving from possibly surprising places. Though elaborated in later parts of the book, the particular shift that we've made in our department—one that I trace to the early influence of the late Jonathan Z. Smith on my own work along with the work of many of my colleagues and which I discussed in the last chapter of *Fabricating Religion* (a book which lays the foundation for the current collection)—was to come to see the item which we study (e.g., some region, document, historic period, group, person, artifact, etc.) as exemplary of something far wider, more general, and thus something that someone else could also find curious though they might be utterly unfamiliar with our document, artifact, etc. For not everyone in our department works on India, let alone the Afro-Caribbean, ancient Greece, or the process of scripturalization (as do Steven Ramey, Merinda Simmons, Vaia Touna, and Richard Newton, respectively [to name but four of my colleagues]), but so long as they use their detailed knowledge of those items as a petri dish, shall I say, where they can experiment with understanding such seemingly mundane things as how groups form, how their members mount or respond to contests, and how such groups eventually come to an end only to be revised and reinvented again and again, etc., then others in the department who are equally interested in those misleadingly simple things but who happen to have training in yet other specialties, studying yet other people, places, and things, might learn something from their work that can be applied from there to here—seeing all of these sites as analogues, if you will.

To refer back to an early piece by Smith on teaching the introductory course, I might rephrase it as follows, with carrying out our research in mind as much as our teaching:

> Each thing taught is taught not because it is 'there,' but because it connects in some interesting way with something else, because it is an example, an 'e.g.' of something that is fundamental, something that may serve as a precedent for further acts of interpretation and understanding by providing an arsenal of instances, of paradigmatic events and expressions as resources from which to reason, from which to extend the possibility of intelligibility to that which first appears to be novel or strange (1991, 187).

This is what we've come to call the examples approach—a thoroughly collaborative approach that, we find, works exceedingly well as long as one can get past seeing the things that we each train so long to study as being inherently interesting and obviously valuable (i.e., studied simply because they exist, as if their own gravitational force somehow compels us to pay attention to them). But getting past that is not a small challenge, for doing so means faculty members must shake off the conditioning of their training, for we've each been contained in increasingly specialized silos for the duration of our graduate programs, and the structure of conferences and academic publishers exacerbates all of this, of course (for why would a nonspecialist in, say, Christian origins or the study of Islam be attending one of *their* panels at a conference, much less reading their work …?). This model of specialization, important as it no doubt is in so many ways, can lead to departments where neighboring faculty often have little if anything in common apart from the hallway their offices happen to share and thus the classes that our students take throughout their degree often end up being discrete, isolated units that have no necessary relevance for each other. (To rephrase: that so-called senior seminars even exist, as some sort of culminating, integrative experience, may tell us all that we need to know about the often-disjointed nature of the rest of their degree.) Instead, moving to a far more generalized level, in which a wide variety of seemingly disconnected, specialized instances can be drawn upon in the service of answering shared questions (in our case, about socially formative processes, or what we mean by social theory), we found that by relinquishing what some others may see as the self-evident value of the objects and peoples they study we gained a much-needed utility and relevance for our work, for seeing it all as exemplary of wider trends and issues allowed us to help each other to carry out what could now be seen as our *shared* work, from research to teaching. Now there's not only a narrative connection between most of the classes that all of our students take but also a shared theoretical problematic and thus focus across much of our research—making collaboration (whether chatting in offices or tackling common projects) a rather natural, daily activity rather than a goal that takes additional effort. (And *this* is what I mean when I say that, ideally, there's some substance behind that branded image on the mugs that we give out to all incoming majors.) As elaborated elsewhere in this book, this shift—admittedly, it's a subtle change but one that is nonetheless still significant and challenging for many to make—is what has helped us to reinvent the study of religion at the University of Alabama. Perhaps it's a shift that can help others as well—if they're willing to entertain seeing the things commonly called religion or faith or sacred or scripture or ritual or …, etc., as being just a little different, and rather more mundane but nonetheless curious, than they might have seemed before.

Fifth and finally: although finalizing this set of papers in the summer of 2020, they were all written, as the acknowledgments signaled, in the pre-COVID-19 world, a time when challenges to the humanities certainly existed, what with changing trends in higher ed funding in the U.S. and throughout North America and the world. But, as I mostly worked from home from mid-March 2020 onward—spending a surprising amount of my time trying to ensure that faculty and students knew what was happening to their spring semester let alone what they could anticipate what their fall might look like—it was painfully apparent that the ground might have shifted out from under us more than any of us currently realize. While the short-term and long-term impacts of the virus on universities still remain to be seen, effects that might ensure that some of the following suggestions are not as applicable as they once might have been, I hope that they at least inspire readers to be inventive and daring in ways that might work best for the situations in which they find themselves—situations that, I fear, may involve continued remote teaching, weathering further cuts, and either more reliance on or perhaps even a loss of the contingent faculty members on which institutions sadly depended for so long. I therefore do not think that what follows is timeless in its relevance or application but I do hope that it is of more value to post-COVID-19 readers than just as an archival curiosity from the early twenty-first century.

So, with all of that having been said, I leave readers to what follows—which, yes, is in part yet another report from the field at large, but one that brings with it a detailed description of how it could be otherwise. For just as with those departments of English that I discuss at one point (the ones that complicated just what reading and meaning and texts and authors and intentions are *while not going out of existence*), I also think that departments of religious studies can thrive while reconsidering just what their members are doing in both their writing and their teaching.

Reference List

McCutcheon, Russell T. 2018. *Fabricating Religion: A Fanfare for the Common e.g.* Berlin: Walter de Gruyter.

Orsi, Robert A. 2012. "The Problem of the Holy." In *The Cambridge Companion to Religious Studies*, edited by Robert A. Orsi, 84–105. Cambridge: Cambridge University Press.

Smith, Jonathan Z. 1991. "The Introductory Course: Less is Better." In *Teaching the Introductory Course in Religious Studies: A Sourcebook*, edited by Mark Juergensmeyer, 185–92, Atlanta, GA: Scholars Press.

Part I **Current State**

1 The Enduring Presence of Our Pre-Critical Past

> No need to remember when
> 'Cause everything old is new again
>
> – "Everything Old is New Again" by Paul Allen and Carole Bayer Sager (1974)

When invited to deliver a paper to the 2019 meeting of the North American Association for the Study of Religion (NAASR) on the topic of the history of the field, I accepted, though I admit to doing so with some small degree of trepidation. I felt the need to say something a little different from what I've already put into print, on a variety of past occasions, concerning problems found in the history of the study of religion—a history that may seem rather distant to us now, given that it was situated in the midst of nineteenth-century European colonialism (see, for example, McCutcheon 2000) or, more recently, in the Cold War politics of two generations ago (McCutcheon 2004). For, as those two citations make evident, I have already discussed the practical implications (both inside and outside of the academy) of how prior scholars approached the study of religion—approaches that were, in the earliest years, grouped together and called either comparative religion or the science of religion. To state it simply, my argument has been that, given my understanding of what it means to study human beings from within the modern research university, some of those approaches are more fitting than others. In fact, as I've also argued, some of these approaches actually undermine the field, at least as I understand it to be properly constituted, despite being offered by their supporters as but one more viable alternative; for I contest the position that holds that virtually any use of the word "religion" in a post-secondary setting, or as part of a piece of research, qualifies as but another instance of the so-called big tent that some think we all inhabit.[1] As with how I discuss definitions in my own introductory classes, then, when it comes to

---

Note: My thanks to Aaron Hughes and Craig Martin for their feedback on an earlier draft of this chapter.

[1] Readers would not be incorrect to read this, in part, as a commentary on the structure and self-understanding of the American Academy of Religion (AAR), the world's largest professional association for scholars of religion. But my experience, over the years, in a variety of other scholarly associations tells me that the troublesome breadth of scholarship included within the AAR is not unique. What's more, to fine-tune my point, even many who adopt the so-called big tent approach can, upon closer analysis, be shown to police a rather narrow range of uses of the term "religion," let alone methods they see as useful for its study, despite the inclusivist claims that they might make.

https://doi.org/10.1515/9783110721713-006

an academic pursuit I would argue that what some now see as the admirable desire to include as much as possible actually hampers the field; instead, when it comes to scholarship, the more precision, the better.[2]

So, having made plenty of such claims in the past about all of this, I felt that this occasion presented an opportunity to say something new ... ; recollecting both Roland Barthes' views on authorship and that strategically brief piece that I've often used in classes, "Borges and I" (1999, 324), I could say that, *qua scriptor*, I certainly know how to write like the author that shares my name, so this—or so I reasoned—might be an ideal moment to go against the grain a bit, to offer something a little unexpected, perhaps in hopes that those who, at least as I see it, stereotype my work as a means to dismiss it, might be surprised, just a little. For along with that surprise there might be a temptation actually to read it for a change and not, as I've seen on many past occasions, assume that a little bit of *Manufacturing Religion* or a chapter or two from *Critics Not Caretakers* (both containing work from more than twenty years ago or more; in fact, the former contains work almost thirty years old), told them all they needed to know about my work.[3] But, sadly, despite this earnest desire, I've decided that I see little new to say when I look again over the work that helped to establish our field but, more importantly, the work that now characterizes large segments of our field, much of it coming from a newer generation of scholars. In both cases, I find myself returning to the same old unresolved themes, since many of the problems that I still find with past practices and the criticisms that I have offered on other occasions strike me as being just as relevant today, when applied to the work that some consider to be at the field's cutting edge.

And so, because it seems to me that the old problems endure, I feel that I have no choice but to use this opportunity to repeat—well, let's just say reinforce, since it seems to avoid the idea of redundancy—what I have said in the past,[4] though exemplifying the recurring challenges of the field at sites that

---

2 Although one might hope that this goes without saying, the either vague, multiple, or even nonexistent definitions of religion that often guide scholarship in our field should make evident that this point bears repeating—something that, thankfully, frequently takes place on Craig Martin's social media presence.

3 A similar motive prompted me to write "I Have a Hunch" for the first workshop of the Yale Seminar in Religious Studies (April 15, 2011), a workshop devoted to the topic of religious experience (and a piece first published in 2012). The paper was disarming enough that, after delivering it, a conference participant inquired more, in all seriousness, about my hunches.

4 Consider this from 2012: "But after looking a little more closely at the work of some of those who are now rethinking their use of the category 'religion,' it has become clear to us that troublesome assumptions persist despite the so-called advances" (Arnal and McCutcheon 2012, 7).

I may not have previously discussed in print. Despite the fact that this chapter first appeared as a pre-distributed discussion paper on a panel devoted to the history of the field (followed by responses from James Edmonds, D. Jamil Grimes, Drew Durdin, and Rebekka King), it is *not about the past at all* (but, come to think of it, when is the past *ever* about the past?)[5]; for despite a wide variety of contemporary writers, notably some who now identify as post-critical or post-theoretical,[6] claiming to have left flawed earlier practices and assumptions behind—after all, who even reads Eliade anymore, one might justifiably ask[7]—the practices and assumptions that continue to drive the field today are, I argue, little different from those that did decades ago.

Before continuing, I should distinguish what I am about to argue from the recent co-written work of two mentors of mine, both from the academic generation prior to my own and both among NAASR's founders: Donald Wiebe and Luther H. Martin. In a 2012 article published in the *Journal of the American Academy of Religion*, they contend that "a history of the development of religious studies as a scientific enterprise in the modern university is an incoherent contradiction that reveals tensions between putative claims to academic status and the actual reality of continuing infiltrations of extra-scientific agendas into the field" (2012, 591).

On this score I differ little from them, though I would add some qualifications. Based on early modern intellectual (and, I would add, political) developments in Europe, a way of conceptualizing and talking about this thing commonly designated by some (but not all—a crucial point) as religion was devised and,

---

[5] See Touna 2017 for but one of the more thoroughgoing applications of this principle to the study of so-called ancient religion.

[6] I take this position to be one that, for instance, highlights the importance of critiques of the category religion yet which nonetheless laments how excessive focus on such critiques prevent us from just getting on with the work of actually studying religion. It is a sentiment that I also find in the work of so-called critical realists; see McCutcheon 2018a, 95–120 for an extended discussion of critical realism in our field.

[7] On a past occasion, my work was criticized as being aimed at outdated straw targets, inasmuch as, or so it was phrased to me then, "no one reads Eliade anymore." (Aside: this criticism, I'd argue, is also evidence of a far too quick reading of some of my work, given that, early on, my focus on Eliade's work [e.g., two chapters in McCutcheon 1997] was always as a particularly condensed and therefore useful illustration of issues found throughout the field, helping to explain his place in the field more as a representative, than a cause, of wider trends that pre- and post-dated him.) I replied by asking if people instead now study the thing they call religion as utterly reducible or at least wholly akin to any number of other mundane elements of human practices. Lacking evidence of such an approach being in any way widespread—for, sooner or later, at least in my reading, religion turns out to be a special case requiring special attention—the focus on Eliade's work struck me, and strikes me, as still having utility.

over the coming centuries, refined and implemented in universities, as a way to generate knowledge about (more likely than not, *other*) people, both at home and abroad, as well as in constitutions and laws by governments, as a way to organize and govern people, until we arrive at today. Now, at least as practiced in the university of modern nation-states, the academic study of religion is seen as somehow different from studies meant to prepare oneself for a professional role as a ritual specialist or so-called religious functionary. Moreover, also in agreement with Wiebe and Martin, this distinction between what an earlier generation (I think here of Ninian Smart, among others) might have characterized as *the study of* and *the practice of* has continually been under attack by those who see such compartmentalization, as they might call it, as inhibiting either the legitimacy or the spread of their interest in the carrying out these practices (a.k.a. undermining the identity and social implications that come from membership within groups that scholars who make this distinction study as nothing more or less than another curious instance of human behavior). Many members of the current generation of scholars proclaim that what was once called the insider/outsider problem[8] or, before that, the theology/religious studies debate is now passé—yet they find themselves still divided between those elaborating and defending the study of/practice of distinction as opposed to those criticizing such work in an effort to erase what they see as an artificially imposed and thus detrimental difference.[9]

However, at least one place where I differ (as might already be evident from some of the above qualifications) concerns what Kocku von Stuckrad, in a reply to Martin and Wiebe's article, rightly (I would argue) identified as a "naïve image

---

[8] Were I to revise the reader on the insider/outsider problem that I edited early in my career (1998), I would add—thanks to a conversation I once had with Jonathan Z. Smith—a chapter on the manner in which this oscillating distinction goes all the way down; for the relative and co-constitutive nature of these two positions ensures that for every asserted inside there is always an outside, meaning that there is no such thing as a true insider or a definitive outsider.

[9] The strategy of the latter group, of course, has been to find a similarity that undermines the presumed difference that animates the work of those who see *studying* as being removed from *practicing*. (To study is itself but a form of practice, some assert, making us all the same, or so they claim.) For example, if the social arrangement that we often call secularism or the viewpoint known as atheism can also be designated *as* religious, or as no less a so-called worldview than is religion, then (or so the reasoning goes) these two must be taught side by side, perhaps with so-called believers of each charged with representing them to students—what some today refer to as "teaching the controversy" or what a previous generation referred to as the pluralistic zoo model of the field, in which a Christian was hired to teach Christianity, a Muslim to teach Islam, and so on and so on.

of the natural sciences that most historians of science would deconstruct today" (2012, 61).¹⁰ Based upon this view, they not only presume that it ought to be inevitable that a rational discourse on religion develops (if not for certain cognitive proclivities, as argued in their 2012 article) but then come to lament their career-long efforts to make it so—a "false and unshakeable delusion" to which they provocatively confess in the above-cited article. While I've argued at length concerning the differences between my own approach and that of at least Wiebe (see McCutcheon 2006),¹¹ this admission, on their part, highlights a key difference that I had previously not considered: what I'll characterize as my own far more pragmatic view of academic intervention and change.¹² For while Wiebe and Martin have confessed to being deluded when they reflect back on their optimism for the development of a truly scientific study of religion, I am instead content in the knowledge that a critical study of religion (a term Daniel Dubuis-

---

10 Several responses to Martin and Wiebe's paper (along with their own replies) appeared separately in both *Religio* as well as *JAAR*; see Part 5: A Scientific Discipline of Martin and Wiebe 2016 for the complete set of these replies and responses.

11 This reply was in response to an article of Wiebe's (2005) in which my work was, in my estimation, mischaracterized in order to compare it favorably to those with whom Wiebe disagreed. Despite this disagreement, however, it should be said that Wiebe, once a teacher of mine at the University of Toronto, and I have maintained a long friendship and productive working relationship.

12 See the final section of this volume for my views on institution-building within the study of religion. With this topic in mind, I think of my own early experiences in the 1980s in what was then called The Centre for Religious Studies at the University of Toronto. This cross-disciplinary graduate unit was autonomous from the then Department of Religious Studies (which drew upon not only U of T faculty but also faculty from the Toronto School of Theology [an association of neighboring Christian theological colleges on the campus of the University of Toronto]). Eventually, those supporting this autonomous model for graduate education lost (in the early 1990s) and the grad unit was absorbed into what became the Department for the Study of Religion, where doctoral students are now "eligible to take a course offered in the Toronto School of Theology (TST), provided it is an Advanced Degree course (5000 level only), and is taught by a TST faculty member who is also a member of the Graduate Faculty of SGS." In fact, according to a 2012 Quality Assessment Report commissioned by the Provost of the University of Toronto, the difference between what takes place at the Toronto School of Theology and the University of Toronto was considered by the reviewers as negligible (see Martin and Wiebe 2016, 325; see also Wiebe 2016). A closer relationship was then represented by the outside assessors as desirable so as to enhance "Toronto's stature as a center of interreligious dialogue" (the report is quoted by Martin and Wiebe 2016, 325–6; the assessors were the late Ellen Aitken of McGill University, David Ford of Cambridge University, and Richard Rosengarten of the University of Chicago). For background, see chapter 13 in Wiebe 1999, "Alive, But Barely: Graduate Studies in Religion at the University of Toronto." See also Hughes 2020 for an overview of the history of the study of religion in Canada.

son, among others, has recently adopted for a specific brand of scholarship on religion, in opposition to what he terms religionists) will *never happen*—at least never happen *en masse* as opposed to being an occurrence in more or less isolated but, in my assessment, intellectually vibrant and, hopefully, influential pockets of the field.[13] For if my analysis of the discourse on religion is persuasive[14]—an analysis that understands the classification of just some or discrete elements of the human *as* religious, in distinction from other elements (which are termed social, cultural, political, ethnic, secular, etc.), as having the effect of arranging and thereby privileging certain aspects of otherwise mundane daily life, in the service of a variety of practical social interests and situations—and, what's more, if the people who continue to elect to become scholars of religion largely come from groups for whom this designation is but a commonsense term in their inherited folk lexicons (making it a way that they too, despite being scholars, arrange and thereby privilege certain aspects of their otherwise mundane daily lives, in the service of their own specific practical social interests and situations), then how could we expect the academic study of religion to be anything other than what it has generally become: a largely normative exercise in the service of reproducing specific understandings of religion so as to normalize specific ways of arranging social actors and thus social life, to the benefit of just some aspects within society? For that's just how the discourse on religion functions—whether used by scholars or anyone else, I maintain. (And by normative I mean far more than the old religious studies versus theology framing but, instead, imply the link between the study of religion as a disciplinary practice, and large scale socially formative exercises aiming to shape the nation in specific ways.) From the well-documented politically liberal and inter-religious dialog model that informs much of the long-standing world religions genre (both the courses and their textbooks; more on this below) to more recent efforts to establish and enhance so-called religious literacy standards throughout society

---

13 Although there are a variety of ways to signal that the study of religion is carried out in a way that differs from an approach that might be characterized as sympathetic to the people under study (such as some calling it the academic study of religion or retaining the earlier term, the science of religion), lately the term "critical" has been favored by some, such as Ramey 2015b. For the purposes of this chapter, I will adopt this nomenclature, noting the importance to distinguish this from the more common understanding of what it means to criticize someone or something. On this distinction, see n. 16 below; see also McCutcheon 2018a, 96 for a discussion of the various uses of this term "critical" in the field today.

14 Aside: see the *Discourse Research and Religion* (edited by Johnston and von Stuckrad—a volume going through an open, online peer review process as this chapter was first being written) for a volume on the breadth of what is today called the discursive approach to the study of religion.

(thereby standardizing and policing an authorized discourse on religion of benefit to certain understandings of the nation; more on this below as well), the academic pursuit known as the study of religion, at least as practiced by many today, in large part constitutes an effort to reproduce and entrench one among many specific ways of using the "religion" category, in the service of a practical political program. For while it would be rare to find a scholar of religion today agreeing that this word "religion" names, say, inferior attempts to mimic the saving grace and love of Jesus as found in Christianity (a use of the term religion that is easily found today),[15] it is not difficult to find scholars who define religion in such a way as to name the presumed non-empirical, essential, and thus universal core of human nature that is, of course, aligned with rather specific social and political goals (yet another use of this word "religion," but one that happens to be in direct contest with the one just identified). While the sort of world that results from the latter strategy may be one in which I would prefer to live, where I would prefer to shop, go to work, and own a house—a point that we cannot overlook, to be sure—the question is *whether an approach to the field that is driven by such preferences or seeks to realize them in practice, no matter how widely they are shared, best exemplifies what an academic pursuit ought to be or ought to be designed to accomplish.* For although I have distanced myself from the way authors such as Wiebe and Martin define science as a disinterested pursuit (not dissimilarly to how I distance myself from those, on the other side of these debates, who portray authors or participants as somehow being disinterested, self-aware, and thus authentic sources of information), I nonetheless share with them the assumption that an academic approach to some topic ought to be distinguishable from engaging in that topic itself, indicating that a degree of distance, irony, or even alienation from personal investments in the topic (what I recall Bill Arnal early on referring to as deracination) is a necessary prerequisite for the academic life.[16]

---

15 I have in mind those positions that opt to classify a specific form of Christianity as somehow superior to those other social movements that are usually known as religions (a latter grouping that could very well include disfavored forms of Christianity, not to mention any of the usually identified world religions), inasmuch as the former is represented as being about a personal relationship, which is then claimed to be superior to what is portrayed as the mere rituals and traditions of other people—a socially invested classificatory move not much different from recent efforts to distinguish mere religion from those supposedly "deeper" or more profound things known as spirituality or faith, let alone much earlier efforts to distinguish "our" religion from "their" superstition.

16 Given how frequently I have heard criticism and critique confused—as if being a critic, as I once opted to call this position, meant criticizing, belittling, demeaning, or disagreeing with people's choices and practices—I feel the need to clarify that alienation, as I use the term

Sadly, I find that just the opposite view is, more often than not, taken, when it comes to our field today, regardless the ink spilt on critical theory in the study of religion—whether in any number of past and easily documented instances (where, for example, but one religion, usually a form of Christianity, was once commonly assumed to be either original or normative and thus the ideal type by which all others could be judged as wanting) or in current practice (where, for example, but one type of Islam is now commonly assumed by many scholars and media pundits alike to be either original or normative and thus the ideal type by which all others could be judged as wanting). I think here of a recent critical reply that Martin Kavka and I co-wrote (2017) to an article published in the *Journal of the American Academy of Religion* (see Nadeem and Farid [2017a]; see also 2017b for their rejoinder), on the colonial-era roots of modern homophobia in parts of the Arab world. Our complaint, though in part about the authors' decision not to define "justice" (a term that they claim to be at the heart of their paper), mainly revolved around the article's move from *description* of a situation to their *advocacy* for how that situation *ought* to change. For the latter is only possible should scholars themselves, in their role as scholars (as opposed to their role as citizens), hold a position on how the groups we study *ought* to treat their members.[17] Given the breadth of positions that one could occupy concerning how the Arab world *ought* to treat homosexuals— and the fact that all of these positions are contestable and debatable by those invested in these issues, each using a variety of devises to authorize their

---

here, does not imply that one has something at stake in the correctness of the position under study. Instead, it merely implies that the scholar sees the practice or the organization as human, all the way down, and ensures that no privileged remainder is set aside, free of historicization.

17 In our field, the claim that we should compartmentalize is often greeted with suspicion, as in Spencer Dew's reaction to Asprem and Taves's claim of "saving our feelings of empathy or opposition for other contexts" (2018, 199; see Dew 2018 for his thoughts on their rigorously explanatory approach). However, the vast majority of scholars likely understand how to present themselves to their students *as* professors as opposed to presenting themselves as, say, siblings or as parents or maybe customers—roles that many of us equally play but only at other times in our lives. In fact, the very setting in which we have debates about compartmentalization, i.e., the modern university, is itself the result of generations of members working to set themselves apart from others for practical effect, and thus we arrive at, for instance, the practice of peer review (a form of self-governance) or even the institution of tenure. So I contend that compartmentalization (and thus the distance from identifying with ones object of study) is a necessary feature of scholarship. The question, then, is the degree to which one compartmentalizes, the practical effects, and how accessible this is to scholars working in various subfields of the academy. For further thoughts on compartmentalization (deriving from a critique of a recent AAR President's "revolutionary love" conference theme), see McCutcheon 2018c, 115–116.

stand in the contest—it struck Kavka and I as inappropriate for this article to have been published in one of the field's leading scholarly journals.[18] That our critical reply was characterized by the original authors, in the opening lines of their rejoinder, as supercilious and then met on social media with accusations that we were yet two more cisgendered white males telling people outside North American and Europe how to act strikes me as but another layer to the problem; for we were under the impression that, as members of the profession, it was well within our rights to take a stand, by means of argumentation and evidence, concerning what should constitute the limits of the profession itself (i.e., what counts as a persuasive argument—the sort of judgment that, presumably, we all routinely make in our capacity as teachers and thus graders). Simply put, the interests of the authors did not strike us as being sufficiently removed from the interests of the groups under study, for their efforts were ultimately directed at—as is so often the case in current scholarship in Islam—changing the groups to suit their own preferences.[19]

Despite the seeming advances in the modern field—what Dubuisson, in the opening sentence to his latest English book, characterizes as "a veritable scientific revolution" (2019, 1)—it seems to me that an effective and always ready rearguard action (as the military tacticians would phrase it[20]) has effectively undermined those gains, domesticated theory, and ensured that, to use Bruno Latour's title (1993) for my own purposes, scholarship on religion has never really been modern—for despite many scholars saying that they've read the critical work, by and large they continue to pursue their studies with colonial-era tools in the pursuit of normalizing their own group's self-interests.[21] So, despite Dubuis-

---

18 The problem, of course, is that as with our field's main taxon, religion, there is also no clear definition of what counts as scholarship on religion and thus what ought to be included or excluded from the pages of peer review journals in the field. Among the goals of this chapter is to take one more step toward clarifying this and, more importantly, to ensure that a younger generation of scholars clearly understands that this issue now falls to them.

19 See McCutcheon 2005 for a small book motivated by the many post-9/11 commentaries on Islam, by scholars, politicians, and the media, which aimed to identify the correct (i.e., peaceful and tolerant) form of Islam, one that was seen to be in step with liberal democratic interests. Such commentaries, by the way, have not lessened in the intervening years.

20 For those unfamiliar with the phrase, it names a defensive strategy whereby a secondary force, in the rear of an advancing front, responds to incursions made against that front or protects it from attacks at the rear, thereby coming in handy should the group be forced to withdraw and retreat. "I've got your back" might be the colloquial way of phrasing this.

21 This has long been apparent to some in the field, when they considered how frequently the work of the late Jonathan Z. Smith is cited appreciatively in the field despite the fact that the critical impact of his work was rarely operationalized. The manner in which critical gains grouped together under the banner of theory have been domesticated and thereby tamed and manson concluding that the results of this revolution "are so considerable that one must here and now envisage new ways to think of the History of Religions," many in the field are instead falling back on lightly revised versions of long familiar (and troublesome) approaches. For, as Leslie Dorrough Smith most recently noted, "although the field itself is now populated by scholars who ... claim a focus on more theories and methodological concerns, ... there is a widespread, uninterrogated, essentialist impulse still remaining in the research of many who claim theoretical savvy" (2019, 1).

To put it another way, it's remarkable how many people in our field still routinely talk about the west and the east, or western and non-western religions, despite all of us having apparently read (and understood?) our Edward Said. Or, consider how Naomi Goldenberg (herself a onetime NAASR president and strong advocate for the governance role of the rhetoric of religion) has described this problem:

> My department colleagues ... are a highly intelligent, accomplished group of religious studies scholars. They are familiar with the substantial body of critical scholarship in the discipline that, for the past two decades at least, has argued ... that "religion" is a modern concept that operates as a distorting anachronism when applied to the study of earlier epochs ... [and] that "religion" has roots in European colonial ambitions and intellectual history... . I do not expect my colleagues to refrain from disagreeing with some or even all of these general tenets of the sub-field of "critical religion." Rather, what I find disconcerting is their choosing to ignore critical approaches to fundamental terms when they are describing religious studies as a discipline (2018, 80).[22]

And, as Ian Cuthbertson observes, in a reply to Goldenberg's above-cited article,

> Colleagues in the religious studies department where I teach will often listen attentively whenever I insist that religion is not a self-evident thing in the world and then shrug

---

aged was a theme of the essays collected together in Hughes 2017 (originally presented as part of NAASR's 2016 annual meeting). By claiming that we've never been modern, I also do not have in mind the sort of argument put forward by Josephson-Storm (2018); interested readers can see my own thoughts on his recent book (McCutcheon 2018b). Concerning Smith's contributions to the field, see Lehrich (2020) as well as the essays collected in Crews and McCutcheon (2020).

22 Her paper opens by describing three learning outcomes created by her department—outcomes that, in her estimation, perpetuate several longstanding assumptions in the field (what Stoddard and Martin, she recognizes, might call clichés [2017]) that remain intact despite being the focus of much critical work (her own included) over the past twenty years. I could add one more: that the use of the category "religion" *distorts*, as Goldenberg phrases it. Although we agree on many things, I would insert more nuanced language at that point, one that avoids the impression that a more accurate or correct description of past events and groups is possible if only we used better and non-anachronistic terms.

their shoulders and proceed with the serious academic business of studying various individuals, tests, and practices in an attempt to determine what these might reveal about religion as a coherent object of study or thing in the world (2018, 103).

So, to elaborate on my thesis concerning what Emily Crews has called "a rash of scholarship that operates blindly when considering 'religion,' failing to parse the many layers of problematic meaning the category religion has accrued" (2018, 117); what Matthew Baldwin characterizes as a "given … that many of our colleagues do ignore and dismiss or minimize," what he also terms "critical scholarship on 'religion' as a category employed in human thought" (2019, 76); and what Craig Martin describes as the sort of "cavalier dismissals" that cause him "anger and frustration" (2019, 152; sentiments shared by Touna [2019, 175]), return, for a moment, to this now-popular idea of the link between the study of religion and advocating for increased religious literacy (an attempt to create increased tolerance in diverse liberal democracies).[23]

While we could mention Stephen Prothero's 2008 book on this topic—whose marketing materials phrase the point of the book as "'We have a major civic problem on our hands,' says religion scholar Stephen Prothero. He makes the provocative case that to remedy this problem, we should return to teaching religion in the public schools. Alongside 'reading, writing, and arithmetic,' religion ought to become the 'Fourth R' of American education."[24]—we could also cite the AAR's just completed three-year initiative (begun 2016 with a $160,000 grant from the Arthur Vining Davis Foundations)[25] to "produce consensus guidelines on religious literacy that administrators and faculty nationwide can draw upon to help shape college curricula"[26] while also drawing attention to Harvard

---

[23] See chapter 10 of McCutcheon 2001 for my earlier critique of the discourse on tolerance in the study of religion.

[24] His interest in this topic continues, e.g., his April 6, 2018, public lecture on "Religious Literacy in an Age of Religious Nationalism" at the University of Kansas.

[25] The foundation was established in 1952 and has a program specifically to fund interfaith leadership as well as religious literacy. It's driven by its "founder's principle that religious diversity is essential to civil discourse within a democracy and that leaders in all walks of life are more effective through an appreciation for the religious views of others" (quoted from https://www.avdf.org/Programs/InterfaithLeadershipReligiousLiteracy.aspx [accessed September 15, 2019]). Davis (1867–1962), the onetime president and chairman of the board of the Aluminum Company of America (Alcoa), was also a large land developer in the Bahamas and Florida before establishing the foundation.

[26] The committee, which also involved a team of respondents and which holds public sessions annually, was led by Eugene Gallagher and Diane L. Moore; learn more at https://aarweb.org/AARMBR/AARMBR/Publications-and-News-/Guides-and-Best-Practices-/Teaching-and-Learning-/AAR-Religious-Literacy-Guidelines.aspx (accessed October 6, 2020).

Divinity School's current Religious Literacy Project[27] along with Diana Eck's much earlier (begun in 1991) and not unrelated Pluralism Project,[28] let alone a variety of departments of religious studies that now see the topic of religious literacy as a thematic engine capable of driving, to whatever extent, their programing initiatives and institutional identity, even mentioning The Open University, in the UK, and its free online short course, "Why Religion Matters: Religious Literacy, Culture and Diversity."[29] This should make plain that one would not be in-

---

The October 3, 2019, press release announcing the completion of their work can be found here: https://aarweb.org/AARMBR/Publications-and-News-/Newsroom-/News-/AAR-Publishes-Religious-Literacy-Guidelines.aspx (accessed October 6, 2020). Its guidelines, while also focused on issues of method (e.g., "Distinguish confessional or prescriptive statements made by religions from descriptive or analytical statements") predictably also focused on acquiring the descriptive details that come with acquiring the world religions discourse (e.g., "Discern accurate and credible knowledge about diverse religious traditions and expressions") (see the executive summary of the report [p. 2]). At the public session I attended, near the start of the group's project, many audience members were frustrated by the manner in which departments of religious studies could be undermined by what then seemed like the committee's interest also to advocate for acquiring knowledge about religions in almost any other disciplinary or course setting—a move that, or so some in the audience argued, could provide warrant for administrations not to support the work of scholars of religion. This made it into their final report nonetheless: "In addition to religious studies courses, religious literacy can also be promoted in other disciplines including (but not limited to) anthropology, archeology, art, biology, criminal justice, economics, education, film, geology, history, humanities, journalism, literature, languages, media studies, music, neuroscience, nursing, philosophy, political science, psychology, social work, sociology, speech, and theatre" as written in the report (p. 4). Ironically, perhaps, as one committee member responded on that occasion, the organization's mission, to promote the public study of religion, does not necessarily require that it promote the academic field of religious studies. It may be worth noting that the AAR's head office in Atlanta recently had an opening for a full-time advocate for the study of religion (though it took an earlier social media backlash to prompt them to consider adding training *in our own field* as a legitimate background for applicants).
27 This initiative was founded, and is led by, Diane L. Moore, cited in the previous note. The project "advances the public understanding of religion with special attention to power, peace, and conflict. Through resources and training for educators and other professionals we explore the complex roles religions play in society" (see the project's self-description at https://rlp.hds.harvard.edu/about [accessed September 15, 2019]).
28 Learn more at http://pluralism.org/about/our-work/history/ (accessed September 15, 2019).
29 To name but a few US departments: Northwestern University grounds its major in the context of Prothero's work on religious literacy (notably his March 19, 2007, appearance on *The Daily Show with Jon Stewart*; see https://www.religious-studies.northwestern.edu/undergraduate/first-year-focus.html [accessed September 14, 2019]). Stanford's Department of Religious Studies' homepage claims that "[r]eligious literacy is key to global citizenship in the 21st century" (see https://religiousstudies.stanford.edu/ [accessed September 14, 2019]). The chaplain's office at Brown University (the proper place for such an endeavor, I contend) sponsors a Religious Literacy Project (see https://www.brown.edu/campus-life/spiritual-life/chaplains/office-chaplains-

correct to understand the effort to increase the public's knowledge of religions—both inside and outside of our classrooms—is now one of the major rationales of the field.[30]

As phrased in a 2015 article in *The Chronicle of Higher Education*, this turn toward teaching religious literacy recognizes "the urgency to make our campuses successful models of communities of diversity and global citizenry that do not ignore but recognize—and draw on—the significance, beauty, and complexity of religion" (Rosenhagen 2015).

That the just-quoted piece was written weeks after the November 2015 terrorist attacks across Paris[31] and in the more immediate context of candlelight vigils held on the author's campus (University of Wisconsin–Madison)—attended, as he describes it in his opening paragraph, by students of a variety of faiths (as well as the religiously unaffiliated)—cannot go unnoticed; for the desire to arrive at a civil and inclusive public square (civil and inclusive as judged by specific

---

and-religious-life/religious-literacy-project [accessed September 14, 2019]). And San Diego State University's Department of Religious Studies offers a fifteen credit hour Global Religious Literacy Certificate. The University of Vermont has a course on the topic, REL 105 Religious Literacy, described as "Religious literacy entails understanding the history and contemporary manifestations of religion, including the central texts, beliefs and practices as they are shaped within specific contexts. Introduces ways of thinking about the public expression of religion and profession-specific engagements with religion;" it also celebrated October 2019 as Religious Literacy Month (see the course description at https://www.uvm.edu/courses/rel_105 [accessed September 15, 2019] and find #RelLitUVM on social media for a list of programing events associated with their Religious Literacy Month). And even such an initiative as the American Religious Sounds Project (a project which seems not to define religion) seems part of this initiative, inasmuch as "the need for understanding religious pluralism has arguably never been greater. Given the remarkable diversity of American religious life and the increasing polarization of our politics, building a civic culture that is inclusive and valuing of all peoples constitutes one of the most pressing challenges we face today" (see http://religioussounds.osu.edu/about-faq#whyReligion [accessed September 15, 2019]). Finally, see https://www.futurelearn.com/courses/why-religion-matters (accessed October 17, 2019) for information on The Open University's online course.

30 It should be noted that the American Academy of Religion's mission statement itself reads as follows: "to foster excellence in the academic study of religion and enhance the public understanding of religion." To that end, it has a Committee on the Public Understanding of Religion, which, among other initiatives, annually awards the Martin E. Marty Award for the Public Understanding of Religion as well as an award to journalists (see https://aarweb.org/AARMBR/AARMBR/About-AAR-/Working-Groups-/Religion-and-the-Public/Committee-on-the-Public-Understanding-of-Religion.aspx [accessed October 6, 2020]).

31 In November 2015, 130 people were killed and 494 people injured in the French capital. The aggressions involved a bombing at a sports stadium and attacks on the streets, restaurants, and a night club.

and usually undisclosed and thereby naturalized standards, of course—*this* is the issue that needs attention) is the driving force behind the religious literacy initiative.[32] Or, as the author, Rosenhagen—himself an ordained pastor in the Evangelical Lutheran Church in America who also holds a PhD from the University of Heidelberg and who was the associate director of the onetime Lubar Institute for the Study of the Abrahamic Religions while now being the director of the University of Wisconsin–Madison's Center for Religion and Global Citizenry[33]—phrases it,

---

[32] A suspicion from the political left (rightly, I would argue) usually greets the discourse on civility when it is wielded by those on the right of contemporary politics, for in such cases it is recognized to be a way to promote a certain sort of order and thereby suppress resistance to it (by ruling such resistance as being out of bounds, because it is "uncivil"—a recent and obvious example in the US would be President Trump's focus on "law and order" in his speeches). For example, consider the reaction by some to the recently founded program for civil public discourse at the University of North Carolina at Chapel Hill, established by its Board of Governors—a board that is understood by some UNC faculty to be at odds with the idea of shared governance (see http://publicdiscourse.web.unc.edu/ or, for a recent article on the program and faculty reactions, see https://www.insidehighered.com/news/2019/09/12/program-civic-virtue-unc-chapel-hill-raising-concerns-about-secrecy-and-funding [accessed September 12, 2019]). The irony, however, is that when the same term "civility"—which, I would argue, is *always* a rhetorical term with socially formative effects—is used by those on the political left it is often left unscrutinized by them, as if it only now just means what it naturally says and is no longer the strategic front for other, undisclosed claims. Case in point: I see little if any critical analysis in the field to the links between religious literacy projects and claims that they enhance some untheorized notion of civility.

[33] Although it closed in June 2016, as described on their now out-of-date website, "The UW Lubar Institute for the Study of the Abrahamic Religions opened in July 2005, testimony to the vision and benefactions of Sheldon and Marianne Lubar of Milwaukee, Wisconsin. Concerned about rising religious tensions worldwide and believing Jews, Christians and Muslims to be capable of prolonged and honest inquiry into both their common heritages and varying perspectives, they imagined a center that would advance mutual comprehension by mingling scholars with the general public, clergy with laity, and members of different faith communities with citizens of Wisconsin, the United States, and the world. Through encouraging people belonging to and/or interested in the Abrahamic traditions to engage each other and to find out more about both of these several traditions and their intersections, the Lubar Institute is dedicated to strengthening the values of religious pluralism so vital for sustaining American civil society and peaceful international discourse." Interestingly, this unit was an institute in the College of Arts & Sciences at the University of Wisconsin–Madison, a public land-grant university in the US. (See https://lubar.wisc.edu/welcome/mission.html for the source of this description [accessed September 21, 2019].) The Center for Religion and Global Citizenry was established on the same campus in August 2017, explicitly as a revised version of the Lubar Institute (see https://religion.wisc.edu/about/ [accessed September 21, 2019). Aaron Hughes's critique of the category of Abrahamic religions (2012) as a socially formative devise used by liberal religious pluralists to establish the basis for interreligious dialog, and thus a category of no analytic power for scholars of religion, deserves mention at this point.

"Colleges need to invest more in their students' religious literacy—not proselytizing, not affirming any particular faith—but simply teaching vital competence about religion and its impact on global affairs that will prepare students for their future while enlightening our civic discourse along the way." Or, as Moore's Harvard project defines religious literacy:

> Religious literacy entails the ability to discern and analyze the fundamental intersections of religion and social/political/cultural life through multiple lenses. Specifically, a religiously literate person will possess:
> - a basic understanding of the history, central texts (where applicable), beliefs, practices and contemporary manifestations of several of the world's religious traditions as they arose out of and continue to be shaped by particular social, historical and cultural contexts
> - the ability to discern and explore the religious dimensions of political, social and cultural expressions across time and place[34]

So, not only do we see in this discourse on religious literacy a normative notion of religion as a constructive (i.e., peaceful, beautiful, and civil) force in human affairs, as well as a politically and theologically liberal understanding of diversity and inclusion, but we also find traditional or what we might better call pre-critical notions of religion as a socio-politically autonomous force that is merely "shaped" by history while "manifesting" itself or its "dimensions" in various discrete locales. In this way, beneficial practical effects are said to be achieved by one or more of the so-called world religions, effects enabled or promoted by our correct understanding of the religions … —*all of which flies in the face of a variety of critical gains made in the field over the past generation or two of scholars.*

To name but one example that might have already come to the reader's mind, the work of such scholars as Tomoko Masuzawa and Suzanne Owen (not to mention about half the authors in Cotter and Robertson's volume [2016])[35]—work specifically on the manner in which the discourse on world religions not only was, from the start, intertwined with very specific colonial governance efforts but which remains invested in a variety of modern political

---

34 Quoted from https://rlp.hds.harvard.edu/our-approach/what-is-religious-literacy (accessed September 15, 2019).
35 I say half because, as elaborated in the afterword that I wrote for the volume, about half the book (much as we see in the religious literacy initiative) is devoted to using the world religions category "better" (e.g., adding more traditions to it that have been, in the estimation of such scholars, inappropriately ignored in the past, such as pagan or indigenous traditions) while the other contributors wish to historicize the category.

projects—goes completely unrecognized and thereby ignored in the religious literacy literature. What is fascinating in all this, then, is that, despite the critical work of such writers and the way that their research seems to have driven much of the conversation in the modern field (or at least in some of its corner), the main problem with the world religions discourse today, at least according to many in our field, is *that people do not know it, and thus use it, well enough.* In other words, the problem is *not* that scholars and the general public at large commonly divide the world into a number of so-called faith traditions (thereby perpetuating a sort of idealism and individualism that each, or so it has been argued, have profound sociopolitical implications) but *that we all don't know the descriptive ins and outs of each.*[36] Recall that, as quoted above, among the goals of Harvard's religious literacy initiative is to enhance "a basic understanding of the history, central texts (where applicable), beliefs, practices and contemporary manifestations of several of the world's religious traditions." What's more, if we add to Masuzawa, Owen, et al.'s critique of the discourse on world religions the work of those engaged in the wider critique of the category religion itself (the genus of which world religions could be said to be but a species), and its practical effects in modern liberal democracies, then we arrive at the curious moment when a portion of the field is working to historicize and thereby limit our attraction to naming something *as* religion or a world religion while much of the field is focused on reviving and securing an undefined notion of civil society by ensuring that the population can—to put it crassly—properly distinguish a Sikh from a Muslim from a Hindu from a Jain from a …, all in hopes, I gather, that a universal oneness among all humanity, and a deference to certain sorts of differences, will become apparent to those sufficiently articulate in the use of this taxonomy.

While I can think of other seeming developments in the field, more of which I will provide in a moment, where a disciplinary past that some of us had thought that we had left far behind turns out, upon closer inspection, to be

---

[36] While I agree that we ought to be careful in the description of other people's claims and actions (with a nod toward Wayne Proudfoot's once widely quoted criticism of what he termed descriptive reductionism, as opposed to his support for explanatory reductionism [1985, 196–7]), this agreement does not prevent me from also reminding scholars (with a nod to a point demonstrated long ago by reflexive anthropologists) that our very questions, assumptions, and categories frame the conversation in ways that often predetermine what our so-called informants or interlocutors say in reply to us (as I elaborate later in this chapter). Our nuanced or sensitive description of others' claims therefore does not prevent our (perhaps unwitting) determining of *how* others are understood in our work—let alone *which* others are even included to begin with.

far more current than we had thought, the contradiction between, on the one hand, contemporary religious literacy initiatives, championed by some of the leading or most influential (or at least well-funded) aspects of the field and, on the other, critical scholars of religion who treat the study of religion as no different than the study of any other domain of human life, should cause us to pause and ask a few basic questions about just how modern this modern field of ours actually is. For the colonial-era world religions discourse that many in our field think they've left far behind turns out to be as relevant and alive as it ever was, whether or not world religions courses continue as the so-called bread and butter classes of departments. (My hunch is that they still are, by the way—this would be an interesting study to tackle.)[37] What's more, the notion of religion as unique and irreducible—a stance associated by many with the now out-of-date though once-prominent Chicago school of thought (though it was never just about Chicago, of course)—remains, I contend, as invigorated and consequential as ever, for it is the assumption that drives the use of the term religion in these literacy efforts;[38] for, as in pollsters collecting data outside voting stations and thereby trying to determine how religious beliefs inform voting patterns, religion is still generally assumed to be a pre-social, non-political disposition that merely has political and social "dimensions" and cultural "expressions" (as per the Harvard Religious Literacy project). Here, as I've identified before, the etymology and modern uses of "express" are helpful to keep in mind, inasmuch as it connotes "speaking one's mind" or putting something non-verbal "into words"—thereby reproducing the common "ghost in the machine" model of the human, whereby a dynamic, prior, and private inner consciousness and meaning is, by means of some secondary and invariably flawed step, said to be conveyed into the public by means of a symbol system that is presumed to exist at a distance from the original, pre-social intention ("That's not what I meant!" is sure evidence of this model, also making plain its agonistic role.). And thus, despite longstanding protests to the contrary, the old Cartesian dualism is as alive as ever in the study of religion—something evident from the very

---

[37] Studying the credit hour production that comes through such courses—a key indicator of a department's vitality—along with obtaining sales information on the still-thriving world religions textbook genre, would provide insight into this. On the enduring (and, I argue, problematic) influence of Huston Smith's still in-print (and lightly revised) 1958 textbook, originally entitled *The Religions of Man* (including its unwavering sales over the years), see McCutcheon 2018a, 46.

[38] Aside: there's even an annual world religions day, established in 1950 by the Spiritual Assembly of the Bahá'ís of the United States and celebrated around the world; see Goldenberg 2018, 85 for a description of a Canadian celebration of the day.

beginning of the popular subfield known as material religion, as in when one of its founders, Colleen McDannell, noted that her topic was "[t]he physical *expressions* of religion" and, in particular, "the material *dimension* of Christianity," thereby prompting her research to have "ranged broadly over many *expressions* of material Christianity" (1995, 1–2, 276; emphases added).

Taking all of this into account suggests to me that, despite the ease with which many in the field convey that they too have read all the critical work and have taken it into consideration, the field has changed very little in the past 150 years. For, citing but one scholar who has already been mentioned above, the distance between Naomi Godenberg's approach to the category religion as a tactical governance device (whereby what she terms marginal, vestigial states are created and policed by dominant populations [2015]) on the one hand, and, on the other, contemporary religious literacy initiatives—which, by the way, Greg Alles has recently described as "not a particularly robust justification for the study of religions" (2019, 11)—is so great that the latter can be considered but one more data point in need of the former's analysis.[39] If anything has changed at all, over this time, it is perhaps the political causes supported by the same old devices.[40]

Before going on to document further enduring problems at yet other places in the contemporary field, let me be clear on the reason for doing all of this. Although I may be incorrect, of course, I have the impression that some members of a younger generation for whose work recent critical gains are important have sometimes naturalized the contemporary place where they do their own work, thereby failing to recognize or appreciate that their institutional and disciplinary space is historically contingent, meaning that its establishment and mainte-

---

[39] See the last chapter to McCutcheon 2003, "Religion and the Governable Self," for an example of my own analysis of the political function of the category religion—an approach certainly related to but not coterminous with Goldenberg's approach.

[40] I admit that I think here of the notion of strategic essentialism and the manner in which a form of essentialism, hotly critiqued by scholars in many cases, can nonetheless be seen by some to be allowed or embraced so long as it is in support of causes or interests which they support; or, as recently phrased by Tong in an article concerned with how scholars can "encounter the [historical] archive on its own terms" (2019, 40), "sometimes it is politically expedient—perhaps even necessary—to adopt essentialist language in order to effect one's political goals" (43). That one's adversaries are just as likely to adopt this technique, arguing just as vehemently for its legitimacy in helping them to achieve their practical goals, ought to be enough reason for scholars of religion to consider how to establish an institutional space where such work is studied rather than used. On this very point, see the persuasive essay by Newton (2020), calling on scholars to avoid essentialism.

nance was hard won, i.e., gained only by previous scholars tackling the work of their predecessors and peers in order to make plain how it was lacking or how it led to a study of religion that was out of step with what they understood to be the usual requirements of scholarship. While I have noted that I do not share Wiebe and Martin's despair over what they described as their delusion, I admit to being concerned that without scholars at all career stages being willing to stand up and make strong statements about the inadequacy of some of their peers' work, the gains that some of us value in our field will, within a surprisingly short time, be lost altogether. For, as just argued, despite many of us agreeing that the world religions genre is an antiquated relic from a prior era, I would conjecture that it is now as vibrant and influential as ever.[41]

Now, I recognize that there are always prices to be paid in engaging the work of others, those whose scholarship strikes one as problematic—prices that vary based on, among other factors, the place of the critic and the place of the one being critiqued. This is what I meant by the *hard-won* gains that we risk taking for granted today. I think here of the earnest warning that my own doctoral supervisor once offered to me, just a short time into my own tenure-track career, concerning the behind-the-scenes work of some of those who were then (and still now) well placed in the field—efforts, as he characterized it, to undermine those with whom they disagreed concerning the shape and effects of the study of religion. I also recall a variety of incidents and interactions in my own career (some of which had administrative and thus institutional force behind them while others were more akin to polite warnings from no doubt well-meaning colleagues)[42] but, far more than this, I also recall the experiences of scholars in the

---

41 At the University of Alabama, where I've worked since 2001, my colleague, Steven Ramey, teaches this course but does so in a way that ultimately problematizes the idea and the course itself for his students.

42 This varies from once being called on the carpet by a department chair, at the insistence of a school's associate provost and also being denied tenure, to being advised by a senior colleague to use the word "approaches" rather than "theories" in a course title (so as not to alienate others), being told by another to place the work of Peter Berger on a syllabus so as to satisfy yet another senior colleague who saw in Berger the pinnacle of theoretical work in the field, having work rejected by a peer review journal for being too critical (cue the policing function of the discourse on civility), being likened to a small dog that has learned a new trick in an article on my work published in that same journal, and having my work trivialized as being mere journalism. Related to this, see Hughes and McCutcheon (2019) for a critical analysis of the discourse on collegiality (an article previously rejected by the *Journal of the American Academy of Religion* because, as we were told by the then editor, it was not about world religions or methods for studying world religions—the only topics the journal apparently published. On another occasion, I plan to elaborate on firsthand reports that have come back to me concerning serious warnings that others in the field, at early career stages (both in graduate school and in teaching posi-

generation ahead of my own, for whom firings (due to what I can only interpret as disciplinary disputes) were not an unusual part of the career for those who thought the study of religion could be something more than interreligious dialog. There are always things at stake, after all, and one would be naïve to ignore that; though the spoils are not that great (at least by some measures), there are spoils nonetheless, and, like all professions, there is an economy of status, rank, security, and perks that governs our institution, much like any other (everything from gaining admission to a graduate program to obtaining employment, let alone a full-time tenure-track position, to finding a position in schools seen as desirable by many, supervising doctoral students, gaining lighter teaching loads, or being recognized for awards). But, writing as someone who is certainly not as far along in the career as such scholars as Wiebe and Martin but who nonetheless is part of the generation whose members are now beginning either to retire or at least consider it, I admit to having concerns for where all this might be going in the near future, a concern which drives my effort to persuade readers that the field is not as far along as some of us might imagine. (We must also recognize that changes over the past decades in how public higher education is funded [i.e., cuts in government support] have led to a situation in which university administrations have not only increasingly relied on tuition revenue but have also opted to employ far greater numbers of [cheaper] non-tenure track faculty [i.e., contingent faculty]. Although the detrimental effect of this policy on young scholars certainly deserves our attention [and is something on which I have written elsewhere (see, for example, McCutcheon 2018c)], I maintain that it has also not helped the specific situation in the study of religion; for it means that far greater numbers of early-career scholars remain in unprotected settings [employed only course-by-course or merely year-by-year], thereby denying them the protections afforded by the tenure system and thereby providing them with little incentive to tackle the work of their elders, with an eye toward the health of the field at large—for, in many cases, those elders are deciding semester-by-semester whether to employ them as adjunct lecturers.)

Should my analysis of the role played by the category religion be persuasive, then we would be well advised to consider that no critical gain will ever be widely influential, let alone permanent. For just as with each new crop of students entering our classes, every new academic generation will bring with it

---

tions), have been given, either in private or public, about associating their work and careers with my own.

long-entrenched habits of thought and action that will require examination and, in some cases, undoing.[43]

As another example of the domesticating nature of the current field, and thus its still rather traditional nature, consider the podcast of the Department of Religion at the University of Virginia. Titled "Sacred & Profane," it now has several episodes.[44] On its homepage (written over a cartoon image of three women taking pictures of themselves at the beach, with one having a darker complexion than her friend and wearing a full body suit now commonly called a burkini while another wears what seems to be a head scarf and gloves), we read: "We may imagine that the sacred is set apart from life, but religion is involved in every aspect of our day-to-day world. How we live together and apart. How we argue. How we flourish. The sacred is the profane." Although I happen to agree that "the sacred is the profane," Bill Arnal and I did not have this particular sense of the phrase in mind when selecting a title for a set of essays that we collected together and published a few years ago (2012). While we, of course, do not own nor can we determine how this phrase is used by others, the difference between these two readings is worth considering, for it is a difference that might not at first be apparent to readers, given how the podcast's use of the phrase seems to be in step with recent scholarship on the role played by classification in the field—and thus open to the possibly arbitrary or at least tactical distinction between those two domains often known as the sacred and the profane.

Now, by that title Arnal and I implied the manner in which naming something *as* religious or sacred or spiritual or contemplative or mystical or … , was itself always a human and thus mundane classificatory act, one with the usual practical motives or effects that attend any act of naming, distinguishing, and ranking (the threefold set of things entailed in classifying something), and thereby (re)producing, negotiating, and contesting identity and place in the world (processes that make it possible to come to the conclusion that we even

---

43 I have noted on other occasions that the introductory class is a place where we would do well to make our students curious, as soon as they arrive in our classes, of their own taken-for-granted practices and knowledge, making their presumptions about the world and habits in the world their objects of study. Or, to borrow Smith's language, gains in such courses often result from defamiliarizing the material for the students.

44 The following example is adapted from a brief blog post, published online on September 1, 2019. Find it at https://religion.ua.edu/blog/2019/09/01/the-sacred-is-the-profane/; find the UVA podcast at https://religionlab.virginia.edu/season/season-1/. (I have seen blogging, over the past several years, as a petri dish where ideas and arguments can be tested, often making them, as in several places in this chapter itself, the raw material for further elaboration at a later time. For more on this, see chapter 10, "Why I Blog," in McCutcheon 2018c.)

inhabit a world, by the way). What we *did not* mean to denote by that phrase was that this thing called religion or spirituality, etc., somehow defied all boundaries and thereby pervades all of mundane life, manifesting itself first here and then there, and thereby informing or influencing seemingly non-religious actions or claims—such as, let's say for argument's sake, taking a photo at the beach. But that's certainly another way one can take that phrase—a way that, in my reading, is in keeping with those who argue that religion is influential of, but uncaused by, the ordinary aspects of our day-to-day lives.

And so, just what is the difference between these two readings?

Well, in the one case, so-called sacred things (the "so-called" is crucial to this use of the phrase) are not in any significant way different—*not whatsoever*—from any other element of the mundane world of human doings, though some social actors who use this term work very hard to create the impression that they are, such as calling so-called religious people on the move "pilgrims" and non-religious people "tourists"—and thus we now study one group differently from the other, given that the former are presumed to be on the move for unique, deeper, or more ethereal and thus non-mundane reasons that so-called sensitive scholars must to take into account. In other words, it would be just a bit insulting to think that that they're "mere" tourists, no? (And here we see but one more traditional element to this still-dominant approach: the privileging of what the observer takes to be just some agents' intentions.)[45] But in the other case, or so it seems to me, this thing called religion or spirituality or ... , is not an identity presumed to be the result of human, structural, or historical action but, instead, is assumed to predate and thereby inform all human actions, resulting in religion or the sacred being "involved in every aspect of our day-to-day world."

---

[45] Of course not all participants whom we study have their stated intentions "taken seriously," i.e., understood to be determinative of how scholars ought to study them. Those whose actions, and claimed rationales for those actions, contest or undermine the taken-for-granted norms of the scholar's own social world are rarely, if ever, taken at face value in scholarship, as scholars usually do when someone claims they are "on a pilgrimage." Instead, understanding the origins or causes of such "obviously" problematic claims and actions is a priority for the scholar (for in such cases, the rationales are often understood by scholars as deluded and the actions deviant— thereby making evident the normative stance that often informs scholarship on marginal groups [whether that stance is intended or not; see Ramey 2015a]). In cases where the scholars' world and expectations are left uncontested or confirmed, the self-understanding of the participant generally sets the terms by which they are to be studied, for otherwise scholars risk adopting what others will likely characterize as an imperialist approach to studying others. That self-interest can be demonstrated to drive the choice of when and where to sanction participants' own so-called self-understandings should cause us to pause and reconsider this whole notion of intention in our field.

Despite the appearance of both stands being informed by the same recent critiques in the field concerning the fluid nature of the boundary between the sacred and the profane (a fluidity certainly not presumed by earlier generations of scholars), this strikes me as a considerable difference in approach and thus a choice that most in the field end up making as they set off to study religion. For in the one case, studying religion will mean learning how "the sacred manifests itself" (to hearken back to more traditional phrasing that, as should have been evident in the earlier discussion of religious literacy, is still as relevant as ever), sometimes doing so in surprising places (the "religion of baseball" approach, we might call it—an approach that shares much in common, I'd argue, with Eliade's once-prominent new humanism, inasmuch as both see the scholar of religion's reach as virtually limitless given that religion informs virtually all aspects of the human).[46] But in the other case, the things that some call religious, etc., will be studied as merely one example of the results of ordinary human actors arranging their worlds in ordinary (but nonetheless curious) ways, by designating something *as* "set apart and forbidden" (to recall an equally old phrasing, but one associated with a rather different tradition of studying sacredness in the field).[47] Maybe people do this to privilege something (or someone) in relation to other things (such as, at least currently in the US, people appealing to what are known as religious exemptions in order to free them from laws that usually govern life in the nation), but it's just as likely that they do it to demote and delimit (such as labeling something *as* religious so as to disallow it, such as, with the US

---

[46] See his essay, "History of Religions and a New Humanism," which opened the inaugural issue of *History of Religions* (1961), reprinted in his essay collection, *The Quest* (1969).

[47] I refer here, of course, to Emile Durkhiem's earlier work, in which sacredness was understood as a contingent identity that resulted from prior human action (i.e., of following a rule system, by which one sets something apart *as* forbidden), thereby making sacred an adjective, i.e., a quality of items in the world, rather than Eliade's use, as I've described elsewhere, in which it is a noun (and thus always preceded by a definite article). In fact, the usage "the sacred" is still easily found to this day, more than likely signifying an approach to the study of religion found wanting in this essay. As but a particularly apt example, consider the historian Nancy van Deusen's *Embodying the Sacred: Women Mystics in Seventeenth-Century Lima* (2017), described by its publisher as follows: "In seventeenth-century Lima, pious Catholic women gained profound theological understanding and enacted expressions of spiritual devotion by engaging with a wide range of sacred texts and objects, as well as with one another, their families, and ecclesiastical authorities …. Through close readings of diverse primary sources, van Deusen shows that these women recognized the divine …. In these manifestations of piety, each of these women transcended the limited outlets available to them for expressing and enacting their faith …."

still in mind, courts banning from public schools, as unconstitutional, the approaches to studying the origin and development of biological life known as creationism and intelligent design)—which is what we'll have to figure out as we dive in to study the larger world that produced these and just these supposedly religious things or people.

It was with this disciplinary distinction in mind that I tweeted a photo not too long ago of a sandwich board advertising "Authentic Mexican Food," in response to a onetime colleague, Emily Crews, who (correctly, I think) observed that "data is everywhere." The question, though, is how can this advertisement be something that a scholar of religion would study? Does the sign have religious aspects and effects that we'll correctly see *as religious* only if we look at it just a bit closer or in the correct manner, in order to see how it corresponds to/overlaps with other members of the broad family known as religions,[48] or, as I'd instead argue, whether the things that we end up calling religion are the result of something no different than the act of setting apart *this* food from *that* food, all in an effort to (as Mary Douglas might have put it) impose a system of order so as to attain some very practical effects (in the case of the sign I just cited, to attract customers and, presumably, make a profit for a restaurant that's in composition with number of others)? For now, the study of religion is but one element of the far wider study of how people identify and order (and yes, contest) the worlds they've made for themselves, a process examined at one particular and manageable place, but with analogues (i.e., data) everywhere (including an ordinary sign outside a restaurant).[49]

To return to my second example, the podcast mentioned above:[50] an approach to defining and studying religion that I consider to be pre-critical (i.e.,

---

48 I insinuate here the role played by the well-known family resemblance approach to defining religion in enabling scholars to see the sacred as pervading the profane. For a critique of the still commonly used family resemblance approach to defining religion, see Fitzgerald 1996.

49 This is what I take Smith to have meant when he spoke of something as an e.g.—a specific instance of a far wider human topic, of interest to the scholar, that could also be exemplified equally well in any number of other places or times, with no one instance being ideal, unique, or prototypical. See the blog for Culture on the Edge (edge.ua.edu), a research collaborative comprised of scholars of religion, for numerous examples of how to make this shift when it comes to studying culture at large and not just that domain often termed religious. See also my own department's Luce-funded initiative (which involves most faculty in the department, under the leadership of PI Michael Altman), American Examples, for another instance of how this model can help us to rethink parts of the field (https://americanexamples.ua.edu).

50 Because it might not go without saying, let me be clear that I am impressed by the work of UVA's faculty and students in producing this podcast, an effort, presumably, to convey their work to wider audiences and publics well outside our usual classrooms. My own department

exemplified decades ago) again lies behind what at first seems to be an initiative that is innovative and thus one that apparently has taken into account some of the most recent critical work in the field. Ironically, I would argue that, as with the religious literacy movement, just the opposite has happened, inasmuch as the phrase "the sacred is the profane" now signifies (at least for some) the former as pre-dating and pervading all of the latter, thereby domesticating and limiting the critical gain associated with understanding those aspect of the human usually designated *as* sacred as being sites where the ordinary acts of signification and contest can be studied.

A third example of the field's rearguard action is the already-mentioned trend, gaining significant speed over the past two decades, toward studying what is now widely referred to as material culture.[51] Whether our field's version of this is known as religion on the ground, material religion, lived religion, embodied religion, etc., this approach is now among the most central for many scholars of religion, and seen by them as provocative and critically edged. It is portrayed by its advocates as historical and rigorously empirical, given its focus on discrete objects, and, because of this, it is usually represented as being at odds with what is portrayed as having outdated idealist connotations: the once dominant text-based model—a model, we are often told, that once lodged the field in mainly studying elite social actors' creation, circulation, and interpretation of texts, doing so at a significant distance from what some now see as the real people and their real lives. As described by Richard Carp, in his entry to Michael Stausberg and Steven Engler's *Routledge Handbook of Research Methods in the Study of Religion*: "At most times and places, only certain elites—usually men—produced tests, while women, the poor and even slaves created material culture" (2014, 475). By applying a method devised by the earlier social history movement among historians, many scholars of religion (especially those in a younger generation) now aim to study religion in the lives of those not previously studied, doing so by means of a home shrine, for example, or at an impromptu shrine on the sidewalk of a busy city, or at a display alongside a busy highway that marks a traffic fatality, to name just three examples that are represented as falling far outside the field's once widely shared focus on the beliefs that were inferred to motivate the actions, associations, and productions of ritual and textual specialists.

---

has taken this seriously as well, from hosting an active blog to a podcast of our own; the blog can be found at https://religion.ua.edu/blog/ and the podcast at https://soundcloud.com/studyreligion.

51 See Baldwin 2019, 80 for a related and detailed critique of the so-called material turn in the study of religion.

But does this apparent emphasis on the empirical and the local/marginal actually free us from what many now see as the old rut of studying disembodied beliefs?⁵² For instance, take the following quotation from the Spring 1997 newsletter of the Material History of American Religion Project, centered then at the Divinity School of Vanderbilt University and funded (like much contemporary scholarship on religion in America) by the Lilly Endowment, and then involving several key figures in the early years of this movement (e.g., Robert Orsi):

> [T]he scholars associated with this project have set out to pay attention to a neglected dimension of the history of religion in America. Too often the story of religion has been told as though it were a matter of thoughts and ideals alone. Material history is embodied history and recognizes that religious people have enacted their spiritual beliefs and religious ideals in a very material world. We are looking at the material evidence, getting into the material, and finding out a great deal in the first year of this project.⁵³

But, given this initiative's effort to distance itself from idealist versions of the field, dare we ask: material evidence of what …? Well, apparently of the beliefs—i.e., "enacted their spiritual lives and religious ideals"—that, in a suitably idealist fashion, are still assumed to motivate people to do this or that with their bodies and thus with their artifacts.⁵⁴ Anyone with an understanding of the assumptions that have driven much in the field might justifiably say, upon reading this: *Plus ça change, plus c'est la même chose, non?* To come at it in a different way: just because we've banished the word "belief" does not mean that material religion studies constitute an advance, for just what is being "enacted" or "materialized" in these objects …? Sooner or later, I suggest, we work our way back to the presumption that individuals have prior beliefs—or, to avoid the systematic and doctrinal overtones of the term "belief," one might instead opt for such terms as "faith" or "experience," to signal something presumed to be more authentic and thus pre-cognitive/pre-social—that are later manifested in tangible items outside their minds (or hearts?)—an idealist presumption, no matter which term one opts for, that has long dominated our field and many others.⁵⁵

---

52 The following derives from an October 3, 2013, post at https://edge.ua.edu/russell-mccutcheon/eliade-has-not-left-the-building/.
53 http://www.materialreligion.org/newsletters/news1/index.htm (accessed September 9, 2019).
54 It is not insignificant that the previously mentioned *AAR Religious Literacy Guidelines* are primarily interested in promoting "informed understandings of belief systems and other worldviews" (see p. 2 of the report).
55 In my more recent work I have purposefully avoided the discourse on belief, whenever possible, and have opted, instead, to discuss claims that situated social actors make. My goal has been to highlight that, as scholars, we not only have no access to beliefs but might also be quite

The gain of the material religion movement, then, is merely to extend this traditional or pre-critical study of non-elite and therefore everyday, common, and often overlooked items—not nearly as significant a gain as its advocates claim.

It needs to be mentioned that the texts that material religion specialists claim we have solely studied in the past *are themselves material items*—a point that seems to be lost on those advocating this position today. (Recall the ease with which Carp, above, distinguished texts from material culture.) What's more, if we take critical theorists seriously, concerning the limitless nature of text, recalling Jacques Derrida's famous quote about texts, let alone the need to address the intentional fallacy in our field, then I'm not really sure how, despite defining our data domain far wider, and thereby switching to pots, rugs, and keychains from books, manuscripts, inscriptions, counts as an improvement over, in Carp's words again, prior "more immaterial and disembodied understandings" (486). For religion is left largely untheorized in all this, with the scholar somehow just seeming to know where to find "the presence of religion in secular cultural landscapes" (486), such as Carp himself who, without defining religion, somehow just seems to know to list together "the taste of a sacred meal, the scent of incense, the feel of rosary beads in one's fingers, the proprioception of one's body in sacred postured or gestures (kneeling in prayer, for example, or making the sign of the cross) or the kinesthesia of one's body engaged in religious activity (for example *sa'y* during the *Hajj*)," all places where this method can be used (475).

My point in all this? I am at a loss to explain how—apart from, say, merely changing the old phenomenologist's word "manifestated" to the now preferred term "embodied" or perhaps "enacted"—this new approach is any different from the old approach that once dominated our field, represented so nicely by the work of those who (yes, like Eliade) drew on hermeneutics, phenomenology, and a late-nineteenth century sort of comparative method intent on finding sameness to come up with a way to somehow "get at" what they considered to be the essential and historically universal *sine qua non* of religion by first studying diverse people's myths, symbols, and rituals (to reference a once

---

mistaken to infer their existence (in our explanatory effort to come up with a unified source for human action and organization) since all we have are actors making claims and counterclaims (i.e., the difference between studying beliefs and studying discourses on belief). The move to claims, influenced by Bayart's work (2005), thereby opens the door to the materialist position that belief (much like claims of authenticity, let alone unbelief) is a rhetorical trope employed by social actors who find themselves in disputes that cannot be resolved in the usual ways, doing so in an effort to justify their previously uncontested preferences and actions by lodging them within the presumably unassailable confines of the private self.

prominent undergraduate course title). For in both cases—phenomenology then and material religion now—"that which presents itself to our senses" (as phenomenologists used to say, as if the world marched toward us of its own accord, with scholars just passively watching or receiving it) is assumed by the observer to be evidence of a something else (there's more than meets the eye ..., as it were), and that "something else" is asserted to be prior and non-empirical and thus only be inferred from our so-called historical, descriptive, and comparative studies. For after all, "[r]eligion is always realized. It is conveyed and apprehended in the sound of music, through prayer, rhetoric discussion, confession and song ..." (Harvey 2014, 502)—but what the prior "it" *is*, that which is claimed to be realized elsewhere, is never in question. Call it faith, call it belief, call it spirit, or call it soul, or even call it meaning, if you will (the last being the preferred term of a number of humanists who study religion), but I'm not sure what difference it makes, for what these two approaches share—material religion and, at least for some, the discredited phenomenology of religion—is a presumption that history is merely an arbitrary, secondary, and contingent stage on which ahistorical and necessary themes and dispositions of universal scope are played out.

(Aside: Given that Lilly supported the above quoted material religion project, maybe none of this should come as a surprise. After all, as the foundation phrases its mission:

> Our primary aim in religion is to deepen and enrich the religious lives of American Christians, principally by supporting efforts that enhance the vitality of congregations. We seek to ensure that congregations have a steady stream of wise, faithful and well-prepared leaders. We also support efforts that help Christians draw on the wisdom of their theological traditions as they strive to understand and respond to contemporary challenges and live their faith more fully. In addition, we work to foster public understanding about religion and help lift up in fair and accurate ways the contributions that people of diverse religious faiths make to our greater civic well-being.[56]

It seems to me that a scholarly approach that heralds the empirical, but which turns out to be in the service of conserving the common assumption concerning

---

[56] Quoted from https://lillyendowment.org/our-work/religion/ (accessed September 9, 2019). Their former website phrased it as follows (emphasizing ministry more and not making reference to "diverse religious faiths"): "The ultimate aim of Lilly Endowment's religion grantmaking is to deepen and enrich the religious lives of American Christians, primarily by helping to strengthen their congregations. To that end, our religion grantmaking in recent years has consisted largely of a series of major, interlocking initiatives aimed at enhancing and sustaining the quality of ministry in American congregations and parishes" (as quoted in October 2013).

the primacy of a non-empirical spirituality and inspiration, can understandably be interpreted to enhance and sustain the participant's viewpoint. The question, though, is whether a mere paraphrase of what people are already saying about themselves and their lives [i.e., that the historical is a mere stage on which eternal themes are played out] constitutes the kind of work that should be considered as falling within the boundaries of scholarship on religion.)

That the so-called material religion approach is but a rebranded phenomenology of religion was confirmed for me with a book that I used in an undergraduate class a couple of years ago: Brent Plate's *A History of Religion in 5 1/2 Objects* (2014).[57] While engaging and therefore nicely accessible to a novice reader, it strikes me as little different from Eliade's *Patterns in Comparative Religion* (1996)—a classic (but, for many, long outdated) study, from 60 years ago, of cross-cultural symbolism and the way in which everything from water to stones can be an active agent that, as phrased by earlier scholars, "manifests the sacred." And so, keeping in mind what I previously characterized as the now widely shared presumption that the approach once represented in Eliade's work is long behind us, it strikes me as significant that on pages 7–8 of Plate's book we find who else but Eliade (a person who, he writes, "thought long and hard about what makes certain activities, gatherings, objects, people, and beliefs 'religious' and not just some other part of mundane existence"), not only quoted appreciatively but, I'd say, being used to anchor the whole exercise that is to come—which also includes a chapter on what I might as well term the agency of, among other objects, stones; for they "can be manifestations of a divine force, provoking people to pilgrimage" (2014, 24), Plate informs his readers.[58] Whether that divine force is mere human projection onto an inanimate world or the human perception of an even deeper mystery is—much like in Eliade's work—left rather vague, at least as I read it. For instance, concerning the Ka'ba in Mecca, Plate writes: "The power of the stone to draw people to it is so strong that a series of silver frames have been placed over it for protection"

---

57 This example derives from a February 26, 2015, post; see https://religion.ua.edu/blog/2015/02/26/the-more-things-change/ (accessed September 10, 2019).

58 Aside: Eliade's continued influence outside our field is easy to document; for example, such works as *The Myth of the Eternal Return* and his *Shamanism* appear alongside the works of Carl Jung and Joseph Campbell in the citations of Karen Armstrong (e.g., 1993 and 2005)—perhaps the widest-selling author writing on religion for the general public—and Eliade's three-volume *History of Religious Ideas* features on Jordan Peterson's list of books that he "found particularly influential in [his] intellectual development" (see https://www.jordanbpeterson.com/books/book-list/ [accessed September 13, 2019]); curiously, one of the books Peterson lists as being "what [people] should read to properly educate themselves" was written by Peterson himself (1999) and, yes, it heavily cites Eliade's work.

(27). How the Ka'ba was signified in the first place, and how that signification has been reproduced and adapted (even contested) over time are not questions this approach aims to investigate.

It was encouraging that a number of my undergraduate students saw problems here as well—understanding that mere descriptions of how people themselves might talk about the world ("I felt drawn to it ...") when scholars ask them questions hardly is a sufficient academic exercise. So, to repeat: despite what many people in our field may claim, Eliade definitely has not left the building, something that is especially evident when we fail to redescribe and theorize the claims made by the people that we happen to study.[59] For while I have no doubt that people the world over *claim* that their objects possess a unique or inspiring gravitational force all of their own (what we could somewhat flippantly call "the power of Christ compels you model," quoting a classic line shouted in unison by priests in the 1973 film, *The Exorcist*), as a scholar working at a distance from these social worlds, I cannot help but see the objects that people routinely surround themselves with as under-determined canvases used for any number of purposes.

So although it may go without saying, it strikes me that the stones are not talking and don't have any power to act of their own accord; instead, we are the ventriloquists throwing our voices—something I admit that Plate suggests, in places ("Perhaps it is the ubiquity of stones in human life ... that has prompted us to bestow certain stones with spiritual power ..." [29] or again, "Individuals as well as communities gather objects, place them in one locations, and allow these objects to hold a significant sacred place in their lives" [31]), but which seems to get lost in all the advice concerning learning to listen to what stones are telling us. For, as far as I can tell, we're talking to ourselves here, making the objects that we surround ourselves with useful props that allow us to portray a monologue as something other than what it is.

---

[59] It may be worthwhile to specify that by redescription I mean Smith's specific sense of the term, something different from how other authors now use the term, such as Goldenberg, for whom it connotes mere repetition of participant claims (2018, 90–2) and Asprem and Taves, who see interpretation (as opposed to explanation) as being synonymous with it (2018, 135). For Smith, redescription signified how claims made in one domain are translated—another term of choice for him—into another, much as Durkheim (as per Smith 2004, 383) could be said to have translated, and in the process redescribed, so-called religious claims into the language of sociology. See Smith 2004, 29 for his own thoughts on the advantages of understanding the goal of our work as redescription, followed by the rectification of the categories we have used to go about our work—a goal that avoids the ontological overtones of much reductive/explanatory work in the field.

While I will leave to others further documentation that the work of Eliade is still an appropriate representative of much of the modern field, no matter how much distance some may claim separates us today from when he first wrote many of his now-famous studies in the history of religions (that is, back in the 1950s)—for example, demonstrating that Tanya Luhrmann's now influential work (e.g., 2012) can also be seen in the same light as Plate's neo-phenomenology would be a project worth tackling—I was lucky enough to have Plate comment on my critique of his book, resulting in a brief online back-and-forth, during which he posted the following comment: "I may be an unwitting Eliadean. So be it."[60] I found this an interesting retort, because, for some time, I've been privately predicting that the work of Eliade would be, or already was, making a return (insert your own "eternal return of the same" asides here). It is a prediction premised on two assumptions that I now offer here.

First, as I've argued elsewhere, a decontextualized approach, such as Eliade's, that reduces—yes, it's as reductionistic as any, just not to naturalistic elements—diverse human actions and claims (i.e., putting moon symbolisms from all over the world alongside each other only inasmuch as they all involve the moon) to a supposedly unified private experience of the thing he called "the sacred" offers an appealing model for anyone trying to overlay a grand, developmental narrative and thus unified identity onto what I'll instead describe as the happenstance of human history and association, as a way to tame and thereby make sense of what others might name as difference, diversity, competition, or even outright contradiction. It therefore offers what many would characterize as an ahistorical response to historical situations (what Eliade referred to as "the terrors of history")—i.e., when contingency seems to defy our efforts to make sense of the world as a predictable, uniform, and thus understandable place. I think that the temptation to make the environments in which we find ourselves cognitively and socially habitable by making the moves that we see in his body of work is great indeed, so one would expect that such approaches would not go away any time soon (even if they are tweaked, just a bit).

(I think here of how, in US courts, intelligent design approaches to the origins of life have been effectively demonstrated to be just a slight revision to the already outlawed [in the public school science class, at least] creationist approaches [they were ruled unconstitutional in Edwards v. Aguillard, 482 US 578 (1987)]. This slight revision to the already-discredited approach was made evident in Kitzmiller v. Dover Area School District, 400 F. Supp. 2d 707 (M.D.

---

60 See the comments posted at https://religion.ua.edu/blog/2015/02/26/the-more-things-change/ (accessed September 11, 2019).

Pa. 2005), a federal court case from the fall of 2005.[61] This regrouping after a loss, only to revise and retry strikes me as an apt image for what's been going on in the field since the late 1980s, when rigorous, and, for some, persuasive criticisms of the phenomenological method were first entering the literature, causing advocates of this approach to retreat and recalibrate their approach.)

But second, the generation of scholars that followed Eliade, those who developed some pretty strong and persistent critiques of his work (both its academic shortcomings as well as the possible sociopolitical motives or effects of such an approach), is now, as noted earlier, either at retirement or nearing the point of retirement in their own careers. This means that the fierce battles over theory and method in the study of religion that were waged beginning in the 1980s—when many of these now-senior scholars were themselves rising to prominence and when the then-dominant Eliadean approach was for the first time seen as a problem—now seem like ancient history to subsequent generations, either the one now starting their careers or the one coming along after that (those in undergrad or grad programs now). And so, once again, we come back to this over-used notion of the eternal return: the sorts of critiques that once seemed to hold this decontextualized approach at bay, to whatever extent, within the academy are now more than likely not read or taught all that much (ignoring something is a power mode of response), which nicely clears the way to, for example, assume that anyone who uses the word "sacred," as either noun or adjective, is seen as doing so in the same fashion, making their works interchangeable. So my argument is that when the persistent urge to dehistoricize in the service of making an authorized place in the here and now meets the eventual or possibly inevitable decline of ardent critiques of how this tendency is enshrined within academia itself, we find scholars there who simply dismiss the critique by replying "So be it" when their work is read as exemplifying what others see to be some of the most problematic features in the field.

The punchline that I keep returning to throughout this opening chapter is therefore rather simple: each academic generation bears the responsibility to continue, to refashion, and to redeploy the critique in key places, in order to maintain an alternative institutional space and a social identity, should any of its members agree that the academic study of religion can or ought to be something other than a learned repetition of the sorts of claims that are often made by the very people whom we study (e. g., claims of transcendental identities and assumptions of human actors being little more than passive recipients of meanings

---

[61] Find the judge's December 20, 2005, ruling at https://web.archive.org/web/20051221144316/ http://www.pamd.uscourts.gov/kitzmiller/kitzmiller_342.pdf (accessed September 12, 2019).

projected from elsewhere). For if our field is something other than undoubtedly well-meaning paraphrases of participant reports, then the argument for that to be the case can probably never be presumed but, instead, must continually be made and remade.

As but another instance of these challenges, take into account the notion of public religion, a topic much discussed by a number in the field today, notably those interested in the role religion plays in social change (a topic of much importance to many scholars today, studying everything from 1979's Iranian revolution to the role of evangelical Christian voters in the 2016 US presidential election). However, much like the problematic notion of material religion, the idea that religions can be either private or public is, I maintain, a troublesome one that we seem not to be able to get beyond. Although the category has a longer history than one might expect,[62] it's a notion given significant steam twenty-five years ago with the publication of José Casanova's *Public Religion in the Modern World* (1994); as described on the publisher's site:

> During the 1980s, religious traditions around the world, from Islamic fundamentalism to Catholic liberation theology, began making their way, often forcefully, out of the private sphere and into public life, causing the "deprivatization" of religion in contemporary life. No longer content merely to administer pastoral care to individual souls, religious institutions are challenging dominant political and social forces, raising questions about the claims of entities such as nations and markets to be "value neutral," and straining the traditional connections of private and public morality.

Instead of assuming that religion is first and foremost an inner experience that (for good or ill) is somehow expressed publicly,[63] whether as some secondary step for the individual or as an historical development (i.e., deprivatization) associated with so-called modernity—a stand associated with what I've elsewhere called the private affair tradition in the study of religion— how would we rethink this entire tradition of scholarship on so-called public religion if we instead un-

---

[62] Martin Marty, writing in the *Encyclopedia of Religion and Society* (1998, 393), notes the appearance of the term "publick religion" in Benjamin Franklin's writings: "In 1749," Marty writes, "the American founder made 'proposals' for an educational academy in Philadelphia. When discussing the study of 'history,' he argued that it would 'afford frequent Opportunities of showing the Necessity of a Publick Religion ,' arguing 'from its Usefulness to the Publick; the Advantages of a Religious Character among private Persons,' and the like." The relations to the more recent notion of civil religion are observed by Marty; on problems surrounding the use of civil religion as a category in the study of religion, see McCutcheon 2003, 279–83.

[63] See chapter 3 for my own views on the socially formative rhetoric of religious experience.

derstood all of daily life to be public (i.e., social and contestable)—always and already?

For maybe religion never was in the private (i.e., either interior or non-political) sphere but, rather, we may have used that word, "religion," and a host of other sociopolitical management techniques, to create the impression of a walled-off and (literally) self-contained realm to which we attached the term privacy, in order to just get some things off the social table—a series of techniques that, in this so-called modern world, no longer seem to be able to separate and contain what they once did (hence the impression that things are now entering the public domain). For social (thus public) roles concerning such things as gender and generation are easily found within the confines of the apparently private home, no? And each of us not only adopts but is framed by the expectations of others, making them part of the seemingly private self that we each apparently think that we have to ourselves alone, no? My point is that the limited (or should we just say the rhetorical) utility of the private/public binary is pretty evident, for each time it is invoked it can easily be collapsed, demonstrating that privacy is itself a social and thus negotiable (i.e., political) construct; yet, despite this evidence, it retains a social efficaciousness (case in point: a rebellious teenager claiming their room is private and, for the good of the family, parents agreeing to this ... , for the most part) that prompts us to keep using this way of asserting "thus far and no further" to our peers.

So what if we just acknowledged all of this and agreed, from the outset, that privacy is invariably a changeable and therefore contestable construct? What would we then make of talking about religion going public ...?

For if this alternative position was our starting point—not that supposedly private things are eventually expressed or manifested so that they meander through or pervade the public but, instead, that claims of privacy are just that, *claims* that are made in specific social situations by specific social actors, the effect of which is either to try to limit what your neighbors see or limit what your neighbors do—then how would we rethink not just what we mean by, but also what we do with, "religion" as well as the other popular signifiers in our field, e.g., experience, faith, belief, feeling, sentiment, and spirituality? And how would we rethink this now-booming scholarly industry on so-called public religion—an industry very much in keeping with traditional views in the field concerning the primarily or initially experiential nature of religion? For now we would no longer have any notion of privacy as naming a substantial thing in the world from which we could then move outward; instead, we'd examine the practical effects of *rhetorics of privacy*. For, to tweak that phrase of Bayart's, all we may actually have are operational acts of privatization.

This strikes me as a dissertation waiting to be written, one that takes the secondary literature on public religion as its primary source, asking *why* this scholarly tradition arose when and where it did and *what* its practical effects have been for how we understand (and regulate) difference in this modern world, as opposed to proceeding, as do so many studies today, with the old assumption that religion has periodically broken into the public realm, for good or ill. The more novel project, I'd wager, would include among its data points much work being done today on religion and law, such as Winifred Sullivan's now influential work where, for example, we read the following: "Religion has proved to be not an irrational private, and authoritarian pre-modern relic destined to fade away, but has proved remarkably vital and ubiquitous, refusing the place assigned it by the modern consciousness" (2005, 152). Religion, here, is not theorized but, in my reading, is instead presumed always to have been on the scene, though being much larger and more dynamic than previous advocates of the secularization thesis once assumed it to be.[64] Instead of theorizing the things that we commonly call religion as themselves being *a product of law* (i.e., the designation is itself a modern tool used in the governance of groups and the management of difference), those in this subfield seem to take for granted that religions exist in the world and are therefore mainly concerned with how best for governments to interact with them (i.e., how to manage the freedom of expression in US political life)—often concerning themselves, in a vein not dissimilar to Cantwell Smith, merely with what to call the prior "it."

I think here of Jennifer Graber's important recent book, *The Gods of Indian Country* (2018), in which religion is identified, in its opening pages, as a word used by "[m]any Protestant Americans in this period [i.e., the nineteenth century] ... to refer to their particular experience of Protestant faith and practice." She then helpfully historicizes the term by noting that because "Kiowas had no word that translates neatly as 'religion,'" her book therefore "do[es] not use the term in my discussion of their ritual practice or understanding of sacred power" (xxi). While supporting this recent turn toward far more careful and historically nuanced work in our field, the issue here, however, is that whether or not *the specific word* "religion" is used by scholars, the parameters established by our *discourse* on religion can still be normalized in our very efforts to historicize the term—for it is the discourse, of which the word "religion" is merely representative, that allows us to so easily identify just some people *as* Protestants (distin-

---

64 In fact, it's the once-prominent secularization thesis that many of these scholars seem to be working against, in an effort to demonstrate the inevitability and universality of religion. I make a related argument in McCutcheon 2014.

guished from Roman Catholics, for example, because of what they *believe* about such theological items as God, Bible interpretation, church authority, etc.), let alone to somehow know that religion is rooted in something called faith and practice that each have something to do with sacrality, etc.—indicating that Graber's move, though helpful, can go so much further in the direction of theorizing "religion." That Graber regularly uses the term ritual as an alternative, and presumably better, term for what the Kiowas were doing (a move similar to Tim Fitzgerald's early work, by the way) while also noting that "ritual" was among the terms that Protestants at the time used to name "Kiowa actions and sentiments" is a useful example of the interesting thing here—it is as if these actions and sentiments are so obviously associated and together distinguishable from others that they require their own name and thus identity. For in the latter usage it is employed in quotation marks and characterized as a label that has "both positive and negative meanings, depending on the context and the speaker" (xxi), while in the former usage there are no qualifications to its use. This leaves the reader to wonder whether, when reading such statements as "When Kiowas migrated south, they brought with them rituals they had learned from their neighbors …" (2) is it there being used as a neutral designator naming what outside observers misconstrue *as* religion or perhaps used in a positive manner to combat past negative uses—prompting further questions concerning whether it is the proper role of scholarship to document and historicize or to correct past usages?

Now, should we make the shift advocated above, then neither will we lament the lack of explicit definition of religion in US law, as do so many of those work in religion and law, nor assume that scholars would be doing better work if we all just jettisoned the term "religion" and inserted some synonym, such as faith, to name what we presume to be the pre-colonial thing that is somehow still and always there. Instead, we'll see in both a tactical nimbleness that the ruling class of the nation-state allows itself, thereby understanding the lack of an articulate definition as well as the presumption of some real internal kernel as a feature rather than a bug in the governing system. For now, on a case-by-case basis, using differing criteria, all depending on the demands of each discrete occasion, some governmental action can be outlawed, because it was judged to be religious or impeded religion, or, instead, allowed, inasmuch as its possibly religious nature was conveniently defined out of existence.[65]

---

65 The examples of the tactical advantage to having no official definition are too numerous to mention, but consider a classic: the city's nativity scene, in the case of Lynch v. Donnelly, 465 US 668 (1984), was primarily understood by the US Supreme Court as an *economic* issue and there-

Before wrapping things up, consider one final example: recent developments in a subfield devoted to the study of belief and unbelief—as a place to see where some of the earlier-named issues all apply. I'll use as my example Lois Lee's *Recognizing the Non-Religious: Reimagining the Secular* (2017).[66] Lee, senior research fellow in the Department of Religious Studies at the University of Kent, is also the project lead on both the Scientific Study of Non-Religious Belief project at the University College London's Institute of Advanced Studies, as well as the Understanding Unbelief program at the University of Kent (both of which are recipients of large grants from the John Templeton Foundation). The co-editor of the online *Oxford Dictionary of Atheism* (2016) and co-founder of the Nonreligion and Secularity Research Network, Lee is a Cambridge-trained sociologist who divides her time between focusing on the study of religion/non-belief and public policy, with *Recognizing the Non-Religious* being the published from of her 2012 doctoral dissertation. If not already familiar with it, those interested in what she rightly characterizes as the fast-growing area of research on secularism and unbelief may welcome her aim to add some precision to what can, at times, appear to be a somewhat confusing research area (e.g., just what does an author mean by "the secular?"). Resisting the temptation to conclude, as some in our field have, that we have now entered a post-secular era, Lee instead tries to offer a more nuanced approach to studying what she considers to be varying types of secularism and, along with it, this thing that many scholars now call nonbelief as well.

Distinguishing between insubstantial and substantial secularism (i.e., between the absence of religion or lack of belief [what some mean by secularism] and that which is non- or possibly even proactively anti-religious—such as the difference between, as she puts it, "being *without* religion ... [and] being *with* something else" [5]), the book's argument lies in the results of recent polls in which the number of those some came to call the unaffiliated, or perhaps the Nones, was surprisingly large and, apparently, growing. This empirical research (e.g., the 2008 British Social Attitudes survey, which reported 37% of respondents to be non-religious) arrived a few years after the already-mentioned secularization thesis had fallen on hard times. Now the question was, or so it seems to me, whether those increasing numbers of people reporting being unaffiliated *undermined* the study of religion, by relieving us of our data and thereby confirming the secularization thesis, or, ironically, *re-invigorated* it inasmuch as those

---

fore not a first amendment issue, i.e., an incentive for people to come to the downtown to spend money during the holiday season rather than the city's endorsement of Christianity.

66 This example derives from a book review, of Lee's work, published in *Religion* (McCutcheon 2019).

attending church, as well as those not (whether or not they report being Spiritual But Not Religious [SBNR]), could all be seen as having what, say, Ninian Smart (and now Ann Taves) once characterized as a worldview. (After all, or so the reasoning goes, those self-identified atheists and agnostics more than likely believe all sorts of things that enable them to organize their worlds, act in them, and thereby live their lives in ways that they see as principled, consistent, or meaningful.) If scholars opt for the latter course, then those studying religion have just as much warrant to study nonreligion as anyone else. (Thus, the field is invigorated.)[67]

Here, by the way, we see how recent critiques of the category religion have been used by those in this growing subfield, inasmuch as the loss of its once-presumed essence and thus distinction from all nonreligious things, now enables those trained to study religion to examine all sorts of things that a previous generation of scholars might not even recognize as a legitimate place to do their work. So, given that it's the latter course (as identified above) that many scholars who study religion have by now taken, they've redefined just what they mean by their object of study and concluded that it's the *function* of the thing formerly known as religion that they actually study and, so along with religion, anything else serving that same world-building/meaning-making function (with a nod to Bill Paden's earlier work) is fair game. And thus, or so I would argue, we arrive back at the religion of baseball model of the field, whereby the critique of "religion" has been used to name even more things as religious.

As previous portions of this chapter should have by now made clear, I am not sympathetic to these developments. In fact, for some time (dating back to early conversations with my colleague, Steven Ramey, who developed his own critical interests in the literature on the Nones)[68] it has seemed to me that, had pollsters *not* posed just this or that question to respondents, we might never have known that there were Nones in need of study—making plain a point Craig Martin has forcefully argued concerning definitions, and thus objects of study, being directly tied to differing human interests (2019).[69] But the ques-

---

[67] Christopher Cotter's book, *The Critical Study of Non-Religion* (2020), stands out to me as being among the most interesting works in this still-growing subfield, inasmuch as its focus is on social actors' strategic use of these designations (religious versus non-religious).

[68] Consider the papers, including Ramey's own presentation, given at the 2013 AAR meeting in Baltimore, Maryland, filmed by Andie Alexander and collected together at https://vimeo.com/showcase/2643896.

[69] Following Edward Shiappa's lead (2003), Martin opts for "wetlands" as his example (2019, 167–8), demonstrating convincingly, to me, that drastically different things in the world *come to be known as* (and, importantly, protected from development) wetlands, all depending whether a

tion here—thinking of both Lee's title and that old nugget about that unaccompanied tree falling in the forest—is whether the unaffiliated were out there patiently waiting to be discovered or, instead, whether they were in fact constituted in the very posing of questions about church attendance and membership. This debate certainly won't be settled here, but it should be pointed out that, depending on how one responds to this choice, the now-significant body of scholarship that has grown around the study of such groups will come to be seen in rather different lights. For we all know, I assume, that, depending on the types of questions one includes in a survey instrument, let alone the way that they are each phrased, pollsters can arrive at all sorts of curious conclusions about the people they poll. So, for example, should we come to the supposedly empirical study of religion armed with "the 'conventional' Western understanding of religion ... as a theistic tradition" (as does Lee [see her glossary's definition (204)]—relying on what I'd characterize as an untheorized, directional qualifier that, as already noted, many of us still use despite Said's critique), then perhaps regular (and precisely *what* do we mean by that?) attendance at a service will (as it often has in the past) constitute the measure of affiliation, thereby helping us to *recognize* the previously undocumented existence of the unaffiliated who were staying home all along. But, given that all of this rests on our definition and starting place, that we may have just *constituted* (as opposed to *recognized*) our seemingly real, empirical object of study should not go unnoticed here (but, lamentably, it usually does, for we easily erase our fingerprints from the scene), as well as the fact that we've just *created* the basis for our own research projects inasmuch as we might now be concerned to study the puzzling fact that the unaffiliated nonetheless report holding views on, say, the afterlife. However—and this is the curious thing in all this, making evident, yet again, how key self-reflexivity could be to our work—had we approached this from the outset by defining religion as, let's say for argument's sake, someone who claims to hold beliefs in an afterlife (hardly an illegitimate definition), then the apparently empirical facts on the ground change quite a bit, since notion of affiliation as some "defining" characteristic utterly disappears and at least one scholarly quandary currently presented by the so-called SBNR along with it; for now many of the respondents distinguished from one another in the scholarly literature by means of our present taxonomies (i.e., those who came to a worship service versus those who stayed at home) might just end up counting as equally and uniformly religious, since

---

conservationist of the George W. Bush administration is using the term; this, by the way, is the "becoming" of which Touna speaks (2019, 179). Accordingly, posing the question "whose interests are being served by this particular definition?" is, Martin concludes, far better query than simply inquiring about "what is a wetland?".

their shared reports of believing in the afterlife override the supposed difference of their institutional affiliation.

But at this point, a second concern arises, one addressed earlier, for I think back to the wording that I just used: "someone who claims to hold beliefs ...." Taking seriously some current scholars' desire for empirical studies (which I read as a response to previous critiques of a past generation's grand theorizing and generalizing), I'd further argue that, as already noted, we never actually study those supposedly ethereal things that we sometimes term beliefs (a term surprisingly neither defined in Lee's glossary, by the way, nor included in her book's index); rather, observers infer their existence from studying the claims that people make in response to the scholar's queries and thus prompts (hearkening back to my earlier point—the sort of self-implicated point that some reflexive ethnographers realized a generation or so ago but of which we continually need to be reminded, it seems). Somewhat like David Hume's (to me at least) persuasive argument about causes, the seemingly commonsense things that we call beliefs can be redescribed as postulations that observers routinely make in their effort to make sense of what they hear people say and see them do, thereby presuming, in a suitably individualist manner, that some inner, coherent, and intentional ghost drives the machine that's doing things out there in the world. In agreement with Donald Lopez, in what I still consider to be an important chapter in Mark Taylor's edited *Critical Terms for Religious Studies* (1998), discourses on belief are best understood as an agonistic affirmation that functions as a boundary device, a verbal flag that we plant to mark who "we" are in distinction from "them." Or, to rephrase, we likely don't have beliefs spontaneously roaming around our heads (or, as noted earlier, in our hearts) until we're asked about them or until we are challenged and/or happen upon someone doing something other than what we have either been taught to do or have become accustomed to doing. And, voila, we suddenly employ this handy discourse on inner (and thus unassailable) sentiments to justify the difference being asserted—"Well..., *I for one believe* that ...."

If beliefs, identities, and questionnaires could be argued to have such a complexly intermixed existence, then I'm not sure what to make of the rapidly growing literature on unbelievers, the Nones, and SBNR. For only if one accepts the so-called conventional Western understanding of our object of study (much as cognitive science of religion scholars do as well, by the way—a development that should no less attract our attention),[70] thereby reproducing a certain commonsense view of the world that only some of us happen to have been raised

---

[70] See McCutcheon 2010 for my own thoughts on problems in the cognitive science of religion.

on, is some of this scholarship even possible. But, for those seeking to historicize these discourses, such work may very end up counting as but one more object of study, further evidence of how scholars at a specific point of time, in a specific place, tried to make sense of a world in which previously useful or at least dominant ways of organizing people and knowledge were in upheaval.

While one could certainly offer further examples for how the modern field, despite many of its critical gains, is largely but a revamped version of its earlier and more traditional self—something that readers who are better versed than I in yet other subfields within the study of religion may be able to do—let me conclude by citing a specific and recent example of the practical means by which critical scholarship is marginalized today.[71] So consider a moment in an online interview with the Duke University's David Morgan, then chair of their department, when he reveals far more than he might imagine:[72]

> Randall Stephens: How do you think theory should inform the study of American religion?
>
> David Morgan: Theory is a great tool, but a lousy end-in-itself. Honestly, I think theory-wonking is pointless. But there is nothing so consequential as the creative revelation that happens when a theoretical model allows us to see our evidence, our questions, and our field with new eyes. It's like waking from sleep. Suddenly, the world is much richer. So it is very important for doctoral students to endure theory seminars. It's a vital rite of passage. It shakes them up, challenges them to recognize the importance of the critical interrogation of the métier they are struggling to master. It's part of the disciplining that makes for good scholars.
>
> We should always read widely and we should be smartly challenged by our students and colleagues. Academics easily miss how dogmatic they can become. I see it all the time. The older we get, the less risky we become. Historians are among the worst in this regard. There is something about the work of historians that makes them theory averse. I'm not sure what it is. I guess they are so taken by their subject-matter and the often deft way they are able to write about it that they mistrust theoretical engagement. But we need not choose between good prose and theory. It is quite true that some of the worst writing

---

[71] Just as the current job market creates conditions in which critical scholarship on religion can be marginalized (as previously discussed), the conditions recently established by the prominence of scholars using social media to discuss their work deserves mention as well; for the very nature of the medium—i.e., pithy or even flippant "gotcha" comments that lack nuance and which are often read quickly or in passing, while a user scans a page for updates—makes caricatures of positions tempting to offer, as if they amount to a rebuttal. For instance, on too many occasions I have read rebuttals to so-called social constructionist positions in our field, posted on social media, that do little more than represent the position in the worst or most outrageous possible light, making it easy to dismiss or trivialize.

[72] This portion derives from a blog originally posted on December 13, 2013. Find it at https://religion.ua.edu/blog/2013/12/13/working-not-wonking/ (accessed September 13, 2019).

in the last century has come from high theory types. But that is no excuse to avoid their work.[73]

As I read it, Morgan—himself a well-known advocate for visual and material culture studies in the field (e.g., 2005)—is articulating a pretty standard realist view within our field: there's obvious stuff that we all know is out there (i.e., "our evidence" or the "subject-matter") and then there are the tools that we use to talk about it in this or that way, tools that may help us to see the it of our studies in a new light. The former is real and primary, whereas the latter is helpful, I guess, but we all know it's merely secondary and nonessential and an excessive focus on the latter can be detrimental to one's work. Thus, only studying the former counts, since people who study the latter are—yes, you read him right—theory-wonking, and thereby engaged in a "pointless" exercise.

This sort of characterization of the work with which one disagrees strikes me as a rather luxurious position to be able to adopt. Because, as someone who thinks of himself as doing work well outside the mainstream, it should be obvious that, despite my own rank in the field, I cannot dismiss (and if you read that quote as anything but an outright dismissal then I think that you're kidding yourself) people who study, say ..., religion and visual culture, by saying that, honestly, they're just descriptivist-wonks who do pointless work. (Even in a more informal online interview, one would likely have to elaborate far more than that for such a claim even to make sense to most readers.) What's more, what if I went on to say that it is quite true (luckily, truisms require no evidence—such as the still current truism that religion is about a deep feeling projected outward later ...) that some of the worst writing (and we all know what counts as the bad writing, right?) in the last century has come from people who do old-school phenomenology but repackage it as trendy "material religion" or "visual culture" and the like. But, as I might imagine myself going on, that's no excuse to avoid such work; so grad students beware: you really should figure out how to "endure"—that's right, endure, as in to undergo a trial, suffer through, persevere, tolerate, put up with—those material or embodied religion seminars because getting through them is a necessary rite of passage ....

No, I could never get away with saying something like that and, what's more, I hope that I would never resort to making such claims, for flippant and unsubstantiated generalizations strike me as undermining the profession, inasmuch as its legitimacy is, to my way of thinking, based on nuanced argumentation. But

---

[73] Find the interview here: http://usreligion.blogspot.com/2013/12/four-questions-with-david-morgan.html (accessed September 13, 2019).

the luxury of dominance ensures that you are exempted from this and so you can get away with off-the-cuff dismissals and the last thing anyone would call you is dogmatic and anti-intellectualist, let alone ask for some a wee bit of evidence and argumentation to support your claims. Instead, I'd conjecture that, to many readers, Morgan's words are probably read as showing an enviable command of the field and a benevolent generosity toward those whom "we" all already know to be, you guessed it, wonking.[74]

Now, I hope that it is obvious that I could not disagree more with Morgan's position. In a blog post from 2013, I tackled this very issue, as it once came out of the mouth of an old-school phenomenologist.[75] My post opened as follows:

> When I was a doctoral student, sometime in the late 1980s, I recall Will Oxtoby (d. 2003)—then a professor at the University of Toronto, member of my doctoral supervisory committee and, a few years later, editor of a very popular two volume world religions textbook—saying that theory was like a snowblower (using a suitably northern analogy to make his point); "it helps you to move things around," he said.

In reply to Oxtoby, I instead likened theory to a snowmaking machine at a ski resort,

> for without the device there is nothing to move around and no hills to be groomed. That is, I started with the assumption that the world does not actively pre-arrange and then present itself to our senses in neatly and naturally packaged units …. So theory is a word that I used not just for explanatory, causal accounts but for the self-conscious examination of the conditions … that make it possible to say that we know something about the world, that something in particular is significant and ought to be talked about.

I then concluded the post as follows:

> So without theory—without a self-consciously employed system to distinguish and then focus attention on a this as opposed to a that—there is, it seemed to me then and still does, nothing to sort through and arrange, for we have no way to mark anything as significant and worth talking about.

---

74 Wonk (noun): "overly studious person" (1962), earlier "effeminate male" (1954), American English student slang. Perhaps a shortening of British slang wonky "shaky, unreliable," or a variant of British slang wanker "masturbator." It seemed to rise into currency as a synonym for nerd late 1980s from Ivy League slang; see https://www.etymonline.com/word/wonk (accessed September 13, 2019).
75 See the July 2, 2013, post at https://edge.ua.edu/russell-mccutcheon/our-primary-expertise/ (accessed September 12, 2019). Portions of this section are derived from that post.

There is much riding, as I then concluded, on that notion of self-consciousness, for, as I already suggested earlier, it seems to me that a scholar's job is to take the usually taken-for-granted and thus unrecognized structures that allow people to arrange and navigate daily life (in the most mundane of ways, which makes them all the more interesting because of how taken for granted they become) and, by looking at them from an ironic distance, make of them items of conversation and debate by placing them alongside other things that we do, ideally doing so in unexpected or provocative ways, in order to see something new that we'd not known before.[76] This is likely why the work of the late Jonathan Z. Smith—who, through an odd quirk of administrative need, was himself a doctoral advisee of Oxtoby's when Smith wrote his (unpublished) 1969 Yale dissertation, "The Glory, Jest, and Riddle: James George Frazer and *The Golden Bough*" (see the preface [p. iii])[77]—has increasingly struck me, over the years, as being so important for a field that has never really shaken off the late-nineteenth century notion of animism (inasmuch as many scholars of religion still seem to presume that the world speaks to them in its own voice, of its own significance). As Smith famously wrote, over thirty years ago, in a portion of text usually quoted for rather different reasons, "the student of religion, ... must be relentlessly self-conscious. Indeed, this self-consciousness constitutes his primary expertise, his foremost object of study" (1982, ix).[78] There's something about those who see themselves as *working*, and not *wonking* (a change of just one consonant makes a considerable difference, does it not?) on the margins that makes them attuned to theory as the means of deciding what gets to count as subject matter and as evidence (or, according to Morgan's interview, who gets to count as a legitimate scholar). After all, as I've also pointed out on past occasions, anyone paying attention to a criminal or civil trial (let alone all those popular procedural cop dramas on Netflix) knows that the juiciest parts are the pretrial hearings, for that is *where they determine what gets to count as evidence*, i.e., what gets to count as something the lawyers can talk about and which the judge or jurors can even know about and thereby consider in coming to their decision; understandably, cases are often won or lost there and not during the trial. Self-conscious lawyers are mindful of this as they walk into court's first day.

---

[76] Which brings to mind Bruce Lincoln's tenth and eleventh theses on method (1996), both concerned with the reasons why the critical distance afforded by the comparative method is necessary for our work.

[77] See Braun and McCutcheon 2018, 47 on Oxtoby's role in Smith's general exams.

[78] I refer, of course, to the now (in)famous *"there is no data for religion"* line that occurs slightly earlier in this book's introduction, and which has (unfortunately, I'd suggest) earned far more attention than the lines just quoted.

So calling a focus on that same moment in scholarship—the means by which signification and identification take place, the set of assumptions that allow us to see ourselves as working in a field to begin with, and when we might contest the presumptions that we each bring to the table before ever getting on with the job of describing something—as pointless wonking is, it seems to me, merely dismissive name-calling that should be considered to be beneath the professional dignity of a scholar. Finding such an attitude throughout the field is then not only a lamentable commentary on the state of our art but, more importantly perhaps, it provides an occasion to examine in detail how what some of us take to be the gains that we've collectively made are curtailed at discrete sites in our profession, not because they are rigorously critiqued and shown to be wanting but because they have been so trivialized as to be ignored, all in the service of portraying a discredited old as new again.

But though the problems endure—ensuring that they will reappear, in some new guise, no sooner than they are critiqued[79]—I'm hopeful that a critical self-consciousness among those who see these gains as worth fighting for will be just as wily and even more resilient. For, in agreement with what Peggy Schmeiser argued in a 2017 paper, "this self-reflection and critique is imperative to the survival of our field and discourses" (2019, 127).

Reference List

Alles, Gregory D. 2019. "Private Money and the Study of Religions: Problems, Perils, and Possibilities." Unpublished paper presented to the annual meeting of the North American Association for the study of Religion, San Diego, CA.

American Academy of Religion. 2009. *AAR Religion Religious Literacy Guidelines: What U.S. College Graduates Need to Understand About Religion*. Atlanta, GA: American Academy of Religion. https://aarweb.org/AARMBR/AARMBR/Publications-and-News-/Guides-and-Best-Practices-/Teaching-and-Learning-/AAR-Religious-Literacy-Guidelines.aspx.

Armstrong, Karen. 1993. *A History of God: The 4,000-Year Quest of Judaism, Christianity, and Islam*. New York: Ballantine Books.

Armstrong, Karen. 2005. *A Short History of Myth*. Edinburgh: Canongate.

Arnal, William E., and Russell T. McCutcheon. 2012. *The Sacred Is the Profane: The Political Nature of "Religion."* New York: Oxford University Press.

Asprem, Egil, and Ann Taves. 2018. "Explanation and the Study of Religion." In *Method Today: Redescribing Approaches to the Study of Religion*, edited by Brad Stoddard, 132–57. Sheffield, UK: Equinox.

---

[79] See Rubenstein 2012, where the discourse on experience is aptly compared to a carnival game in which toy moles keep popping up out of their holes no matter how many times you've whacked them.

Baldwin, Matthew C. 2019. "Objects and Objections: Methodological Reflections on the Data for Religious Studies." In *Constructing "Data" in Religious Studies: Examining the Architecture of the Academy*, edited by Leslie Dorrough Smith, 73–100. Sheffield, UK: Equinox Publishers.

Bayart, Jean-François. (1996) 2005. *The Illusion of Cultural Identity*, trans. Steven Randall et al. Chicago: University of Chicago Press.

Borges, Jorge Luis. 1999. "Borges and I." In *Jorge Luis Borges: Collected Fictions*, trans. Andrew Hurley, 324. New York: Penguin.

Braun, Willi, and Russell T. McCutcheon, eds. 2018. *Reading Smith: Interviews and Essay*. New York and London: Oxford University Press.

Carp, Richard M. (2011) 2014. "Material Culture." In *The Routledge Handbook of Research Methods in the Study of Religion*, edited by Michael Staussberg and Steven Engler, 474–90. New York and London: Routledge.

Casanova, José. 1994. *Public Religion in the Modern World*. Chicago: University of Chicago Press.

Cotter, Christopher R. 2020. *The Critical Study of Non-Religion: Discourse, Identification and Locality*. London: Bloomsbury.

Cotter, Christopher R., and David G. Robertson, eds. 2016. *After World Religions Reconstructing Religious Studies*. New York and London: Routledge.

Crews, Emily. 2018. "Perhaps Action Enough." In *Method Today: Redescribing Approaches to the Study of Religion*, edited by Brad Stoddard, 114–8. Sheffield, UK: Equinox.

Crews, Emily, and Russell T. McCutcheon, eds. 2020. *Jonathan Z. Smith: A Career and its Consequence*. Sheffield: Equinox Publishers.

Cuthbertson, Ian Alexander. 2018. "Preaching to the Choir? Religious Studies and Religionization." In *Method Today: Redescribing Approaches to the Study of Religion*, edited by Brad Stoddard, 96–105. Sheffield, UK: Equinox.

Dew, Spencer. 2018. "'Constitutional God-Given Rights': Explaining Religion and Politics in the Malheur Occupation." In *Method Today: Redescribing Approaches to the Study of Religion*, edited by Brad Stoddard, 158–67. Sheffield, UK: Equinox.

Dubuisson, Daniel. 2019. *The Invention of Religion*, trans. Martha Cunningham. Sheffield, UK: Equinox Publishers.

Eliade, Mircea. 1961. "History of Religions and a New Humanism." *History of Religions* 1/1:1–8.

Eliade, Mircea. 1969. *The Quest: History and Meaning in Religion*. Chicago: University of Chicago Press.

Eliade, Mircea. (1958) 1996. *Patterns in Comparative Religion*, trans. Rosemary Sheed. Lincoln, NE: University of Nebraska Press.

Fitzgerald, Tim. 1996. "Religion, Philosophy and Family Resemblances." *Religion* 26/3:215–36.

Goldenberg, Naomi R. 2015. "The Category of Religion in the Technology of Governance: An Argument for Understanding Religions as Vestigial States." In *Religion as a Category of Governance and Sovereignty*, edited by Trevor Stack, Naomi Goldenberg and Timothy Fitzgerald, 280–92. Leiden: Brill.

Goldenberg, Naomi R. 2018. "Forget About Defining 'It': Reflections on Thinking Differently in Religious Studies." In *Method Today: Redescribing Approaches to the Study of Religion*, edited by Brad Stoddard, 79–95. Sheffield, UK: Equinox.

Graber, Jennifer. 2018. *The Gods of Indian Country: Religion and the Struggle for the American West.* New York and London: Oxford University Press.

Harvey, John. (2011) 2014. "Visual Culture." In *The Routledge Handbook of Research Methods in the Study of Religion*, edited by Michael Staussberg and Steven Engler, 502–22. New York and London: Routledge.

Hughes, Aaron W. 2012. *Abrahamic Religions: On the Uses and Abuses of History.* New York: Oxford University Press.

Hughes, Aaron W. 2017. *Theory in a Time of Excess: Beyond Reflection and Explanation in Religious Studies Scholarship.* Sheffield, UK: Equinox Publishers.

Hughes, Aaron W. "Reflections on 'Thinking with Jonathan Z. Smith.'" *Religious Studies Project* (blog). November 11, 2019. https://www.religiousstudiesproject.com/podcast/reflections-on-thinking-with-jonathan-z-smith/.

Hughes, Aaron W. 2020. *From Seminary to University: An Institutional History of the Study of Religion in Canada.* Toronto: University of Toronto Press.

Hughes, Aaron W., and Russell T. McCutcheon. 2019. "Epilogue: The Gatekeeping Rhetoric of Collegiality in the Study of Religion." In *Constructing "Data" in Religious Studies: Examining the Architecture of the Academy*, edited by Leslie Dorrough Smith, 267–90. Sheffield, UK: Equinox.

Johnston, Jay, and Kocku von Stuckrad, eds. 2021. *Discourse Research and Religion: Disciplinary Use and Interdisciplinary Dialogues*, 7–21. Berlin: Walter de Gruyter.

Josephson-Storm, Jason. 2018. *The Myth of Disenchantment: Magic, Modernity, and the Birth of the Human Sciences.* Chicago: University of Chicago Press.

Kavka, Martin, and Russell T. McCutcheon. 2017. "Justice, That Fraught Idea: A Response to 'The Normal and Abnormal.'" *Journal of the American Academy of Religion* 85/1:244–54.

Latour, Bruno. 1993. *We Have Never Been Modern*, trans. Catherine Porter. Cambridge, MA: Harvard University Press.

Lee, Lois (2015) 2017. *Recognizing the Non-Religious: Reimagining the Secular.* New York and London: Oxford University Press.

Lehrich, Christopher I. 2020. *Jonathan Z. Smith on Religion.* New York: Routledge.

Lincoln, Bruce. 1996. "Theses on Method." In *Method & Theory in the Study of Religion* 8:225–7.

Lopez, Donald. 1998. "Belief," In *Critical Terms for Religious Studies*, edited by Mark C. Taylor, 21–35. Chicago: University of Chicago Press.

LoRusso, James Dennis, ed. Forthcoming. *On the Subject of Religion: Charting the Fault Lines of a Field of Study.* Sheffield, UK: Equinox Publishing.

Luhrmann, Tanya. 2012. *When God Talks Back: Understanding the American Evangelical Relationship with God.* New York: Knopf.

Martin, Craig. 2019. "'The Thing Itself Always Steals Away': Scholars and the Constitution of Their Objects of Study." In *Constructing "Data" in Religious Studies: Examining the Architecture of the Academy*, edited by Leslie Dorrough Smith, 151–74. Sheffield, UK: Equinox Publishers.

Martin, Craig, and Russell T. McCutcheon, eds. 2014. *Religious Experience: A Reader.* New York and London: Routledge.

Martin, Luther H., and Donald Wiebe. 2012. "Religious Studies as a Scientific Discipline: The Persistence of a Delusion." *Journal of the American Academy of Religion* 80/3:587–97.

Martin, Luther H., and Donald Wiebe, eds. 2016. *Conversations and Controversies in the Scientific Study of Religion: Collaborative and Co-Authored Essays by Luther H. Martin and Donald Wiebe*. Leiden: Brill.

Marty, Martin E. 1998. "Public Religion." In *Encyclopedia of Religion and Society*, edited by William H. Swatos, 393–4. Walnut Creek, CA: AltaMira Press.

Masuzawa, Tomoko. 2005. *The Invention of World Religions Or, How European Universalism Was Preserved in the Language of Pluralism*. Chicago: University of Chicago Press.

McCutcheon, Russell T. 1997. *Manufacturing Religion: The Discourse on Sui Generis Religion and the Politics of Nostalgia*. New York: Oxford University Press.

McCutcheon, Russell T., ed. 1998. *The Insider/Outsider Problem: A Reader*. London: Cassell.

McCutcheon, Russell T. 2000. "The Imperial Dynamic in the Study of Religion: Neo-colonial Practices in an American Discipline." In *Postcolonial America*, edited by C. Richard King, 275–302. Champaign, IL: University of Illinois Press.

McCutcheon, Russell T. 2001. *Critics Not Caretakers: Redescribing the Public Study of Religion*. Albany, NY: State University of New York Press.

McCutcheon, Russell T. 2003. *The Discipline of Religion: Structure, Meaning, Rhetoric*. New York and London: Routledge.

McCutcheon, Russell T. 2004. "'Just Follow the Money': The Cold War, the Humanistic Study of Religion, and the Fallacy of Insufficient Cynicism." *Culture & Religion* 5/1:41–69.

McCutcheon, Russell T. 2005. *Religion and the Domestication of Dissent or, How to Live in a Less Than Perfect Nation*. New York and London: Routledge.

McCutcheon, Russell T. 2006. "A Response to Donald Wiebe from an East-Going Zax." *Temenos* 42/2:113–29.

McCutcheon, Russell T. 2010. "Will Your Cognitive Anchor Hold in the Storms of Culture?" *Journal of the American Academy of Religion* 78/4:1182–93.

McCutcheon, Russell T. 2012. "I Have a Hunch." *Method & Theory in the Study of Religion* 24/1:81–92.

McCutcheon, Russell T. (2010) 2014. "Religion Before 'Religion'?" In *Chasing Down Religion, In the Sights of History and the Cognitive Sciences: Essay in Honour of Luther H. Martin*, edited by Donald Wiebe and Panayotis Pachis, 285–301. Thessaloniki, Greece: Barbounakis Publications. Reprinted by Equinox Publishers.

McCutcheon, Russell T. 2015. "Afterword: Reinventing the Study of Religion in Alabama." In *Writing Religion: The Case for the Critical Study of Religion*, edited by Steven W. Ramey, 208–22. Tuscaloosa, AL: University of Alabama Press.

McCutcheon, Russell T. 2018a. *Fabricating Religion: Fanfare for the Common e.g.* Berlin: Walter de Gruyter.

McCutcheon, Russell T. 2018b. "On the Myth of Disenchantment." *Harvard Theological Review* 111/4:610–7.

McCutcheon, Russell T. 2018c. *"Religion" in Theory and Practice: Demystifying the Field for Burgeoning Academics*. Sheffield, UK: Equinox Publishers.

McCutcheon, Russell T. 2019. Review of Lois Lee, *Recognizing the Non-religious: Reimagining the Secular. Religion* 50/2:309–11.

McCutcheon, Russell T. 2021. "Learning to Code: Digital Pebbles and Institutional Ripples," In *Introduction to Digital Humanities: Research Methods in the Study of Religion*, edited by Christopher Cantwell and Kristian Petersen, 319–337. Berlin: Walter de Gruyter.

McDannell, Colleen. 1995. *Material Christianity: Religion and Popular Culture in America*. New Haven, CT: Yale University Press.

Morgan, David. 2005. *The Sacred Gaze: Religious Visual Culture in Theory and Practice*. Oakland, CA: University of California Press.

Nadeem, Mahomed, and Esack Farid. 2017. "The Normal and Abnormal: On the Politics of Being Muslim and Relating to Same-Sex Sexuality." *Journal of the American Academy of Religion* 85/1:224–43.

Nadeem, Mahomed, and Esack Farid. 2017. "A Rejoinder to 'Justice, That Fraught Idea.'" *Journal of the American Academy of Religion* 85/1:255–60.

Newton, Richard. "Racial Profiling?: Theorizing Essentialism, Whiteness, and Scripture in the Study of Religion." *Religion Compass*. Accessed July 21, 2020. https://onlinelibrary.wiley.com/doi/full/10.1111/rec3.12369.

Owen, Suzanne. 2011. "The World Religions Paradigm: Time for a Change." *Arts and Humanities in Higher Education* 10/3:253–68.

Peterson, Jordan. 1999. *Maps of Meaning: The Architecture of Belief*. New York and London: Routledge.

Plate, Brent. 2014. *A History of Religion in 5 1/2 Objects*. Boston, MA: Beacon Press.

Prothero, Stephen. 2008. *Religious Literacy: What Every American Needs to Know—And Doesn't*. New York: HarperCollins.

Ramey, Steven W. 2015a. "Accidental Favorites: The Implicit in the Study of Religion." In *Claiming Identity in the Study of Religion: Social and Rhetorical Techniques Examined*, edited by Monica Miller, 223–38. Sheffield, UK: Equinox Publishers.

Ramey, Steven W., ed. 2015b. *Writing Religion: The Case for the Critical Study of Religion*. Tuscaloosa, AL: University of Alabama Press.

Rosenhagen, Ulrich. "The Value of Teaching Religious Literacy." *The Chronicle of Higher Education*. December 2, 2015. Accessed September 16, 2019. https://www.chronicle.com/article/The-Value-of-Teaching/234393.

Rubenstein, Mary-Jane. 2012. "The Twilight of the Doxai: Or, How to Philosophize with a Whac-a-Mole(TM) Mallet." *Method & Theory in the Study of Religion* 24/1:64–70.

Shiappa, Edward. 2003. *Defining Reality: Definitions and the Politics of Meaning*. Carbondale, IL: Southern Illinois University Press.

Schmeiser, Peggy. 2019. "Governance and Public Policy as Critical Objects of Investigation in the Study of Religion." In *Constructing "Data" in Religious Studies: Examining the Architecture of the Academy*, edited by Leslie Dorrough Smith, 127–35. Sheffield, UK: Equinox Publishers.

Smith, Jonathan Z. 1969. "The Glory, Jest, and Riddle: James George Frazer and *The Golden Bough*." PhD dissertation. Yale University.

Smith, Jonathan Z. 1982. *Imagining Religion: From Babylon to Jonestown*. Chicago: University of Chicago Press.

Smith, Jonathan Z. 2004. *Relating Religion: Essays in the Study of Religion*. Chicago: University of Chicago Press.

Smith, Leslie Dorrough. 2019. "On the Grammar of Teaching Religious Studies." Unpublished paper presented to the annual meeting of the North American Association for the study of Religion. San Diego, CA.

Stoddard, Brad, and Craig Martin, eds. 2017. *Stereotyping Religion: Critiquing Clichés*. London: Bloomsbury.

Sullivan, Winifred. 2005. *The Impossibility of Religious Freedom*. Princeton, NJ: Princeton University Press.

Tong, M Adryael. 2019. "Categorization and its Discontents." In *Constructing "Data" in Religious Studies: Examining the Architecture of the Academy*, edited by Leslie Dorrough Smith, 38–47. Sheffield, UK: Equinox Publishers.

Touna, Vaia. 2017. *Fabrications of the Greek Past: Religion, Tradition, and the Making of Modern Identities*. Leiden: Brill.

Touna, Vaia. 2019. "Scholars and the Framing of Objects." In *Constructing "Data" in Religious Studies: Examining the Architecture of the Academy*, edited by Leslie Dorrough Smith, 175–82. Sheffield, UK: Equinox Publishers.

van Deusen, Nancy E. 2017. *Embodying the Sacred: Women Mystics in Seventeenth-Century Lima*. Durham, NC: Duke University Press.

von Stuckrad, Kocku. 2012. "Straw Men and Scientific Nostalgia: A Response to Luther H. Martin and Donald Wiebe." *Religio* 20/1:55–61.

Wiebe, Donald. 1999. *The Politics of Religious Studies: The Continuing Conflict with Theology in the Academy*. New York: St. Martin's Press.

Wiebe, Donald. 2005. "The Politics of Wishful Thinking? Disentangling the Role of the Scholar-Scientist from that of the Public Intellectual in the Modern Academic Study of Religion." *Temenos* 41/1:7–38.

Wiebe, Donald. 2016. "Questioning the Quality of the Quality Assurance Process in Ontario's Universities." *Academic Matters* May: 19–22. https://academicmatters.ca/questioning-quality-quality-assurance-process-ontarios-universities/.

Part II Critical Shift

2 Classification Matters or, Why You Should Care About Scholarship on the Category Religion

I have written this chapter with an intended audience in mind who might have better things to do than to stay up to date with the latest news from the academic study of religion—a field in which it is all the more challenging to stay current given that, in English alone, it goes by a variety of names, including religious studies, comparative religion, the history of religions, as well the academic study of religion, the science of religion and, most recently for some, the critical study of religion (or simply critical religion). Now, those who are just mildly aware of the field—and those with greater investments might have just perked up a bit at the mention of it being a *field*, inasmuch as there's an ongoing debate as to whether it is a cross-disciplinary field or a discipline, with North Americans generally favoring the former while many Europeans prefer the latter—might be reasonable to assume that by "debates" I mean the once-animated dispute over whether or not theology is properly considered to be a part of the study of religion (a dispute on which I was weaned while a graduate student, at the University of Toronto, in the late 1980s, what with one of my supervisors at the time, Donald Wiebe [himself a Lancaster PhD (1974), under the supervision of the late Ninian Smart], being among its most active participants). I say "once animated" because it strikes me that, though it is easy to find some people still discussing it, this is no longer an issue that defines the field; for, all depending on with whom you speak, it might become obvious that, yes, that particular battle has been won and so, of course, theology is but one more component of the study of religion (take, for example, the American Academy of Religion, the largest professional association in the US, and its explicit commitment to, as they [as well as many departments] routinely call it, "religious studies *and* theology" [emphasis added]). Or, directing your query to yet someone else (such as myself, for example), you might instead learn that this classic way of dividing up the pie, theology versus the scientific study of religion, is rather misguided inasmuch as classical humanistic approaches to the study of religion—though not explicitly theological, they tend to see in religion a site where the enduring, and therefore timeless, human spirit is creatively and meaningfully manifested—are, in my view, no less ahistorical and normative than are those identified as outright the-

---

Note: My thanks go also to Andie Alexander and Brent Nongbri for comments on an earlier draft of this chapter.

ology (regardless the brand), making it rather pointless to distinguish the two. And if you speak to those who, recalling a once but, in my assessment, no longer prominent understanding of science, aim for some sort of disembodied objectivity in their work, they'd likely lump my own work on the politics of classification systems in with those they'd refer to as theologians, thereby defining the field so narrowly as to exclude what many of us now do when we say that we're studying religion. All of this makes the once-prominent theology versus religious studies debate misleading at best. To rephrase: longstanding approaches to the field that see in religion but one more site where a disembodied thing called human nature expresses itself, let alone more recent approaches that find in religion a cognitive puzzle to be solved by appeals to psychology, genetics, and brain sciences, are, to my way of thinking, both just as troublesome as are approaches aimed at discerning how some timeless and universal thing called the sacred is supposedly manifested first here and then there (an approach associated with the work of the late Mircea Eliade, of course, but one which, I'd argue, is just as prominent today in so-called lived or material religion approaches). For, in all of these cases, scholars take a rather modern designator—the very word religion itself—and the things that we commonly use it to name, as obvious and self-evident, as if they are all naturally and thus properly distinguishable from other things in our lives. And it is this matter of distinction, and the practical implications that come with it, that has recently drawn the interest of a growing number of scholars. So, to return to where I started: those who haven't been carefully monitoring developments in the field might not be aware that far more than an argument over the place of theology has been taking place in the study of religion over the past few decades.

I'll therefore take the occasion of this chapter as an opportunity not just to summarize some of these more recent debates in the field but also to translate their significance to readers who, not unlike many of our colleagues, may assume that the study of religion is, predictably perhaps, all about studying religion (by which I mean describing the worldwide diversity and similarities among people's beliefs and practices). What I hope will become apparent throughout is that, at least for some of us, an important shift over the last decade or two has been the realization that *the study of religion isn't really about religion at all*, whatever that may or may not be defined as being (since there are almost as many definitions of religion as there are definers, no?). Instead, freed initially by a strong critique of what we used to call *sui generis* religion (that old but powerful idea that religion was utterly unique and therefore couldn't be understood correctly as *anything but religion*), some have now concluded that the study of the things designated as religion is but an example—an e.g., citing the late Jonathan Z. Smith's preferred phrasing—useful in studying *people:* what they say, what they do, how they organize, and what they leave behind after they're done saying and doing and organizing. And among the curious things that some of those people do is to make claims about a subset of their sayings, their doings, their relics, and their organizations being somehow set apart from all others, something marked by calling them "religious." Thus—and again, for some of us in the field today—the study of religion offers an opportunity to study how people classify, rank, organize, and thereby come to know and act in the worlds that classifying something *as* religious helps to establish and then represent as persuasive and authoritative—a system no doubt linked to other common and everyday distinctions as us/them, in/out, private/public, safe/dangerous, citizen/foreigner, allowed/disallowed, and, yes, sacred/profane. And so, with all of that having been said, I would hope that this chapter's title now makes just a little more sense, for not only do I think that classification systems matter—that is, have practical consequences, making them far more than just mere names that we only later attach to things—but also that those who are not deeply immersed in at least some current developments in the study of religion may come to see it as a particularly good place to illustrate and explore this point, making plain, once again, that the study of religion isn't really about religion.

Now, again appealing to those with just a passing acquaintance with the field, the position that I've just outlined may sound rather counterintuitive. After all, many of us likely just assume that we all know what religion is, feeling quite comfortable using the term to carve up our day-to-day world at what we generally presume to be its joints (recalling that famous line from Plato's *Phaedrus* [265d–266a]); and so, like that associate justice of the US Supreme Court talking about obscenity, we all more than likely think that we know it when we see it. (I'm here citing the words of Potter Stewart, of course, in the well-known case of Jacobellis v. Ohio [1964], which reversed a lower court's conviction of a movie theatre manager who had been charged with possessing and exhibiting obscenity by showing Louis Malle's then-provocative 1958 film, "Les Amants.") Thus, a newspaper with a religion section that's set apart from the local political or sports stories, not to mention the personals and the want ads, surely makes good sense to many of us, as does the ability for a town council to treat a bowling alley, a pub, or a hospital as somehow different from a mosque, a church, a temple, or a synagogue—with the latter grouping striking us as naming the members of an obviously common class of items, given something that they apparently all share (with us coming up with the name "houses of worship" to name them all). In fact, our knowledge of religion—dare I call it folk knowledge, and risk inviting you to see yourselves and your own commonsense practices as our object of study?—is so firmly established that we might greet as absurd anyone who wishes to argue that just because we're accustomed to calling certain things religions this taxonomic habit doesn't make them any more religious than anything else.

What should by now be clear is that my hope is to persuade readers that such a counterintuitive approach is not absurd at all. Quite to the contrary. Say we start from the position that sees not religion but the *discourse* on religion—which encompasses both the word itself along with the vocabulary associated with calling something a religion (by which I include such signifiers as faith, belief, experience, tradition, myth, ritual, magic, superstition, etc.) as well as the practices and institutions that help us to take this thing we call religion for granted as an item of our intellectual and social landscape. Starting from the position that sees not religion but the *discourse* on religion as a fairly recent historical occurrence of practical effect allows us to ask a whole new set of questions about how people like us continually create, govern, and police the usually taken-for-granted environments in which we live our lives, arrange our affairs, distribute our resources, and establish and contest our identities, doing so by designating and then treating certain things in the past or present *as* religion.

In order to make this argument, I'll presume that a once (and, no doubt for some, still) dominant version of the field (that I've already critiqued in detail in the previous chapter) is known to you—the one in which the study of religion is understood as descriptively chronicling, at a variety of places and times, the many variants of an inherent trait of the human, usually represented as an internal feeling or private experience that, sooner or later, is expressed outwardly by means of those things commonly called myths, rituals, and traditions. Being comparative at its heart—hence the choice of comparative religion for the field's early name in the English-speaking world—scholars in this vein aimed to look beyond the evident differences to find the universal sameness that they presumed to be the basis for all religion, which, in turn, was assumed to provide insight into our most basic and thus universally shared humanness. Now, some of you may already know that comparative religion, as it was once called, was a colonial exercise of the late-nineteenth century, something identified by a variety of recent scholars. But what you may not have considered is that today's still-prominent world religions class and textbook genre, not to mention current calls to enhance so-called religious literacy, can be understood as a survival, in the classic anthropological sense, of that much-earlier age of expansion, when reports from euphemistically labeled "explorers" and "missionaries" concerning the alien and exotic customs they encountered in the colonies made their way back to curious minds in European centers of learning, reports that challenged the leading thinkers of the time (not to mention the politicians and the people once in charge of the business world) to figure out how "us" and "them" were (or, as they so often concluded, were not) related to one another. With the invention of the category of world religions (first originated by later-nineteenth century Dutch and German theologians, but quickly adopted by others), our intellectual predecessors were able to distinguish what were understood as merely national or ethnic religions from those that had successfully spread worldwide (making their way from "them" to "us," as it were). Thus, a modern, global, organizational concept was born that, though the rationale of its use has certainly changed over the past century or more, still allows us to group together otherwise diverse and separated (whether in space or time) people, places, and things in terms of what we interpret as their universally shared philosophically idealist content—simply put, because we seem to have decided that people first of all *believe* things (about such things as gods and ancestors, about something ethereal that outlasts the individual's body, about the beginning of the universe and the end of time, and about the reason we're all here—what Douglas Adams succinctly summed up as life, the universe, and everything). Then, second, because we've apparently concluded that these same people then act out their prior beliefs in unique public ways (via such things as ceremonies, rituals, and myths), it's seen as not just worthwhile to group together all the similar-looking systems that result from these two assumptions (and thus something called Hinduism is not just born but can be spoken of in the very same breath as something called Judaism or Islam) but, as part of that same sorting and grouping activity, we've also decided that it's a good idea to separate them all, as a group, from what we see as the far more ambiguous world of politics and history, given the generally agreed upon timelessness and purity of the former and the contingent messiness of the latter.

So, presuming that, like most members of our own society, you're up to speed on the common usage of the general term religion, or using the more particular term world religions, let alone the way that we make claims about the supposedly uniform identity, across changing time and place, of the members of that family (e.g., Buddhists believe X, Christians do Y, and Sikhs wear Z, etc.), what you may not know is that, beginning an academic generation or so ago, some scholars started to rethink these almost self-evident assumptions and conclusions in rather significant ways. Now, by this I don't mean the influential work of the late Wilfred Cantwell Smith (who died in 2000, having played a foundational role in both McGill's program in our field, in Canada, as well as Harvard's). Although his early 1960s project did indeed critique the category religion, it did so in order to replace it with a term that, or so he argued, was even better for naming the unique thing that he somehow already knew to be in need of a name. For those unaware of his work, Cantwell Smith, in a book entitled *The Meaning and End of Religion*, argued that our common, Latin-derived word, religion, inappropriately named what he claimed to be two separate things: the initial experience or, as he preferred to call it, faith in transcendence, as well as the tradition that resulted and accumulated only later, deriving from the eventual expression of that prior faith; calling it all religion, or so he concluded, incorrectly conflated the original cause with the secondary effect. Calling into question Cantwell Smith's undefended assumption that there was some self-evidently distinguishable kernel inhabiting the heart of that class of objects known as religions, the scholars whom I have in mind went looking elsewhere for their inspiration—finding it in the work of social theorists interested in how groups are formed. I'm referring to a scholarly tradition into which I place myself, one that resulted, eventually, with the work of Tomoko Masuzawa in the US (such as her 2005 book *The Invention of World Religions*) as well as the current work of such people as Naomi Goldenberg in Canada, Tim Fitzgerald, Malory Nye, Suzanne Owen, and Richard King in the UK, Teemu Taira in Finland, or Brent Nongbri, now in Norway, not to mention some of the authors collected together by Christopher Cotter and David Robertson (the founders of the Religious Studies Project podcast, by the way) in their 2016 edited volume, *After World Religions*. Although it's not difficult to find scholars who criticize our current use of the world religions category for being too narrow and thereby excluding other things that they somehow know to rightly need a place within it (such as Pagan religions or indigenous religions), the group that I'm describing takes a rather different approach, one that is nicely summed up by the subtitle of Masuzawa's book: *How European Universalism Was Preserved in the Language of Pluralism*. For, unlike Cantwell Smith, these scholars are not looking for the correct or a better way to name the thing formerly known as religion but, instead, are interested in our very tendency—noting that it is a very specific "we" who betray this tendency, by the way, given that the word or concept of religion is hardly universal among humankind—of assuming that a clearly delineated subset of human claims, actions, and organizations *ought* to be distinguished from all others by being represented as somehow having austere, serene, or pristine origins or contemporary uses. (I think here of the interest of Vaia Touna, my colleague at Alabama, in the practice of labeling certain things in the ancient world *as* religious.) Starting instead from the assumption that *all* human claims, practices, and institutions are inextricably part of situated history (by which I mean, building on the work of the late French scholar, Roland Barthes, the world of contingency and happenstance, where no social actor possesses the omniscience of a novel's narrator and all claims and associations are contestable and invested), these scholars became intrigued that social actors sometimes invoke the voice of another, as in attributing some practice to "tradition," let alone "the gods" or maybe even "the law," but inevitably doing so in their own voice, since it's the only one that we've got. (I think here of the 1970s US comedian Flip Wilson [d. 1998] and his once-iconic character Geraldine, who, having made a transgression of some sort, regularly exclaimed, "The devil made me do it.") This double-speak, if we can call it that (or perhaps ventriloquism is a more apt analogy?), struck some scholars as a way of disowning the situation and interests that routinely animate our claims, not unlike how someone grading essays might draw attention to a writer's use of the passive voice, which removes agency and thus accountability from the narrative, such that saying "someone was hit by a car" seems to imply that the car somehow did it on its own. Seeing representations of invariably historical claims and practices as if just some of them could be grouped together as uniquely distinguishable from all others as itself being an effective authorizing technique that, if it works, transforms the contingent into the necessary and the debatable into the authoritative, the scholars to whom I'm referring concluded not only that Geraldine's attribution of agency to the devil (if you recall Flip Wilson's routine, mentioned just a bit ago) was—pretty obviously, I guess—a handy way to dodge the implications of her own choices, but also that the designation of certain claims, practices, and institution, whether now or in the recent or distance past, *as* religious, *as* sacred, or *as* spiritual *has the same privileging effect* for the claims, practices, and institutions so named. For, at least as it has developed in European- and then North-American-derived, modern liberal democracies, the term, though commonplace in folk discourse, is actually a technical legal category, one that is enshrined in governance documents and which therefore comes with a variety of practical benefits, such that an uncontested claim that some disclosure, item, action, or group is religious results in a privilege for those engaging in it—such as the widespread practice of classifying such institutions as churches, at least for the purpose of taxation, as nonprofits instead of as businesses.

Now, you may have caught that I just made reference to something happening *if* claims worked and *if* they go uncontested, something that reminds us that, should we always see them as historically situated, such claims should be understood as *always* being contestable, inasmuch as they originate from but one of almost innumerable positions that an interested and invested social actor might occupy—something not all that apparent when we hear someone say, "God demands," "The Constitution says ...," or even "Tradition dictates ...." But, again starting from the assumption that what we study is always human, and thus contingent and situated through and through, means that we, as scholars, will continually look for the authorizing mechanisms that allow *this* to be seen as persuasive over *that*—that is, the devises whereby the many ways of doing something are policed and narrowed to *just these* practices and *just these* institutions or, in a word, the production of those continually tweaked conventions that we come to represent as authoritative, uniform, and timeless *traditions*.

If you've stuck with me so far, and if the sort of work that I've been describing is either somewhat or completely new to you, then you may need a practical example or two to see the relevance of this shift in scholarship that I've been describing. Hearing that the very designation or treatment of something *as* religious, *as* sacred, is one among many socially formative techniques of governance used to make a certain sort of mundane, day-to-day life possible and persuasive can sound rather abstract; and, given how firmly committed many of us are to instead understanding these designations to be inherently linked to some unique feature of the items so named, well, as already indicated, this alternate position can seem counterintuitive, at best, or maybe even a little absurd. For who would be prepared to see, let's just say, a church as just another social institution within a community, one among many others, all of which are working to normalize certain sorts of social relations, in competition with other institutions which are themselves trying to establish yet other ways of arranging social life ...? (Come to think of it, those organizations called churches are awfully interested in such seemingly mundane things as who you can marry, when you can have sex, when children should be treated as adults, etc.) So, while I could invite you to consider, for example, a 1984 US Supreme Court decision in which the court decided that it was allowable for public funds to be used to set up and maintain what was pretty obviously an explicitly Christian nativity scene in the downtown shopping district during the Christmas season (the already-mentioned case of Lynch v. Donnelly 465 US 668). Why? Although the US Constitution's First Amendment makes pretty clear what some, echoing the text of a letter written by Thomas Jefferson, have called a wall of separation between church and state (a wall that, in practice, is far more porous than you might at first imagine), the crèche was characterized by the justices as being more *economic* than *religious*, given that it was part of a wider (dare we say secular?) effort to attract shoppers to the downtown, "to let loose with their money," as a witness, quoted in the Court's decision, had phrased it. But instead, I'll cite some more recent and maybe more relevant examples in which the social management taking place via the category religion (a way that our societies rules things as being either in or out of bounds) may be a little more familiar and thus a little curious to you.

So consider Asma Uddin's 2019 book, *When Islam Is Not a Religion: Inside America's Fight for Religious Freedom*. Anyone familiar with European and North American news over the past few decades—not to mention other parts of the world, such as what's going on, since about 2014, in China with the Uyghur population, let alone the ways in which Islam has been represented over the past several hundred years throughout Europe—will know that politicians, journalists, and intellectuals alike have expended considerable energy to normalize a certain type of Islam (one that is seen to be in-step with so-called liberal democratic values, such as tolerance) in opposition to a type that is seen to be in direct (and, at times, violent) competition with the so-called West. (That the West/East distinction is itself among the management tools used in these disputes should be obvious to anyone who read, and retained, their Edward Said, by the way—making it a no less socially formative, and not merely descriptive, designation. Sadly, though, I see this distinction often used today by scholars, with little to no nuance.) Thus the terms "political Islam" and "Muslim extremism" were born, as normative ways to distinguish certain sorts of Muslims from others, under the presumption that Islam, being a religion, ought properly to inspire only inner emotions and quietist dispositions; variations from that norm, whether Muslims in Europe or the Middle East or even Buddhists in Indonesia, are candidates for the designation "terrorist," inasmuch as their practitioners are portrayed as "appropriating" or, more popularly, "hijacking" the religion in question. Uddin's book, focused on cases in the US, examines wholesale efforts to discount Islam as a religion, such as movements to deny building permits for mosques in various parts of the country, such as the case of the Islamic Center of Murfreesboro, Tennessee, which, back in 2010, sought to expand its facility. Given the manner in which the so-called free exercise clause of the US Constitution's First Amendment is understood to ensure that government remove itself from its citizens' religious lives—"Congress shall make no law respecting an establishment of religion or prohibiting the free exercise thereof ..."—losing the designation of religion would lead to the loss of some pretty obvious benefits for Muslims in the US, such as the equal protections clause of the Constitution (i.e., the Fourteenth Amendment) no longer applying, let alone possibly changing their status with regards to human-rights protections, making it possible to legally discriminate and deny services to them. As already referenced, this all hinges on the role this word religion plays in the US government's founding document, prompting us to distinguish between how people might use the term religion in daily life as opposed to how it functions as a governing category in law. Uddin's book, then, is a handy catalogue of recently devised tactics, on the part of some, to manage Islam within the US by representing it instead as a dangerous political ideology intent on undermining the rule of law.

But what I find most interesting is how, in a recent interview with this author that was posted at the Religious Studies Project (on June 24, 2019), the interviewer seems incapable of understanding the category "religion" to function in precisely this manner—something more than apparent to those who went to court to stop the expansion of the Islamic Center's facility, by the way, since they saw undermining the linkage between Islam and its status as a religion as an effective way to oppose their neighbors' different way of life. Instead, I'm guessing that the interviewer more than likely assumes that the word religion names some obvious feature or aspect that Islam, of course, shares in common with all of those other things that we call religion. For, while discussing the 2010 court hearing in the case of the Islamic Center of Murfreesboro's desire to expand its building, Uddin said:

> in the course of that six-day hearing it was argued very explicitly ... , and there's always been a long time when these arguments have implicitly been made that Islam is not a religion, but these words were actually stated in court. And the argument was, essentially, that all the different protections that houses of worship get under the law do not apply in that case because Islam is not a religion.

To which the interviewer, Benjamin Marcus (himself at the Religious Freedom Center in Washington, DC, working on religious literacy initiatives) replied, sounding somewhat incredulous, "And, I assume that .... Did the judge say anything, provide any good questions ... that would try to undermine that argument? Or did the judge just let that go forward unchallenged?" Here is the moment where I think we see the practical, governance effects of the category religion in a liberal democracy bumping up against the commonsense understanding of religion that operates in much of our day-to-day lives, for the interviewer just naturally seems to assume that the judge *should* intervene in such an argument—"I assume that ... " he starts off, after all, making plain the expectation that a judge *ought* to be undermining or challenging this position (though he catches himself and revises his initial declarative statement by reinventing it as a question). And after Uddin outlines some of the "outrageous questions" posed in that courtroom to defendants by the critics of the mosque, Marcus adds, "Wow! So what do you find most alarming about this move to redefine Islam as something other than a religion ...?" Now, while you may all probably agree that Islam *is* a religion, I would hope that you would not greet all this with a "Wow!" but, instead, see in both your own classificatory agreement as well as this one episode from Tennessee two instances of social actors strategically using what is at hand—in this case, a designation with practical, legal consequences—to achieve either a variety of social goals (whether your own or those of but one of Murfreesboro's rather conservative subgroups), thereby seeing the category religion as an organizational tool that, when awarded, brings benefits and, when withheld, denies protections. To repeat: although *you* may wish those privileges to extend to the Muslims members of the city of Murfreesboro, this does not mean that it is not worth understanding how the tug and pull of social life within a group is negotiated and managed *by means of this common designation.* (Aside: the new Murfreesboro Islamic Center opened on August 10, 2012, after the US federal government's Department of Justice intervened, and on June 2, 2014, the US Supreme Court declined taking the opponents' request to appeal, putting an end to the legal dispute.)

And so, as I noted earlier, studying religion is not really about religion at all; instead, as made pretty evident in this case from the American South, studying how this category religion is used, in seemingly mundane day-to-day situations, is all about how societies establish and contest themselves.

As a second example—with a nod to the US Supreme Court decision involving the nativity scene that I mentioned just a bit ago—consider those occasions when the benefits come *not* from bestowing but, instead, from withholding the category religion. Now, so far I've proposed that, in liberal democracies such as our own, the category, once entrenched in law, as it often is, provides a mechanism to privilege certain sorts of claims or behaviors among others. But that's only half of the story, because, as with all privileges, such benefits come at a price. The question is whether a community is willing to pay that price in exchange for the perks that being designated as a religion entail. I think here of historic commissions that exist in many towns, those bodies that decide on which neighborhoods or even which buildings will be awarded a status that sets them apart from all others, inasmuch as they are said to represent the history of the community. While such designations are generally seen as prizes to be won, they also mean that changes to your home, whether repairs or renovations, must now meet the expectations of a committee, concerning such things as allowable exterior paint colors or types of roof shingles. (I recall here the April 27, 2011, tornado that tore through my own city and, at least as compared to us and the damage to our little home at the time, the difficulties and limitations that a friend had in fixing their home, given that, unlike our own, it was on the city's so-called historic register.) While this might be a small price to pay for the additional home value entailed in such listings, it nicely illustrates that no benefit is free of cost—so too in the case of the category religion; for once this designation is bestowed, a variety of practices might be allowable—practices that, in regular social life, might not—but one can only engage in them in a rather strictly policed manner, concerning when and where and who gets to do it (whatever the it is). Sure, in the US, the Afro-Caribbean syncretistic tradition known as Santeria was designated as a religion in another famous US Supreme Court decision (1993's Church of the Lukumi Babalu Aye, Inc. v. Hialeah, 508 US 520), but that doesn't mean that members can indiscriminately kill (i.e., sacrifice) chickens, anywhere and anytime they like. No, but they *can* do it as part of their ceremonies, at specific times and in specific places, free from the sorts of animal cruelty and food handling laws that might govern slaughtering chickens otherwise.

So if benefits and costs attend such designations, it might be incorrect only to assume that being called a religion is beneficial; perhaps, as suggested in the case of the nativity scene, the benefit sometimes comes from *not* being a religion (for, in that case from Rhode Island, the dominant group in the city got to have seasonal symbols displayed at the public's expense, but only when they were understood as economic instead of religious). And so, with historic commissions in mind, especially given that they are sometimes called heritage sites (I think here of everything from the English Heritage Trust, a charity that runs a variety of historic sites throughout the country, to the small town of, say, Cleveland, Mississippi, whose Heritage Commission ensures that, according to their website, the "[p]roperty owners within Crosstie Historic District enjoy the advantages of increased economic value and a built environment protected from unsympathetic changes"), I turn to my second example: the manner in which things others might routinely call "religious" can be strategically redefined as "heritage" or even culture when dominant groups within communities seek to banish something called religion from public space but without undermining their own interests. What I have in mind here can be exemplified in a wide variety of places, from the heritage signified by the wooden crucifix, complete with a crucified Jesus on it, that still hung for some time above the speaker's chair in the legislature of the Province of Quebec, in Canada, despite the pending secularism legislation introduced by the provincial government. (That it was eventually removed in June 2019 is a testament to the limits to which such classificatory schemes can sometimes be stretched.) Known as Bill 21 l, it bans public employees from wearing overt religious symbols during work hours. (This past June, however, it was reported that this and other crosses, hanging in Quebec courts, would come down once the bill becomes law, in June 2020—but we'll see if that happens ...; it is a bill, by the way, that has been strongly criticized by others in the country.) I could easily add to this list: as but one example, consider the German region of Bavaria, where crosses are now considered part of their cultural heritage and not as religious symbols, thereby allowing the government to mandate that, as of June 2018, Christian crosses be placed prominently in all public offices while other people's religious symbols are banned from the public space. That some church leaders see this as a crass appropriation by the state of their own religious symbols adds complexity to the example, of course, demonstrating nicely that the authority that results from our efforts to set things (and people) apart is itself contestable. But my larger point concerns how this artful redefinition (by the invention of such qualified designators as "conspicuous religious symbols," which function similarly to "political Islam") allows a dominant group to display only its treasured identity markers, at a taxpayers' expense that's shared by all, while still allowing them to portray themselves as tolerant and thereby respecting that much celebrated liberal value of religious diversity—all by, at least in this case, artfully withholding the designation religion from their own treasures.

I know that this is only two brief examples—though there are so many more we could draw upon, such as the current practice of attributing religious motives to one's desire to, for example, deny services to customers with whose lifestyles one disagrees, so as to steer clear of otherwise relevant anti-discrimination laws or how people can designate their refusal to give their children vaccines as being based on a "sincerely held religious belief." (I think here of recent efforts in the US to overturn Obama-era protections and instead allow "faith-based adoption organizations" to deny LGBTQ couples the right to adopt children.) What I hope to have demonstrated by means of these examples is that the category has utility in this modern world of ours, *not*, as many might at first think, for naming something ethereal and thereby inherent to the items being named as such but, rather, for walling things off from one another, so as to promote or demote them in relation to other things in society, all depending on the social interests of the speaker. Making this shift in how we understand this category to work—from assuming that it names some prior religious identity to seeing it as identifying for a variety of socially formative purposes—is part of what Daniel Dubuisson, on the opening page of his most recent English book, *The Invention of Religions* (2019), has called a "veritable scientific revolution ... in the departments of 'Religious Studies' in many North American universities along with some of their British counterparts." That this revolution is largely unknown to people outside the field is something that I've sought to correct here, by trying to make evident that how we name and organize our worlds not only matters —something that's pretty evident to almost anyone when they consider themselves to have been mis-identified in some manner—but that this can be illustrated by our usually taken-for-granted habit of giving so-called religious names to things that can be understood in a variety of other ways (inviting us to consider precisely what is to be gained by adding that adjective "religious" as a qualifier to their names). That the category religion is up to something, making it not just a neutral descriptor of obvious spiritual and thus apolitical, otherworldly states and dispositions, is all I've hoped to persuade you of—and I mean here *all* of its uses, and not just some that we judge (and dismiss) as crass or insincere—something you might recall the next time you see the term in even its most benign uses, thereby making you just a little curious about what all might be going on when we extract things from our everyday, mundane, and historical lives by ascribing to them religious names, sacred identities, and thus timeless and uncontestable value.

3 Shifting From Experience to the Discourse on Experience

> In the evening, I went very unwillingly to a society in Aldersgate Street, where one was reading Luther's Preface to the Epistle to the Romans. About a quarter before nine, while he was describing the change which God works in the heart through faith in Christ, I felt my heart strangely warmed. I felt I did trust in Christ, Christ alone for salvation; and an assurance was given me that he had taken away *my* sins, even *mine*, and saved *me* from the law of sin and death. (Wesley 1988, 249–50)

These are the familiar words attributed to John Wesley (1703–1791), in what scholars call his conversion narrative, concerning an experience that reportedly took place during a meeting (somewhat like what we'd refer to as a modern-day Bible study) in London on the evening of Wednesday, May 24, 1738. At that time, Wesley, the son of a minister, was himself a Church of England minister who had recently returned from a (not altogether successful) three-year assignment as a missionary in Savannah, Georgia (at that time a British colonial possession). Reporting that he had "continual sorrow and heaviness of heart" on the days preceding that evening meeting in late May, Wesley recounts in this famous journal entry how—as that evening's speaker was addressing Martin Luther's commentary on Paul's letter (or, from the Greek, epistle) to the early Christians who were in Rome—he had experienced a "strange warming" of his heart—a phrase that has become rather famous since then, especially among historians of Methodism, the originally British but now worldwide Protestant denomination that John and his younger brother Charles (1707–1788) went on to establish. According to his journal, this sentiment or feeling—something which, in this tradition, is clearly differentiated from the cognitive content of knowledge, often termed "belief"—was followed by John Wesley's awareness of the role that Jesus Christ had played, through his life, death, and resurrection, in guaranteeing Wesley's own salvation from, as he puts it, "the law of sin and death."

Although many other examples could be supplied, we have here one of the better-known accounts of an interior sentiment or affectation (that is, an experience, a feeling, or an emotion—hardly synonyms, to be sure, but all used to name this pre-social perception) that, to the person who reports having had it, defies explanation. It carries with it what they might describe as a fullness or an immediacy of awareness that, or so the reports usually go, makes it stand out as unique and thus distinguishable from the other sorts of sensations that people regularly report having—such as the experience of hunger, thirst, joy, boredom, or even fear. Despite what insiders from a variety of cultures may call such exemplary moments in their awareness—if they do in fact possess a framework within which such things not only count *as* things worth paying attention to but also stand out as worth reporting—in the academic study of religion scholars commonly call such sentiments "religious experiences," and those who study them have, for some time, been interested in comparing such reports, looking for the various cross-cultural and trans-historical similarities and differences in the content and form of such reported experiences, in hopes of drawing conclusions about either how religion works or how the human brain does.[1]

So, with this initial piece of data in hand—our data being Wesley's journal entry concerning the "strange warming" of his heart—a simple question presents itself: what are we to do with the fact that some people report having had such experiences? Moreover, just what *is* an experience and what sense does it make to talk, as many scholars do, about such things as *unmediated experiences*—that is, internal states or dispositions that apparently result from nothing observable in the empirical world (unlike, say, the experience of heat which is presumably *mediated* by sensory preceptors and neurons as you grab the hot handle on the frying pan)? For that matter, what *is* a strange warming of the heart? What might cause it? Come to think of it, what does it mean to have a heavy heart? Was Wesley speaking metaphorically (better put, *writing* metaphorically, for all we have is a text and no one is actually speaking here—an important point to which we will return), as in when people commonly associate their heart with emotions, such as claiming to have a broken heart? Or was he speaking literally about sensations taking place in his upper chest, as in when people today talk about experiencing heartburn (which certainly does not involve the heart at all)? Somehow, I suspect that the latter doesn't quite capture what Wesley was trying to put onto paper—though, could physiological or physiological studies help shed light on what *caused* his experience? After all, as the noted US neurologist Oliver Sacks once phrased it, "with no disrespect to the spiritual, ... even the most exalted states of mind—the most extraordinary transformations—must have some physical basis or at least some psychological correlate in neural activity" (2007, 41). But if Wesley was writing metaphorically—a technique we commonly use to place two otherwise unlike things beside each other, to say something about the one by transferring properties associated with the other—then to what were his metaphors "warming" and "heart" actually referring?

These are the sorts of questions that have occupied the attention of many scholars and may very well be the questions that some readers wish to pursue. Those looking for a start on such answers would do well to read Ann Taves's

---

[1] This, of course, is the classic use of the comparative method, akin to a late-nineteenth century usage, in which essential similarity is sought amidst historical and regional difference.

still-important survey of the literature (2005), along with Martin Jay's detailed survey of various uses of the notion of experience in modern scholarship and literature (2005), not to mention Jensine Andresen's edited collection of essays for a sample of how some cognitive scientists are today approaching the topic (2001). But before attempting to answer these questions, we ought to step back and consider whether it is even correct to assume—as those who try to answer such questions commonly do—that such a thing as language (e. g., whether spoken in words or, as in Wesley's journal, written in a text) *refers* to something outside of itself, as in when we commonly assume that "cup" (whether the sound you hear when it is spoken or the shapes you see when it is read in print) *refers* to some property internal to that object that so many of us hold in the morning, filled with coffee (that is, the very property that makes it a cup and not a bottle, pen, or paper), or when we assume that the quoted words that opened this chapter *correspond* to an utterance that originated from an historical agent named John Wesley, who lived in England more than a couple hundred years ago. In fact, is it even correct to assume that his words—and perhaps this assumption is why we even call them *his* words—correspond not simply to an utterance that somehow flowed from his lips or, in the case of our quotation, from his pen, but that they also correspond to a meaning and an intention that he presumably had somewhere in his head (notice how meanings are in the head while emotions are in the heart)?[2] Reading these words—*his* words—is therefore thought to provide the careful reader with access to a meaning—*his* meaning—that Wesley had in mind when putting pen and ink to paper; a private meaning only he possesses, akin to his private experience, that he exhibited publicly through the medium of language. As I have written in the past, this is the old "What did Shakespeare mean when he wrote ... ?" approach to studying meaning—the common approach that we so easily find in everyday life. According to this model, writers and speakers *express* (a key word that deserves our attention here) their meanings in a code (in our case, it is called the English language, which is symbolized in arrangements of characters that we call letters or in combinations of spoken sounds that we call phonemes) that, when heard or read properly, enables a listener or a reader over two hundred and fifty years later to understand themselves as knowing what someone named Wesley experienced and then meant when he spoke about his heart's strange warming. Without this

---

[2] Given how some now consider cognition to be a phenomenon associated with the whole human organism (so-called embodied cognition), it is not difficult to imagine a day in the future when our commonsense tendency to associate thought with the head, and the brain in particular, will be seen as no less curious that how we today think of those ancients who once supported the theory of bodily humors.

assumption (that something eternal lurks behind the letters and the sounds, something that directly links the reader to the writer and the listener to the speaker—what theorists would simply call the *sign* that links the *signifier* to the thing being *signified*), it would make little sense to ask about what either Shakespeare or Wesley meant when he wrote either this or that, for both of them are long gone and all that remains is a text in front of diverse readers— the collection of signs in ink on paper or pictured in shades of light and dark on a computer screen—that has passed through innumerable hands and before countless eyes before our own.

Despite the widely shared nature of this approach, is this the way experience, language, and meaning-making actually works? Is experience something inside a person, owned and only later shared by a person, and is meaning somehow disengaged from the words on a page and the sounds that we hear, such that the sounds and the ink can come and go but the meaning they represented remains forever? If so, then the text of Wesley's opening quotation might function like an arrow leading away from his experience, on that fateful evening in May, and to the reader, wherever and whenever they may be, efficiently communicating across time something unique about this strange feeling that he had. But if meaning and experience *do not* work in this fashion, if they are not some sort of inner, pure, and eternal thing, exclusive to the subject and only later symbolized publicly in inevitably fallible language, then too quickly moving from reading words on a page, overhearing words spoken orally, or watching people doing things, to concluding that texts, sounds, and behaviors provide direct access to some inner world of timeless significance betrays a serious flaw in scholarship.

To rephrase: perhaps we could say that if you follow the everyday, commonsense model of meaning-making (which is often called the correspondence or the referential theory of meaning), then claims of religious experience will of course be understood as signaling a pre-verbal and thus pre-social moment that is only later expressed publicly, and always done so only to varying degrees of satisfaction (which is none other than the old, "I can't quite put it into words" approach to how meaning works). However, if we adopt an alternative theory about how meaning-making takes place, and, by doing so, further complicate meaning's relation to those supposedly internal states or dispositions that we commonly know as either experiences or beliefs—a theory to be discussed below in more detail—then we will have to take seriously that, as once phrased by Ludwig Wittgenstein, "the expression of belief, thought, etc., is just a sentence;—and the sentence has sense only as a member of a system of language; as one expression within a calculus" (1965, 42). To put it another way, notations on a page or sounds coming from the mouths of people may only be just that: notations and sounds that may refer to nothing other than the rules of the symbol systems in which they occupy a place—rules that we, as the people who develop and use them, employ to distinguish which markings and which sounds get to count as languages to which we pay attention and which are seen and heard as mere marks and sounds that can be ignored. If this is the case, then both markings and soundings are not neutral collections of signs that re-present (as in the sense of presenting the something to which they are said to correspond) an otherwise unavailable inner world to outsiders. If so, then they do not provide the reader or the listener (no matter how careful they may be in their descriptive and interpretive work) with direct access to any pre-verbal or pre-social meanings that were lurking in someone else's head.

If this alternative approach to meaning-making is our starting point, then the question "Do you know what I mean?" may not be about the meaning at all, regardless what the person asking the question may think when saying it. Instead, such a statement may actually be an invitation to determine whether speaker and listener share, and thus play by, the same set of linguistic rules—what Wittgenstein earlier called a calculus. And the common reply to such a question, yes, "I know what you mean," may merely establish that that the listener and the speaker do indeed share the same rules and are thus members of the same group. Case in point: consider an example I once discussed in the past: the widely parodied "eh?" (pronounced "ay") which is often used by Canada's English speakers (a trait picked up from the British, but which is also found in US English, where "huh?" seems more prominent). Walking around Toronto or Calgary, it would not be unusual to hear someone say, "Nice weather, eh?" But the person saying this is not, in fact, posing a question. For, despite the upward inflection as their sentence ends, one would never expect to find "eh?" used at the end of a sentence that put forward a controversial claim—one that risks the sort of disagreement that marks a break or a gap in social life. That is to say, the linguistic signal "eh?" functions for Canadians much as "or what?" functions in English slang, as in "Is this great weather or what?" These are both occasions to solicit agreement from the person with whom one is having a conversation—"Yeah, it's great weather" is therefore the expected, and thus the correct, answer. Important to recognize is that this exchange is therefore not about the weather, for the observation on the quality of the weather simply provides an occasion for group building and identification. The sentence that ends in the rising inflection "eh?" (sometimes associated with raised eyebrows) is therefore a way to invite, perhaps even to force, agreement and thus solidarity from another, by putting forward a claim already known to have the agreement of your conversation partner—it is already known because you each already understand the other to be a member of your group, sharing your tastes, your sensibilities, your expectations, and most importantly, your language. This agreement therefore is a mark of shared social affinity: "Are we both in the group who think that the weather is pleasant today?" to which someone answers, "Yes, we are peers." "Eh?" questions are simply occasions for grooming the group and certifying your place within it.

If queries about the weather may not actually be about the weather, then could experience talk not be about the experiences either? For if we follow Wittgenstein, then regardless what people making claims of having had an experience may think, like all instances of language, their claims may be nothing more or less than evidence that the writer or the speaker are properly schooled in using their group's language rules—using the rules does nothing more or less than use the rules, thereby reproducing and reinforcing them, and in the process reproducing and reinforcing the identity of the group that results from those who use them.

The sounds and the markings therefore don't refer to anything outside of the fact that the speaker and listener, the writer and reader, are equally competent to put their shared rules into practice—much as readers of this text are doing right now. In this case—recalling an earlier example—if I write "cup" (as I have just done, and which readers have just read), it may tell us nothing about some feature of an object on my desk that makes it naturally distinguishable from all other objects also on my desk. Instead, writing and reading "cup" may tell us everything about our (that is, the writer and the reader) common place within a rule system which happens to distinguish "cup" from "cap"—not to mention "cop," "cot," "cut," "cat," etc.—a distinction that we reproduce and teach to newcomers because we find it useful, not only because the system of distinction helps us to find the thing into which we pour our coffee in the morning but, more importantly perhaps, because it facilitates our cooperative activities with others ("I'll have a cup of coffee" we say as we step up to the counter). Participating in such systems is therefore not just a way to get that coffee but a way that we continually reinvent ourselves as a "we" and an "our."

Of course, this theory of language will probably frustrate those who employ the commonsense view of words as neutral signs that directly correspond to intangible ideas in the real world. But, for others, the fact that users of our language system have so successfully schooled each other in "seeing" a cup when hearing the sounds or seeing the text represented by "cup"—sounds and symbols repetitively driven into us, from an extremely young age, by those around us, those who made us what we are today—makes language, meaning, experience, and social identity all the more interesting, I'd argue. For despite my assurance today that a cow is a cow and that it says moo, I also happen to know (because I've seen others do it to their children) that well-meaning adults leaned into me, as a very young child, and repeatedly told me, likely with great enthusiasm—"The cow says moo. The cow says moo ..."—while probably pointing just as repeatedly to a drawing in a child's story book or to an object outside the car window. Would that sketch in the book, that object on the other side of the farmer's fence, have naturally been something worth paying attention to without, as a very young child, being forced to, without being given a name for it, and without being told of a whole series of interconnected relationships that it had with other names ("farmer," "farm," "horse," "barn," "milk," etc.) that had been repeatedly given to me in precisely the same manner? Without initiation into this particular linguistic and social calculus, would I have *experienced* the cow and its moo? Or would they have both been among the many irrelevant items in a hectic world in which I had come to pay attention to things perhaps unimaginable to those intent on seeing certain objects *as* cows and hearing certain sounds *as* moos?

Apparently, experience can be a lot more complicated than was first apparent when reading that quotation from John Wesley, for it now seems possible that the internalization of a previous calculus—dare we just call it a discourse?—developed long before we each arrived on the scene and into which we were initiated by others, ensuring that none of my experiences are simply my own. Thus, instead of talking about "his experiences" and "his meanings," as we did earlier when discussing what Wesley wrote, we might better phrase it as *their* or even *our* experience and *their* or *our* meaning, inasmuch as the larger frameworks that determine what gets to stand out *as* an experience and what gets to count *as* meaningful are public and therefore collective and always contestable. And it is not just that "cup" or "cow" do not necessarily point to something internal to those things we call cups and cows, for everything that has just been said (or, again, should I say written?) equally applies to *all* of the other words in the preceding paragraphs. For example, whether I used it in my own text, or whether used by Wesley—as in the phrase, "I felt my heart strangely warmed"—we may have no choice but to ask: To what does "I" and "my" refer? Does it point to something unique inside of me (for the first-person pronoun has appeared numerous times throughout the chapter, such as referencing previous my writings) or merely to shared assumptions and social rules common among those who constitute my peers?

The essays selected for the anthology that I co-edited with Craig Martin, and for which an earlier form of this chapter stood as the introduction (all of which were intended for a reader new to these issues but motivated enough to tackle some complex issues), explored this very complexity—from, for example, pieces by Joachim Wach (1951), who headed up the University of Chicago's History of Religions program prior to Eliade's arrival, and Diana Eck (2003), interested in universals on which a shared social affinity can be based, to Robert Desjarlais (1997), aiming to prompt readers to rethink their sometimes too easy identification with others, and Joan Wallach Scott (1991), asking historians to shift from looking for experiences in the archive to studying the discourse on experience itself. Therefore, readers expecting to find a selection of articles in the vein of Wesley's journal—that is, a collection of articles narrating religious experiences that people claim to have had—will likely be disappointed by that book. It asks them to do considerably more critical thinking on the topic by seeing its opening selections (in which we find examples of the widespread view of religious experience being uncaused by other sorts of experiences and yet universally shared among all human beings) as data in need of analysis. To do so, the volume then turns to a selection of essays that each call into question these very assumptions, making not experience, let alone religious experience, the focus of study but, instead, the discursive conditions that enable, and the social effects of making, such claims. It's for that reason that the collection opens with Raymond William's brief but still crucial study of the two contrary senses in which this word "experience" has been used in the English language—what he termed experience-past and experience-present. For the modern sense of experience as naming a private affectation or sentiment of fullness and immediacy—what Williams calls experience-present, which is just as Wesley used the term and much as many people today now use the term—is, he argues, a fairly recent linguistic invention. So Williams also draws attention to another notion of experience as naming the cumulative and empirically evident result of past situations. In fact, it is this latter, older sense of the term, as naming something public and observable, that occupies the majority of *The Oxford English Dictionary*'s many different definitions for the word (citing examples from as early as the fourteenth century). So, despite the popularity today of assuming that experience denotes an interior disposition available only to the participant—such as those who might nostalgically look back on their school days, longing for "the student experience"—we still have no difficulty understanding a job ad that specifies that applicants need to have "work experience." For in this case, experience names something evident and documentable that accumulates over time (hence Williams names it experience-past), something empirical and therefore public (for I can hear whether you know how to play the piano and I can taste whether you know how to cook), something that is not an invisible affectation but something that can be done with the body (such as the skills required of the job), something that we each can therefore observe so as to confirm whether you have it or not. So while I can see whether you know how to do long division, I certainly can't see Wesley's strangely warmed heart.

Two items are crucial to entertain at this point. First of all, whereas experience-present is private and unavailable for empirical (that is, sensory) confirmation (i.e., one cannot confirm that Wesley's heart was indeed "strangely warmed"), experience-past is very public and therefore available for empirical confirmation (i.e., one can easily verify whether a novice professor has teaching experience). These two different usages of the term are therefore quite the opposite of one another, each functioning as part of very different discourses. Second, if we accept Wittgenstein's earlier assessment of claims of belief as being nothing more or less than utterances that can be heard and sentences that can be read, then claims of experience-present are, after all is said and done, just that—*claims* and, as claims that can be understood, they must, as already noted, operate by the shared calculus or discourse that we call language, rules that are thoroughly public and social (after all, neither you nor I invented the grammar that we use to make sense of this very text). The point? Experience-present can be understood as but an instance of experience-past. To put it another way, the ability to have an experience, much less to report that one has had one, is itself evidence of one's prior participation in a certain sort of social world, one comprised of specific rules that can themselves be observed, taught, recorded, and compared to the rules of other social worlds. Experience-present may therefore be an internalized residue of a prior and thus past social world, invented by others and that, through the actions of others, has imprinted its calculus on us—or better put, *within* us.

Now, of course, this is certainly not the way that the people who make disclosures about their experiences usually think of them—and the question is whether their self-representations (e.g., I think this, I saw that, I meant something else) limit how scholars can examine people's claims and the actions about which they may make claims (e.g., I did this because ...). Case in point: I have no doubt that John Wesley wasn't assuming that his claim to having had an unique experience at a meeting on Aldersgate Street was nothing but an example of how arbitrary signs are connected up in complex systems to form language—a system which is meaningful only so long as more than one person accepts the arbitrary arrangements and combinations that we know as text and grammar. Not at all! Instead, I presume (a key part of the analysis here is that this is my presumption) that he, much like the person who assumes "cup" somehow points directly to that thing still sitting on my desk, took for granted that his journal entry was somehow in step with a stable reality in the world, one to which only he happened to have direct access. After all, it was his own heart that was strangely warmed. But is this description of his assumptions entirely correct? For, come to think of it, if he really did believe that only he had access to this interior disposition, then what sense would it make for him to come home, put pen to paper, and write about it, for writing places indicators of this supposedly private disposition into a public domain? So while he may have likely, and perhaps quite sincerely, understood himself to have undergone something unique to himself, that cannot be the whole story.

What if we assumed, instead, that the private place from which Wesley's feeling supposedly originated was not limited to him. What if it was somehow shared by others, such as those also attending that evening meeting, or those who might someday read his published journals? What if we assumed, much like those who today talk about human nature as being something unique to each individual (i.e., to each "I") yet shared by *all* individuals (i.e., by the "we")—thereby making them all equally individual *and* equally members of that family we know as humanity—that the site of Wesley's private disposition of assurance was also present, though just as private, within everyone else? Now, it starts to make sense for him to write about it, while still being unable to put "it" into words adequately, for now the thing which his writing expresses might be something of relevance to people other than Wesley himself. "Know what I mean?"

So if we're trying to be descriptively accurate when coming across people using the term "experience" in that sense that Williams termed experience-present, we likely have to address two things that these people seem to assume: (1) that although their sense of an interior sentiment is autonomous, or disconnected from being caused by the mundane or empirical things of usual day-to-day life, it is nonetheless also (2) universally shared by (all or at least some) others who are likewise thought to have a similar private, interior space (what scholars sometimes call subjectivity) where such emotions reside. And this is just what we see happening when, in response to the question "Know what I mean?" we commonly see someone reply by simply shaking her head, up and down or side to side. And, as if by magic, without the so-called meaning ever being put on the table—placed in public, for scrutiny and possibly for dispute—something seems to have been mysteriously transported, as if by telepathy, between these two otherwise distinct hearts and minds. "Yes, I know what you mean" or "No, I do not."

Throughout the history of that field that we know as religious studies, the academic study of religion, comparative religion, or even the science of religion (the last two names for the field were once more popular than they are now), we come across scholars who, much like the people they study, presume just this: that their object of study is an internal yet universal state (whether emotional, as in an experience or faith, or cognitive, as in those things referred to as beliefs) that can only be accessed by means of its various expressions or—using a term favored by those known as phenomenologists of religion (descriptivist scholars interested in doing comparative work, looking for cross-cultural similarities)—its manifestations. These manifestations are generally found in specific sorts of narratives (called myths), certain types of behaviors (called rituals), and a host of other media, from art to hand gestures (all called symbols). In fact, these three items—myth, ritual, symbol—were once (and, in some university curricula, still might be) the basis for common course titles, in which the variety of manifestations studied in a semester were thought to betray a common core, or, using a term often used in philosophy, what is usually termed an essence.

Likened to the core of an onion—inasmuch as it is the only thing remaining when one peals back its many layers—the essence is that without which something would not be what it is. For example, we might say that the color of the onion—or so the argument goes for those who define things (like onions or cups on my desk) by identifying their essence—does not make it an onion, for red onions are no more or less onions than those that are yellow or white or green (what we also call scallions). Color comes and goes (i.e., color is contingent), suggesting that it is not a necessary, or essential, trait of the onion. Perhaps size, shape, or taste is a better candidate for an onion's necessary trait. Or perhaps the way we use them? Where they are grown? A little thought on the subject makes it clear that none of these features is required for something in the world to count as an onion, for different onions taste differently, have different shapes and sizes, and can be used in any number of ways—but that doesn't mean that any of them are less of an onion. Much as an onion's empirically observable characteristics (size, shape, color, etc.) can all differ, though the item is still an onion, many scholars of religion have assumed that, like the onion-ness that remains when its various observable layers are each removed, there is a nonempirical core that remains once the unnecessary (that is, changeable) traits of religious beliefs, behaviors, and institutions are gone.

This strategy for defining something as a this and not a that usually goes by the name of essentialism; in the study of religion, in which we find so many different variations in people's beliefs and actions, the essentialist approach has, for the past few hundred years, settled on private experience as the true essence of all religion. And because the inner world is so often thought to take priority over the outer world, these initial, pre-social experiences come to be understood as the source, the cause, of all that follows them; first comes faith, as the scholar of religion Wilfred Cantwell Smith might have phrased it, and only then come the traditions and the institutions. Therefore, despite the many observable differences in the claims people make, the way they do things, and the sorts of groups they form to pass along their traditions, beliefs, and rituals, much as with onions there must be something in common (or so it is thought) in order for us to recognize all of these things *as* religious. And that thing they all share turns out not to be a *thing* at all; instead, it is an internal state, an intangible disposition, a subjective immediacy of awareness that all people are said to have and thus to share. Though expressed in a multitude of ways, that which motivates these varied expressions, that which is first felt internally and only then manifested externally, is said to be a common and thus necessarily shared.

One of the better-known examples of an early scholar of religion adopting this approach was the German Protestant scholar Rudolf Otto (someone whose work is much outdated, despite some, such as Robert Orsi, still claiming him to be a relevant writer). Working in an intellectual tradition not unlike that of his predecessor, the German romantic, Protestant theologian Friedrich Schleiermacher, Otto shared important assumptions about the empirical unavailability of experience in common with his contemporary, the American psychologist William James, and set the stage for the later work of such scholars as the influential Chicago historian of religions, the Romanian-born Mircea Eliade. Otto concluded that those things which we call religious are religious not because of any external or observable trait that they may or may not have—for, after all, place that thing called an altar in a different setting, and do different things with it, and you won't likely continue to think it's an altar but simply a table or a desk. Instead, items in the empirical world simply provide an occasion or a site for the expression of what he held to be a prior and timeless inner awareness that is projected outward from the individual and into the world. And for Otto, this inwardness awareness is an experience of the numinous, a now well-known term that he coined from the Latin word *numen* (presence or power), naming one's inner awareness of being in the presence of the compelling yet fearful mystery of it all.

That it is awfully difficult to study a mystery (after all, where does one begin and how does one know where to end?) seems to have been overlooked by the many people influenced to this day by Otto's work. However, the problems do not stop there, for there are other implications of this still-common position for scholarship on religion. For example, in the opening lines of chapter three of his important book, *The Idea of the Holy* (as the title was translated from the 1917 German original, *Das Heilige*), Otto famously writes the following:

> The reader is invited to direct his mind to a moment of deeply-felt religious experience, as little as possible qualified by other forms of consciousness. Whoever cannot do this, whoever knows no such moments in his experience, is requested to read no farther; for it is not easy to discuss questions of religious psychology with one who can recollect the emotions of his adolescence, the discomforts of indigestion, or, say, social feelings, but cannot recall any intrinsically religious feelings. We do not blame such an one, when he tries for himself to advance as far as he can with the help of such principles of explanation as he knows, interpreting "aesthetics" in terms of sensuous pleasure, and "religion" as a function of the gregarious instinct and social standards, or as something more primitive still. But

the artist, who for his part has an intimate personal knowledge of the distinctive element in the aesthetic experience, will decline his theories with thanks, and the religious man will reject them even more uncompromisingly.

Drawing on the common analogy of art and religion—inasmuch as people sometimes assume both to be concerned with unique feelings that cannot be fully explained by appealing to any of their observable causes—Otto's position is clear: *to be, or to feel, is to know*. Those who do not possess "an intimate personal knowledge of the distinctive element" of the object under study therefore have no choice but to remain silent when it comes to discussing it. Such scholarship on religion is deeply influenced by an intellectual movement we know as Romanticism—a philosophical, artistic, musical, and literary movement that originates in some eighteenth-century Europeans' negative reactions to the scientific rationalism of the Enlightenment. Religion cannot be explained—or so the argument goes—it can only be felt. Practiced in this way, the study of religion amounts to a form of participation, inasmuch as the scholar is assumed to share in the experiences of the people under study—at least enough to feel and understand them in order to represent them accurately.

But in what other area of the university, in which other scholarly discipline, would we play by such rules—would we associate identification and membership with scholarship? For must one be an ancient Greek to study ancient Greece? Must one be a Communist to study Communism? What about marine biologists and what they study? No doubt there are those in other fields who, along with Otto, think that being a participant gives one a privileged viewpoint. For instance, take the more recent academic fields that are today called area studies, where one can easily find professors who maintain that, for example, women have a privileged insight when it comes to the curriculum of a women's studies class. But perhaps, instead of studying the supposed content of experience, as with a previous generation of scholars, we ought to shift the ground as we did with the Canadian "eh?" just as recommended by Wittgenstein, and take seriously that claims of experience are just that, *claims* and, as claims, they are public, they are negotiable and contestable, and they are *doing* something while coming out of a specific situation and context. And because they are doing something, those making the claims are social actors and their claims are a form of socially formative action that can be studied. And it is this doing, the establishing of a zone of social privilege—the thing that results from claims about the unique nature of "women's experience" or the "American experience"—that can attract the scholar's attention. Of course those making the sorts of claims that we find in Wesley's and Otto's texts more than likely wish their beliefs, behaviors, and institutions to be treated in a special way (aside: to set apart is among the ancient

Latin roots of the modern word "sacred"), but I do not think that scholars ought to be bound by the wishes of the people whom they study (recall, here, the last of Bruce Lincoln's still-relevant and usefully provocative "Theses on Method").[3] In fact, this is *the* issue that operates in the background of all of the essays in this book.

But why should we proceed as if people are *not* the experts on their own experiences? While I could cite a number of examples to persuade readers that experience is a social product, that without a grid provided for them from the outside (let's say, by a writer such as myself, removed from the world they take for granted), they may not be *experiencing* themselves in either this or that way in the present moment (say, *as* a reader, *as* a student, *as* a teacher, *as* a female, *as* a male, etc.), consider instead a brief but useful example from Wendy Brown's important book, *Relating Aversion: Tolerance in the Age of Identity and Empire* (2006). Brown, a political scientist, is interested in the history and current effects of what is now an almost taken-for-granted theme of life in modern social democracies: that we must *tolerate* each other's differences. That there are some things which many—though, significantly, not all, and *that's* the point!—of us agree we must *not* tolerate (such as those behaviors we label as crimes) makes it evident that the limits of toleration (or, to put it another way, the boundaries of the group which tolerates and what is tolerated) are contestable, that they change over time, and that they must therefore be tweaked, repaired, built, and rebuilt.

With this in mind, consider Brown's helpful example of the Museum of Tolerance in Los Angeles, part of the Simon Wiesenthal Center. A portion of the museum is devoted to exhibits documenting the horrors of Nazi Germany's attempt to eliminate Europe's Jewish population—exhibits that, as with many modern museum exhibits, prompt visitors to move through carefully recreated settings, to interact with multimedia presentations, and thereby to be enveloped by an ever-growing narrative about events in the past and the significance they ought to be seen as having in the present. "The installation culminates," Brown writes,

---

[3] "When one permits those whom one studies to define the terms in which they will be understood, suspends one's interest in the temporal and contingent, or fails to distinguish between 'truths,' 'truth-claims,' and 'regimes of truth,' one has ceased to function as historian or scholar. In that moment, a variety of roles are available: some perfectly respectable (amanuensis, collector, friend and advocate), and some less appealing (cheerleader, voyeur, retailer of import goods). None, however, should be confused with scholarship" (Lincoln 1996, 227).

with our literal descent into a concentration camp-like space, replete with barbed-wire; entrances that separate the adult and able-bodied from children, the aged, and the infirm; and uneven rough cement floors. We issue into the cold, cavernous space of a gas chamber where, for a very long time, we watch images of the camps as actors read the words of inmates and survivors.

"At this point," Brown concludes, "we are no longer mere witnesses to the Holocaust but are *inside* the experience" (139). In support of her point, Brown quotes two previous visitors, writing in the guest book at the end of the exhibit: "I had read some things about the Holocaust, but had never seen it first hand," writes one, and another says, "now I know how it must have felt."

But there's just one problem, a particularly nagging problem, when it comes to the manner in which these visitors have experienced the terrors of the Holocaust. As Brown rightly observes, none of the visitors has actually seen anything other than the museum exhibit, for, in case we need reminding, she adds: "what we are seeing is staged rather than real;" and "this 'experience' is a facsimile" (138, 139). The awareness that so sincerely moved the museum's visitors—what to them more than likely is perceived as vivid, authentic, and therefore rationally persuasive and emotionally compelling—was, as the observer and the museum curators know, manufactured for them, over half a century and a world away from the events that it claims to re-present; it was done so by the same sort of careful planning and attention to detail that one finds in any modern multimedia and immersive exhibit, whether it be a museum, an amusement park, or a motion picture. The visitors have quite obviously never left sunny LA; yet to those writing in that guest book, they have somehow been transported back in time, to some core moment a world away—a moment they seem to think of as unchanged despite being recreated in a museum exhibit. Could there be any better example of the manner in which experiences are conjured within prefabricated grids and settings, making experience an artifact of a prior social world?

But to press the point still further, what are we to make of the presumption that, whether or not we can access it, there's a pristine "core moment" somewhere out there, in the dimly lit past? Could it be the case that this very sense of an original, even if we agree that it is irretrievably separated from us in time, is just as much a product of a calculus in the present, comprised of specific expectations, assumptions, sets of interests and needs that may have little or nothing to do with their so-called origins? For instance, consider that group commonly known in US history as "the founding fathers." What did they found? Certainly not the contemporary country known as the United States of America, for the nation-state that exists today was beyond the wildest dreams of political actors in the mid-to-late eighteenth century. Certainly, from the point of view of the present, their long past actions were *necessary* to establish the new nation-state (e.g., their writing a constitution), but they were hardly *sufficient*, for none of those social actors could anticipate issues in the future (which indicates the crucial role of the US Supreme Court in bridging the gap between distant past and unanticipated future, for this is the body responsible to apply a late eighteenth-century text to ever changing present day circumstances). Their unknown future (they lacked foresight) became our known past (because we possess hindsight), thereby allowing us to look backward in time *as if* those past actions led to our present. But because the contemporary moment is comprised of countless present situations, each populated by and indicative of the desires of countless different social actors, in any number of different situations and all looking backward in time for some hint of justification for the particular present *as they wish it to be*, we can see how that thing that we once understood simply as a uniform and tangible past actually turns out to be filled with innumerable actors doing a variety of things for any number of reasons. The past, then, becomes an almost limitless (i.e., it is limited only by memory and documentation) repository from which contemporary actors can pick and choose at will to suit their purposes (and thus we arrive at the position of those who argue that the past is a present phenomenon, a position not unfamiliar to those who argue that experience is a product of discourse, by the way). No doubt, many things were begun in 1776, but should one desire to draw attention to the longevity of certain US political institutions, then a relatively small number of events in that year stand out as significant—significant because of the current desire, not significant in and of themselves. In precisely this way one can argue that the past is an ever-changing construction of the present—ever changing because the present is so diverse and is itself always changing (that is, the present has a nasty habit of continually becoming the past, which opens the way for yet another unanticipated future to become a new present).

To apply some of this, consider one of my own school's football players whom I still recall being interviewed some years ago on the local evening news, at a press conference prior to Alabama's annual October game against the University of Tennessee—among our archrivals. When asked what it was like to play a game in Knoxville's famed Neyland Stadium—with over 100,000 cheering fans, all wearing orange and white—he replied by saying that the only thing that he could compare it to was "what the gladiators and lions experienced in the Roman coliseum." Much as with the museum's visitors, we must not overlook the fact that, despite his claims, no actual time traveling has taken place; instead, this player's sense of being in ancient Rome was likely a product either of Hollywood special effects magic (had he seen Russell Crowe star in the 2000 film *Gladiator?*) or the imagination of historians hoping that their reading of such things as ancient inscriptions, statues, and architecture might hold up their weighty claims about such things as "the Roman experience." Moreover, today "ancient Rome" comes to stand for so many different things (I think here of the contests over the "whiteness" of the ancients and their statues),[4] all because of the many events that have transpired long after it and which were necessarily unknown to the people who actually lived in that place during that time (such as seeing Rome as but one of many so-called "great civilizations" that have risen and fallen over the past several thousand years, including many whose life spans long post-dated Rome's own inevitable decline). So it seems very likely to me that, for this football player back in 2006, the English sign "gladiator" (the Latin *gladiatōrēs*, swordsmen, comes from *gladius*, meaning sword) more than likely signifies things that are very different from what it may have meant for the slaves, criminals, war prisoners, and some free men as well who were put in the position of having to fight for their lives. What it meant for such people is, I would suggest, largely if not completely lost to time. The result is that all we have left is someone in the present using such signs as "gladiator" and "ancient Rome" to accomplish social work in the here and now.

But whether grounded in the fictions either of Hollywood or of scholarship, we must not overlook that this player's presence on that field in Knoxville apparently becomes understandable to him—becomes something we might call an *experience*—only once it is juxtaposed to the calculus of this facsimile, somewhat akin to those who, in the immediacy of the shocking (i.e., without precedent) attacks in the US on September 11, 2001, were only able to make sense of that day's events by comparing the chaos of the real to facsimiles and fabrications: "It was like a movie," they all said when interviewed by reporters on the scene, no doubt referring to Hollywood's long tradition of disaster films set in busy US cities (depending on their generation, everything from 1974's *Earthquake* and *The Towering Inferno* to *Independence Day* [1996], *Armageddon* [1998], and *Deep Impact* [1998] likely constituted their reference point). This confirms not only that, as scholars of religion are apt to say (with a nod to Jonathan Z. Smith but also Alfred Korzybski, from whom Smith borrowed this designation), we must not confuse our map of the territory (such as a description of an action, which is a mere representation) with the territory itself (what constitutes the original presentation of the act) but also that there is in fact no pre-mapped territory, no original, and thus no direct experience of a real world, without the application of a prior, constructed map that not only exists at a distance from that which it

---

[4] See, for example, Sarah Bond's article (2017) and the controversy that attended her work (e.g., Flaherty 2017).

eventually represents but, *more importantly perhaps*, a map whose use actually transforms the generic, chaotic, and thus unknowable limitless background—somewhat akin to white noise or the brute and unorganized stuff of existence—into a delimited and thus manageable domain that can be conceptualized and only then experienced and known, so that one can now experience oneself as being either "in place" or "out of place," either "early" or "late," either one of "us" or one of "them." For as Smith himself phrased it in the closing line of his essay, "Map is Not Territory," "maps are all we possess." Or, as the anthropologist Gregory Bateson once phrased it:

> We say the map is different from the territory. But what is the territory? Operationally, somebody went out with a retina or a measuring stick and made representations which were then put on paper. What is on the paper map is a representation of what was in the retinal representation of the man who made the map; and as you push the question back, what you find is an infinite regress, an infinite series of maps. The territory never gets in at all …. Always, the process of representation will filter it out so that the mental world is only maps of maps, *ad infinitum*. (1972, 454–5)

So the question is whether, as scholars, we're content to take the museum visitors' and the football player's—let alone anyone else's—claims of experience at face value, simply collecting and cataloguing them, or whether we're interested in how they could come to understand themselves and their relations to others in just this or that way. If the former, then we'll go on assuming either that something in the exhibit captures the essence of what it must have been like to be a victimized Jew in late 1930s and early 1940s Europe or that something on the football field captures the essence of the brutal ancient coliseum where slaves battled for their lives. But it seems that we have good reason for *not* doing such speculative work and for making a shift—after all, as scholars, we know that even if such originals ever did exist (and, if so, which of the many experiences from that time get to count as definitive of that moment?), they are long lost to history; we therefore have no standard against which to compare these people's claims, preventing us from ever knowing how accurate they really are. It's something akin to the troubles of the earlier example, of "You know what I mean?" followed by an agreeable head nod—such action effectively bypasses ever really testing just what the meaning is.

So, just as Wittgenstein suggested, the head nodding, the museum visitors writing in the book, and the college football player likening himself to an ancient fighter, might not actually be about the supposed one-to-one correspondence between the claim and the thing that it is said to represent. If so, then perhaps Wesley's report of his having experienced a strangely warmed heart had little to do with what he might have thought he felt and what he might have thought it meant. Perhaps the British historian of the English working class, E. P. Thompson, in his once-groundbreaking book, *The Making of the English Working Class* (1980), was onto something in thinking that the early appeal of Wesley's Methodism was to be found in England's dire social context at that time—for example, the terrible living and working conditions of the Industrial Revolution, which was then beginning to transform a previously dispersed, rural, agriculturally based economy to a condensed metropolitan manufacturing economy. Perhaps this was the social context—much as Wesley's "continual sorrow and heaviness of heart," as he phrased it in his journal, provided psychological context for his own experience—that allowed people at that time to come to experience themselves *as* sinners, *as* needing trust, assurance, and salvation from torment and death. Perhaps this is what prompted them to attend Wesley's highly popular and emotionally ecstatic tent meetings in which their emotional lives, individual value, and group solidarity was expressed and wildly celebrated by means of what Thompson, provocatively applying Karl Marx's still well-known critique of religion as an "opiate of the masses," describes as "a ritualized form of psychic masturbation" (405).

So, having begun with quoting Wesley's disclosure of an experience, I close with a scholar's analysis of the social, political, and economic causes of a heart's strange warming. If readers have stuck with me so far and are now able to entertain experience as the seemingly private residue of an all too public thing—something that has a history and which can be understood to be a product of a prior calculus (whether it be linguistic or sociopolitical)—then we have come some distance. For there may be no more compelling example of just how different scholarship on experiential claims may be when compared to those making the claims themselves, indicating that, despite the apparent sincerity of the people making claims about their feelings, sentiments, dispositions, faith, and even beliefs, the scholar who shifts their focus may learn that something else might be going on.

Reference List

Andresen, Jensine, ed. 2001. *Religion in Mind: Cognitive Perspectives on Religious Belief, Ritual, and Experience.* Cambridge: Cambridge University Press.

Bateson, Gregory. 1972. *Steps to an Ecology of Mind: Collected Essays in Anthropology, Psychiatry, Evolution, and Epistemology.* New York: Ballantine Books.

Bond, Sarah. "Why We Need to Start Seeing the Classical World in Color." *Hyperallergic* (blog). June 7, 2017. Accessed April 29, 2020. https://hyperallergic.com/383776/why-we-need-to-start-seeing-the-classical-world-in-color/.

Brown, Wendy. 2006. *Relating Aversion: Tolerance in the Age of Identity and Empire.* Princeton: Princeton University Press.

Desjarlais, Robert. 1997. "Rethinking Experience." In *Shelter Blues: Sanity and Selfhood Among the Homeless*, 10–7. Philadelphia: University of Pennsylvania Press.

Durkheim, Emile. (1912) 1995. *The Elementary Forms of Religious Life*, trans. Karen Fields. New York: The Free Press.

Eck, Diana. 2003. "Bozeman to Banaras: Questions from the Passage to India." In *Encountering God: A Spiritual Journey from Bozeman to Banaras*, 1–21. Boston: Beacon Press.

Flaherty, Colleen. "Threats for What She Didn't Say." *Inside Higher Ed.* June 19, 2017. Accessed April 29, 2020. https://www.insidehighered.com/news/2017/06/19/classicist-finds-herself-target-online-threats-after-article-ancient-statues.

Jay, Martin. 2005. *Songs of Experience: Modern American and European Variations on a Universal Theme.* Berkeley: University of California Press.

Lincoln, Bruce. 1996. "Theses on Method." *Method & Theory in the Study of Religion* 8:225–7.

Otto, Rudolf. (1917) 1958. *The Idea of the Holy: An Inquiry into the Non-Rational Factor in the Idea of the Divine and Its Relation to the Rational*, trans. John Harvey. London: Oxford University Press.

Sacks, Oliver. "A Bolt from the Blue." *The New Yorker* (July 23, 2007):38–42.

Scott, Joan Wallach. 1991. "The Evidence of Experience." *Critical Inquiry* 17/4:773–97.

Taves, Ann. 2005. "Religious Experience." In *Encyclopedia of Religion*, edited by Lindsay Jones, Vol. 11, 7736–50. Detroit: Thomson Gale.

Thompson, E. P. (1963) 1980. *The Making of the English Working Class.* London: Penguin.

Wach, Joachim. 1951. "Universals in Religion." In *Types of Religious Experience: Christian and Non-Christian*, 30–47. Chicago: University of Chicago Press.

Wesley, John. 1988. *The Works of John Wesley. Vol. 18. Journals and Diaries I (1735–8)*, edited by W. Reginald Ward and Richard P. Heitzenrater. Nashville: Abingdon Press.

Wittgenstein, Ludwig. (1958) 1965. *The Blue and Brown Books: Preliminary Studies for the "Philosophical Investigations."* New York: Harper Torchbooks.

4 "There's No Original in This Business"

> The conceptualization and representation of the past is fraught with difficulty, not simply because of the ambiguities and paucity of data but because the construction of history, written or oral, past or present, is a political act. (Whitelam 2001, 11)

As evidence of the impact that Jonathan Z. Smith's writings have had on my own research and teaching over the past nearly thirty years—such as his call for scholars to be critically self-conscious (as written in that much-cited introduction to *Imagining Religion*)—I've written on a variety of occasions about the practical implications of the categories that scholars use when going about their work. I have in mind the habit of calling this or that thing (that we might observe firsthand or read about) "a ritual," "a myth," "a tradition," or "a scripture," along with designating someone that we meet as being "a Hindu," "a Muslim," or "a Christian," not to mention "a believer" or "faithful." What's more, there's the related problem of anachronism that has occupied a good deal of my thinking, something that results when we casually use those same categories, many of which are pretty obviously modern and therefore recent innovations, to identify various doings or people in the recent or distant past, people that we moderns infer to have once existed from reading a text, an inscription, or interpreting some other item of material culture that we've unearthed or just stumbled across. Thus, or so the careful scholar might conclude, there's more than might at first meet the eye to making what might otherwise seem as uncontroversial claims about something being "an ancient Greek myth" or "Sumerian religion;" for, upon closer examination, such claims turn out not to be merely the innocent or neutral descriptions that we at first might have taken them to be (with another nod to what I've learned from Smith) but, instead, theory-laden and thus invested redescriptions that bring something perceived, at first, to be alien to us within the orbit of the knowable. The problem, though, is that the investments are all undisclosed and, because of that, they're efficiently naturalized since we fail to see them as operating at a distance from the world that they claim to describe.

While I welcome the fact that I am now hardly alone in offering such analyses (most recently, I think of such scholars as Matthew Baldwin [2019] and Peggy Schmeiser [2019] as joining the ranks of such critical voices, with Vaia

---

Note: My thanks to Barbara Krawcowicz for inviting me to write the original version of this chapter and also to my colleague Vaia Touna for reading and commenting on an earlier draft of this chapter.

Touna [2017a] counting as an strong example of the sort of work we can do if adopting such a shift), until fairly recently these critiques have struck me as being limited to the margins of the field. While such critical work existed, yes, and sometimes appeared in print in mainstream journals and in books from what many read as prestigious presses, it was not necessarily seen by many scholars of religion as something that one needed to take all that seriously.[1] So this growing body of literature was hardly seen as just that: a coherent and active body of literature, on a series of interrelated topics and field-wide problems, that could be read and mastered let alone applied to novel cases so as to refine our shared scholarly work. Instead, as is so often the case with grad school seminars on method and theory, it has been seen as something to get behind you as quickly as possible—a rite of professional passage, as it were.[2] Much as I once wrote regarding those who, early on in their own essays and books, quote what many read as Smith's more famous line from that same opening to *Imagining Religion* cited earlier (i.e., that quoting him on religion being a creation of the scholar's study was a genuflection that sanctified the fact that those quoting him usually then went on to do their work as if they'd never read Smith on this point [McCutcheon 2008, 8]), it seemed that those who *did* take notice of what we might just call the category and the anachronism critiques often did so in order to minimize and dismiss both, allowing them just to get on with understanding things as they pretty much always had. For what better response to the claim that "religion" is a fairly recent invention can there be than simply pointing at a reference to a god or a cosmic origins tale in some ancient text while repeating Dr. Johnson's famous stone-kicking retort to Bishop Berkeley: "I refute it thus?" That the almost intuitive association, at least for many of our peers today, between claims concerning the exploits of what some scholars term non-obvious beings and all of the many other things that some of us today so commonly assume to just naturally comprise that family called religion is a linkage that *we*, the readers of these texts or the interviewers of people, *are*

---

[1] In fact, Baldwin (2019, 74) reminded me recently of how, in his presidential address, even the onetime American Academy of Religion (AAR) president, Tom Tweed—someone whose work is associated positively with theory, at least for some—represented such criticisms as "intemperate" among the "like-minded" who inhabit a "corner" of the field; see Tweed 2016.

[2] For instance, David Morgan (the scholar of visual culture and religion) said in an interview that "it is very important for doctoral students to *endure* theory seminars" (emphasis added). Find the interview from which this quote is taken at http://usreligion.blogspot.com/2013/12/four-questions-with-david-morgan.html (accessed October 1, 2019).

establishing ourselves, is something that necessarily goes unnoticed in order for this realist retort to win the day.[3]

But, often, this naïve realism still wins the day.

For example, consider a recently published reply by M Adryael Tong to a paper written by Annette Yoshiko Reed (2019), both of which were originally presented at the 2017 meeting of the North American Association for the Study of Religion (NAASR). Having made the argument that so-called word studies (such as etymologies of the category religion), though increasingly prominent, hardly exhaust the many other ways that scholars might study how people organize and signify their worlds, Reed's paper was met with four replies, one of which, by Tong, argued, "By emphasizing methodological differences—in addition to ideological differences—among historical texts, we resist overly simplistic narratives and allow ourselves to encounter the archive *on its own terms*" (Tong 2019, 40; emphasis added). I admit that I find this claim rather curious in that it strikes me as uncritically repeating assertions made sixty years ago, or more, by scholars who were then advocating for studying religion *on its own terms* (i.e., critics of so-called reductionism, like Mircea Eliade, among others, who asserted that religion was a unique experience requiring unique hermeneutical methods for its proper study). In doing so, it overlooks (thereby dismissing, I'd add) decades of critical work that has made more and more apparent to scholars (not just in the study of religion) that no one ever comes to the material that they study as if they were themselves a blank slate confronting pristine originals. Instead, what gets to count as items populating the so-called archive is itself predetermined by sets of prior assumptions and practices on the part of the scholar—ironically, something forcefully argued in Leslie Dorrough Smith's editor's introduction to the very book in which Tong's paper appears.[4] But such crit-

---

[3] For example, few scholars would argue today that definitions are actually constitutive of their objects of study—i.e., change the definition and we will then end up studying different things; instead, most scholarly definitions, if they're even stated explicitly, are arrived at descriptively and thus inductively, given that the scholar already somehow just knows which things are the religious things and then sets about to find the elements that several of them more or less share (and thus the comparative method is still often used to identify essential similarity, just as it was in the late-nineteenth century), which ends up being used as the definition of the group.

[4] Recounting working on her dissertation at the University of California, Santa Barbara, as well as reviews of the book that eventually resulted, Smith observes (in the former case) that her interest in what she came to term chaos rhetorics was not seen as legitimate data and (in the latter) that the book's reception has generally steered well clear of noting her wider point: that scholars of evangelicalism themselves employ these same techniques to constitute their own objects of study (Smith 2019, 1).

ical work notwithstanding, Tong seems to be saying that a real world of the past just awaits its proper study, if only scholars could shed their preconceived notions, employ a variety of approaches, and thereby understand it as it was inherently meant to be understood (i.e., on its own terms).

While the work of J. Z. Smith, among others, has significantly helped some in the modern field to get to the position where they can read such realist claims as being rather problematic, it strikes me that the task now is to continue to develop, apply, and, most importantly, teach (i.e., pass along to a new generation) those earlier critiques, knowing that those who see such critical work as hampering their own commonsense approaches will continue to advance their uncritical claims—and the sheer number of such noncritical voices in the field often gives the impression that this position is just intuitively correct—something I hope the first chapter made abundantly clear. To rephrase: with each new generation joining the work of scholarship, we will more than likely find untheorized, everyday realism reasserted again and again. This means that we must continue to press the case since those with whom we argue will not rest theirs. To rephrase the point, as I have remarked on past occasions, among the biggest recurring challenges in the field is the manner in which a widely popular folk discourse on religion, popular among a specific group, is often elevated, with very little or even no fine-tuning, to the status of a technical discourse in the field; this is because our work on religions, myths, rituals, traditions, etc., often proceeds by means of what many in the field understand to be everyday categories of—at least to them—obvious meaning and commonsensical application. Defamiliarizing students from their taken-for-granted knowledge (to borrow another term often used by Jonathan Z. Smith—something he reported doing on the very first day of his classes [Braun and McCutcheon 2018, 70]), upon joining any one of our classes (and thereby making them curious about their own assumptions about the world), is therefore among the first things that a professor likely needs to tackle in order to initiate them into the study of religion as a discourse no less technical than any other field in the contemporary university.

Instead of making this argument yet again at one of the sites where I often have, such as the category religion itself, I'd like to shift the ground a little and consider what we might learn if we instead applied it to one that I have been using rather uncritically up to this point in this chapter and one that is employed by almost all scholars as they go about their work: that time and that place that we call the past. For, despite many in the academy now being suspicious of how narratives are intimately related to the production and circulation of both knowledge and power, the ease of assuming the linear development of time, just naturally and inexorably flowing from left to right (at least for us English readers), and thereby steadily and surely moving from the ancients to us moderns—with the former understood as "influencing" or "leading to" the latter—is one that remains foundational to our work in the academy; and, because of that, it deserves more critical attention than it has usually received. That some of this work was indeed done some time ago, when justifiably strong critiques of earlier scholars' claims concerning "the primitives versus the civilized world," is encouraging, of course, for it made painfully evident that once taken-for-granted orderings of time come with ranked investments in the contemporary world (investments often of considerable consequence); but such critical self-reflection should not stop with considering only how either a ritual specialist or an elder tells a tale about the ancestors or the terribly flawed manner in which our late-nineteenth-century predecessors studied those they once designated as "the primitives."

Case in point, consider Reed's already-mentioned article, which identified a variety of other analytics that scholars might consider using when studying how groups make their worlds knowable and actionable, such as "the practice of creating narratives that remap synchronic diversity onto chronological time" (2019, 11). That her article then routinely classifies the sites where she goes looking for this narrativization technique as pre-modern or antiquity is, as best as I can tell from the essay, not seen as but another instance of this same approach (i.e., they instead seem to be used as realist descriptors of obviously past states of affairs). The message conveyed therefore seems to be that, while scholars are able to identify when other people work at "creating abstract categories and/or totalizing systems of taxonomic distinction to organize and explain their encounters with difference" (Reed 2019, 13), our own efforts are somehow immune to such critical reflection—given that it would probably not be difficult to argue that such designators as pre-modern and antiquity are themselves part of a chronologized narrativization that some of us today happen to use to make sense of ourselves as modern, doing so by establishing relationships of similarity and difference, causality and influence, between "now" and a distant "then" and thus "us" and the distant "them."

To begin to think through how we might more consistently and thoroughly apply our own critical tools in a self-reflexive manner—something I very much associate with a research agenda that takes Smith's contributions, at least as I read them, seriously—I turn to two recent books concerned with how scholars of religion can better approach their studies of the ancient past: Brent Nongbri's *Before Religion* (2015) and Carlin Barton and Daniel Boyarin's *Imagine No Religion* (2016). Thinking back to the marginalized place of much recent critical work, reading these books makes it feel as though something has shifted in our field (something more than evident also in Daniel Dubuisson's latest English book [2019]). For here we have, in the case of *Imagine No Religion*, two senior and well-respected area specialists taking very seriously the critique of how modern categories inform (or, as they might say, obscure—and the difference between these two representations is the issue in need of consideration) our modern understanding of the past while, in the case of *Before Religion*, a section of what was once a larger dissertation (and thus from an earlier-career scholar) applies the critique of "religion" to how we might begin to better understand a variety of sites from our archive of the past.[5] What's therefore worth noting, I think, is that the critique of the category religion has, with the publication of these two books, been marked as something to be addressed, in detail, by scholars at both ends of our careers' broad spectrum—and also by those who work in area studies that once might have been seen as semi-autonomous fields of their own.[6] This development suggests to me that we ought to pause, at least for a moment, to consider our field's future; for in rethinking their respective topics in the light of this critique, the authors of these two books are among a growing number of historians and textual specialists who, I would argue, are beginning to understand just what is at stake if the project that some of us have outlined were to take hold in the academic study of religion. For they are not just aware that a large body of literature on this topic now exists (something that, judging by the literature cited, seems more apparent to Nongbri than Carlin and Boyarin, I admit), but they also seem to understand that grappling with the implications of this critique is now something that can no longer be ignored or simply glossed over.[7]

But what makes Nongbri's and Barton and Boyarin's books interesting for me to compare is not how similar they are (which, as already noted, seems to

---

[5] In the interest of full disclosure, I was among those invited to blurb Nongbri's book and I have written elsewhere on Barton and Boyarin's book (see chapter 2 in McCutcheon 2018).

[6] In my experience, it is not difficult to find a scholar of the Hebrew Bible or New Testament who does not identify as a scholar of religion but who, instead, sees these as entirely different fields. In fact, the whole point of Arnal's essay (the last chapter in Arnal and McCutcheon 2013) is to propose that it could be otherwise.

[7] In fact, Nongbri's book provides, I would argue, one of the most helpful introductions to the category critique, which at least dates to the work of Wilfred Cantwell Smith in the early 1960s (though his inflection of it was certainly normative and theological) and Jonathan Z. Smith as well, of course, but which today includes such authors as Tomoko Masuzawa, Timothy Fitzgerald, Richard King, Naomi Goldenberg, Suzanne Owen, Teemu Taira, Craig Martin, Bruce Lincoln, Malory Nye, etc. Notable is also the work of Kevin Schilbrack; for though unsupportive of this critique, he is among the few who have taken it seriously enough to have repeatedly engaged it in print, e.g., Schilbrack 2010, 2012, and 2013. For my own reply to his work (and for a general critique of the now popular critical realist stance), see chapter 6 in McCutcheon 2018.

remain as popular as ever among scholars) but how, under some scrutiny from his reviewers, the former reversed himself on a key point central to the book, suggesting what I think to be a far more interesting and productive direction for the field. But before elaborating on that difference, consider what the books share in common: both are premised on the assumption (dare I call it a hope?) that, akin to Tong's already quoted realist claims, a *more careful* examination of the ancient sources will allow us to leapfrog over our colleague's flawed readings and interpretations (caused by such things as their inappropriate use of the modern term religion when reading their ancient sources), which will allow us to understand the ancients more accurately. This is rather obviously signaled in the subtitle of the Barton and Boyarin's volume (*How Modern Abstractions Hide Ancient Realities*) as well as in the important closing pages of Nongbri's book, where his conclusion's final paragraph recommends dropping the word religion when describing items from the ancient world and, instead, finding new ways to describe them so that the material is "disaggregated and rearranged in ways *that correspond better* to ancient people's own organizational schemes" (2015, 159; emphasis added). For both books, then, the solution to the challenge of anachronism and the prominence of modern categories is a form of critical realism, whereby one recognizes that, while our word religion may not be out there in the ancient material, the people responsible for producing that material nonetheless did or felt things that corresponded to what we mean by religion, and we could have access to it all if we could just read our sources in the proper fashion. Thus, what we have here is what I might as well call the "cake and eat it too" strategy, whereby the critical viewpoint is applied *but only so far*, for were one to take Nongbri's own admission seriously—such as when he wrote, "All of our concepts are modern and hence anachronistic when applied to the ancient world" (158)—then the idea that we, today, could offer alternative readings that somehow corresponded more closely to ancient people's own self-representations would be seen as a sheer fantasy. (Why? Because we lack time travel and thus the ability to arrive at the authentic original, should such a source have ever even existed, that we could then use as the authoritative standard against which to judge the adequacy of our readings.)[8] So although both books are generously detailed, engaging the critique over the length of an entire manuscript, they each strike me as amounting to an effort to constrain the cri-

---

8 This is none other than the classic functionalist response to the work of the previous generation of Intellectualists, such as criticisms of E. B. Tylor's famous speculations on the basis of religion in dreams. See my own edited volume, *Fabricating Origins* (2015)—notably the afterword—for an accessible introduction to the problems associated with scholarly discourses on origins.

tique that some of us have offered concerning our field, by limiting it to a word, religion, rather than seeing the critique of the category religion to be but one component of a far broader examination of our now well-established method for studying others in a fashion that is inevitably socially formative for ourselves and our own worlds. For in both cases, people removed from us are nonetheless presumed to be accessible to the careful reader—should we read "their" material in the correct fashion, that is. And the result of such careful readings is that *they* happen to have arranged their worlds and understood themselves pretty much as *we* happen to arrange our worlds and understand ourselves today.

The moral of the story? Although it might be intellectually sloppy to call it religion, there's undoubtedly an it there, nonetheless, and the challenge is to find a better word for it. And so the important scholarly shift that I presumed that I saw in these recent works turns out to be not as significant as I had first thought.

This sort of work therefore strikes me as a strategically partial implementation of the critique that some in the field have offered over the past two decades; it is a type of scholarship akin to those who posit religion to have existed prior to the invention of the term used to name it (what I've elsewhere called religion before "religion"—i.e., "they" just called it something different from "us" [McCutcheon 2010]). But in this case, even when authors are willing to acknowledge that the conceptual tools that we use to organize human affairs into seemingly distinguishable (and thus knowable) domains are our own situationally specific devices (e.g., our propensity not just to identify but to distinguish religion, or what some now call spirituality or even personal religion, from politics, for example),[9] some nonetheless yet maintain that behind or prior to our tools there resides some sort of pristine experience, identity, or meaning that we, as scholars, can access (presumably with even better tools at our disposal, such as more accurate categories and a better understanding of the ancient context)—thereby providing access to that which had previously been obscured (hearkening back to Barton and Boyarin) by our mistaken readings (such as Tong's thoughts on the archive being read on its own terms). But, as already indicated, such a stance strikes me as theoretically troublesome, inasmuch as it must assume the existence of some sort of transcendental viewpoint that is conveyed yet conserved over time and distance, providing historians with unmediated access to the past, inasmuch as the anachronistic shortcomings of *other* people's scholarly tools somehow do not apply to our own.

---

9 See chapter 1 of Touna 2017a for a helpful critique of this notion of personal religion.

With this ironically ahistorical historian's strategy in mind, consider a third recent book on the ancient world: Nickolas Roubekas's *An Ancient Theory of Religion* (2017). As described on its back cover, the book "examines a theory of religion put forward by Euhemerus of Messene (late 4th-early 3rd century BCE) in his lost work Sacred Inscription," doing so in a manner that finds fault with variety of other writers' applications of the ancient approach. However, as argued so well by Touna at a Society of Biblical Literature panel on the book (see Touna 2017b), the only manner in which an argument concerning the more correct reading of this ancient source can be effective is if readers (apparently following Roubekas himself) completely forget what they just read on the book's own back cover: *the original work is lost!* So what is of importance to see, in keeping with the manner in which the critical turn in the field is sometimes acknowledged but simultaneously marginalized by writers, is that just as historicity seems to be *elevated* (in identifying the flawed, because contingent, even self-serving readings of one's interlocutors) it is also *ignored*, inasmuch as an utterly absent original (known to us, today, only by much later references to what turns out to have been copies of copies of copies, all of which spanned several hundred years) is thoroughly overlooked. Only in this way can a scholar be concerned with recovering what Euhemerus *really meant* and *really thought* (i.e., cake and eat it too).[10]

This limitation was apparent to me from the outset for, on May 17, 2016, I wrote a long email to the author, providing feedback on one of the pre-publication chapters (i.e., what later became chapter 6 in the published book) that Roubekas had kindly sent for my comment. After an opening salutation, the initial paragraph (with original typos corrected in this quotation)[11] reads as follows:

---

[10] Please note that I am not going so far as to invoke the intentional fallacy at this point, something that could, however, easily be cited as an impediment to ascertaining what either an ancient or even contemporary author *really meant*, even if a supposedly pristine, original document was said to exist.

[11] The opening line of my email in part read as follows: "I've not proofed this email so it might be full of typos .... " That I, as the author of this present chapter, have opted to revise my own original email (which, apart from mistyped words, used such shorthands as chpt for chapter, Xian for Christian, coz for because, and E for Euhemerus as well as E'ism for Euhemerism, etc.)—thereby producing a version that better suits the more formal scholarly requirements of the present occasion—should make evident a point being argued throughout this chapter: the original is gone (i.e., a product of this footnote's meta-narrative) and all we have are readers in the present working with what happens to be at hand and exercising choice for current practical purposes, sometimes uses a rhetoric of origins to authorize (by seemingly erasing or naturalizing) those choices.

> Overall, it is ironic—no?—that you critique/identify the use of rhetorics of authenticity in the work of early Christians yet an important distinction to you seems to be Euhemerus's own Euhemerism as opposed to Euhemeristic sources that don't get it right (the bulk of this argument is obviously in your earlier chapters but you make reference to it in this chapter). I have in mind what you term well into the chapter, improper Euhemerism or second-hand Euhemerism, or near the end what is termed a Euhemeristic source versus Euhemerus's own work, ancient Euhemerism (i.e., what you also term Euhemerus's Euhemerism). Or when you say, near the end, that later writers "cherry picked." But isn't all citation cherry picking … ? You cite my comments on authenticity, understandably, because that helps your case … That's how texts/argumentation works, no? But saying it in this case seems to function to delegitimize these authors and then certify your work, presumably with the original text … Thus you work to say that they didn't actually read the original is part of this [strategy]. So there is the original, the authentic Euhemerist theory as opposed to adaptations or revisions to it …. I think this is something worth mulling over, since it seems that you have a realistic view of history operating here; there was a guy named Euhemerus who wrote this or that and which meant this or that and you interpret the writings in the correct way as opposed to these early Christian writers who interpret it in a self-serving way … But what if it is self-serving all the way down—including scholars?! Thus, your very use of the presumption of an actual Euhemerus who meant this or that would now be seen as an identification strategy of your own, by which you distinguish yourself as a critical historian from all those sloppy self-interested Christian apologists …. Something that seems to be at the core of your approach [and] worth thinking through …

Of note is that this problematic approach to how we come to know that thing called the past, identified in what was admittedly just a chapter draft, made it into the published book. For example, consider the following: "[T]he utilization of a second-hand, distorted euhemerism needs to be seen as a precious tool in the ongoing process of (Christian) identity formation during the first centuries after Jesus's death" (Roubekas 2017, 124). That all readings are secondhand—let alone third and fourth and, etc., all having arisen from copies of copies of copies, with long-absent originals, much like intentional authors, existing only in the reader's mind—is necessarily unaddressed in such a claim, as are the no less socially formative purposes supported by modern readers and writers who employ the trope "the past" to legitimize their contemporary work. All of which persuades me that, as sophisticated as we think our category critiques sometimes are, and as much as we nod to those opening lines of Smith's from over thirty years ago, there still exists significant opportunities to do better work in the field. For after all, how can one judge distortions when the original is gone, or might have never existed to begin with?

And with that, I return to the significant (and, for me, encouraging) difference that I find in Nongbri's work. While he at first seems to have been in agreement with this speculative quest for origins (in that words other than "religion" might better suit what the ancients were actually up to), he has nonetheless come to understand the difficulty posed by this simultaneous embrace/denial of historicity; for, in his reply to a series of blog posts discussing his own book,[12] posted originally throughout February and early March 2017, Nongbri wrote as follows:

> There is a price to pay when we make accusations of distortion. In historical argumentation, when we say that one interpretation constitutes a distortion of this or that aspect of the past, we may be easily taken to imply two things: that there is something out there to be distorted and that there is some viewpoint that could provide an *un-distorted*, or at least a *less distorted* interpretation. And this raises the question of how we determine relative levels of distortion. Is it by reference to some "thing itself" out there in the world? If so, how do we "get at" the thing itself in the past, or even in the present?[13]

As he then went on to elaborate:

> Although the book avoided the term "distortion," I've been convinced by discussions with Vaia Touna and others that *Before Religion* wasn't entirely successful in navigating this cluster of methodological problems. At the conclusion of the book, I wrote as follows:
>
> ... it is crucial to understand that this is not simply a problem of finding another concept or word that covers the same ground as "religion," of finding a better word for it. The whole point is that, in antiquity, there never was any "it" there to begin with. The different type of descriptive accounts that I have in mind would allow what we have been calling "ancient religions" (that is, the contents of all those books called Mesopotamian Religion, Religions of Rome, Ancient Greek Religion, etc.) to be disaggregated and rearranged in ways that correspond better to ancient peoples' own organizational schemes. (*Before Religion*, 159)
>
> I see more clearly now how this final appeal to produce accounts that "correspond better to ancient people's own organizational schemes" raises the same set of questions as those provoked by the notion of "distortion" above. If I could revise the book, I would definitely reconsider the way I use the language of *correspondence*. Nevertheless, I still do think we can talk about the past, and adjudicate better and worse understandings of the past.

And how, exactly, does Nongbri think we can accomplish this? By turning our attention to our own discourses rather than to the supposedly pristine objects assumed to precede them. As he puts it:

---

12 See https://religion.ua.edu/blog/tag/words-and-things/ for the set of posts, with contributions from Shannon Trosper Schorey, Andrew Durdin, Adrian Hermann, Richard Newton, Matt Sheedy, and Anders Klostergaard Petersen.
13 Posted at https://religion.ua.edu/blog/2017/03/01/on-religion-words-and-things/ (accessed January 9, 2018).

I think we would do well to turn our attention from "the past itself" to the rules that historians make for themselves regarding how we talk about the past. Just as texts don't contain their own interpretations, words don't have any particular necessary connection to the material world. Broad social consensus exists for the meanings of most words, and so we don't generally think about our own role in maintaining that status quo ... So, my working assumption now (until I'm corrected by further conversations with colleagues!) is that our words really do make our worlds, so we have the responsibility to try our best to use words as thoughtfully as we can.

While there still remains much to converse about with Nongbri (such as what constitutes our "best" try and what the ends of such a scholarly turn may be), he has moved what I see as a considerable distance as a result of his previous conversations, going from the widely used criterion of correspondence to an approach premised on the socially formative nature of scholarly discourse—a move that, I would contend, puts him rather at odds with both Roubekas's attempt for the correct Euhemerism as well as Barton and Boyarin's attempt to reveal how ancient people actually thought about themselves. And it is just this distance, and thus Nongbri's willingness to take both history and the situated position of the historian seriously, that encourages me about where at least some part of our field might be going. And I admit that work by some today, notably by some of the earlier-career scholars who are reflecting on what to do with what J. Z. Smith has left us, adds to this encouragement.

In closing, I should acknowledge that, for some, this will surely be an unsatisfactory note on which to end, i.e., being content with studying *discourses on the past* as opposed to somehow moving beyond or behind them in order to study the archive "on its own terms," so as to more satisfactorily access *the actual archive of the past*. But the position to which Nongbri has moved strikes me as an entirely fitting view for the scholar to adopt, inasmuch as it presumes from the outset that the past is just that, *quite literally past*, i.e., done with, over, at an end, and that all that therefore remains are potentially random material items (for who knows why just these things happen to remain, let alone how much was even there to start with) that we, in the present, signify in a variety of ways in order to breathe our own life and thus meaning into them. The omniscient narrator's stance is so tempting to adopt, of course, and so effective at normalizing our own viewpoint, that we often fail to take seriously just how removed from us this thing called the past actually is—so removed, in fact, that it is quite literally gone and unknowable (making the antecedent to the pronoun "it" itself unsignified and that preceding sentence itself a speculative claim). To make this point with students, I've sometimes proposed that they consider what happens to our knowledge of the past when, say, a small rural church which houses one-of-a-kind birth or marriage records burns down or when a tornado or flood destroys all of a family's photo albums and keepsakes. In such cases, we come to inhabit a position where (recalling the ironic way in which the once-controversial US Secretary of Defense, Donald Rumsfeld, might have phrased it) *we actually don't know how much we don't know.*

Or, from personal experience, I could cite my last remaining older sister and myself going through our father's possessions shortly after his death, in the late summer of 2019. Despite having listened to tales of family lore over the years and despite being but one generation removed from the artifacts we were sorting, we had no idea whatsoever who the people were in the photo albums from the 1930s, let alone why this or that particular item had been saved by him in the files and boxes that we were going through. While we could seek out cousins who might retain some of this knowledge, thereby identifying a few of the people or events, how much more problematic is this signification when the time spans hundreds or even thousands of years, when the originals cease to exist altogether? (But note: even with the so-called original photos in our hands, many of which bore our late mother's faded handwriting on the back, we still didn't know what to make of them.) In our case, the result was that most of it was given away to charity or just thrown out, with some, perhaps out of either guilt or hopefulness, tucked away in boxes that now inhabit closets in each of our homes, with us completely and unavoidably unaware of any significance it had for our parents—or, better put, *may* have had, because our father, for all we know, may have himself forgotten *that* he even had it or *why* he had it. For he too might have retained things based on who knows what motives after our mother's death back in 1996. For example, did he even know that their first bankbook, as a married couple, from 1946, was in one of those small metal strongboxes that he kept locked in his own closet? And because I'll never be able to find an answer to that question, the issue, for the critically minded historian, is *why did I keep it* and *what am I to do with it now* …?

Of course adopting this thorough-going historicist position—a position not that different from deciding that all we have to study is not religion but, rather, the discourse on religion—means that the standard mechanisms on which scholars have often relied to authorize their work over against their many other contemporary competitors (e.g., claims that "our" reading recovers some author's original intentions for, unlike "their" reading, it "is in the spirit of" either this or that norm or so-called classic or authoritative tradition or figure) will no longer be heard as persuasive. Even claiming something to be a primary, versus a secondary, text will now be an issue in need of examination, given that it would be wise to assume that so-called primary texts have more than likely gone through innumerable editors' hands and thus editions on their way to our desks. For now, once-commonplace appeals or claims will be seen to be but instances of data along with all other instrumental uses of past in the present (to allude to the helpful work of Bruce Lincoln [e.g., 1989, 27–37]). That scholars of so-called ancient religion are now beginning to confront some of this, inasmuch as the rug provided by the seemingly universal category religion has been pulled out from under them, therefore strikes me as an exciting moment in the field, inasmuch as it challenges them to live up to Smith's already-mentioned call for scholars to be "relentlessly self-conscious," a trait that, as he went on to argue, "constitutes ... [our] primary expertise" (1982, xi). For if the past does not mysteriously linger, speak for itself, or somehow set the terms by which it ought to be understood, but, rather, has indeed passed us by, then we are left with studying the ingenuity of always-present actors, working with who knows what yellowed and cracked materials, but always doing so for inevitably present purposes—ourselves as scholars among them. (For further elaboration on this point, see McCutcheon 2003.) And given the multitude of contemporary social actors and their varied situations and interests, this seems to me to be more than enough for us to study, leaving this category of origins to those actors' own rhetorical toolboxes. For after all, as Thompson has reminded us, "Origins belong to the intellectual and literary worlds, not to the world of events, either political or social" (Thompson 1999, 31). Or, as Smith himself once remarked in a wonderfully candid interview, when addressing the topic of translation: "there's no original in this business" (Braun and McCutcheon 2018, 12).

Reference List

Arnal, William E., and Russell T. McCutcheon. 2013. *The Sacred is the Profane: The Political Nature of "Religion."* New York: Oxford University Press.

Baldwin, Matthew C. 2019. "Objects and Objections: Methodological Reflections on the Data for Religious Studies." In *Constructing "Data" in Religious Studies: Examining the Architecture of the Academy*, edited by Leslie Dorrough Smith, 73–100. Sheffield, UK: Equinox Publishers.

Barton, Carlin A., and Daniel Boyarin. 2016. *Imagine No Religion: How Modern Abstractions Hide Ancient Realities*. New York: Fordham University Press.

Braun, Willi, and Russell T. McCutcheon, eds. 2018. *Reading J. Z. Smith: Interviews and Essay*. New York and London: Oxford University Press.

Dubuisson, Daniel. 2019. *The Invention of Religion*. Sheffield, UK: Equinox Publishers.

Lincoln, Bruce. 1989. *Discourse and the Construction of Society: Comparative Studies of Myth, Ritual, and Classification*. New York: Oxford University Press.

McCutcheon, Russell T. 2003. "Filling in the Cracks with Resin: A Response to John Burris." *Method & Theory in the Study of Religion* 15/3:284–303.

McCutcheon, Russell T. 2008. "Introducing Smith." In *Introducing Smith: Essays in Honor of Jonathan Z. Smith*, edited by Willi Braun and Russell T. McCutcheon, 1–17. Sheffield, UK: Equinox.

McCutcheon, Russell T. (2010) 2014. "Religion Before 'Religion'?" In *Chasing Down Religion, In the Sights of History and the Cognitive Sciences: Essay in Honour of Luther H. Martin*, edited by Donald Wiebe and Panayotis Pachis, 285–301. Thessaloniki, Greece: Barbounakis Publications. Reprinted by Equinox Publishers.

McCutcheon, Russell T., ed. 2015. *Fabricating Origins*. Sheffield, UK: Equinox.

McCutcheon, Russell T. 2018. *Fabricating Religion: Fanfare for the Common e.g.* Berlin: Walter de Gruyter.

Nongbri, Brent. 2015. *Before Religion: A History of a Modern Concept*. New Haven CT: Yale University Press.

Reed, Annette Yoshiko. 2019. "Partitioning 'Religion' and its Prehistories: Reflections on Categories, Narratives, and the Practice of Religious Studies." In *Constructing "Data" in Religious Studies: Examining the Architecture of the Academy*, edited by Leslie Dorrough Smith, 9–26. Sheffield, UK: Equinox Publishing.

Roubekas, Nicholas. 2017. *An Ancient Theory of Religion: Euhemerism from Antiquity to the Present*. New York: Routledge.

Schilbrack, Kevin. 2010. "Religions: Are There Any?" *Journal of the American Academy of Religion* 78/4:1112–38.

Schilbrack, Kevin. 2012. "The Social Construction of 'Religion' and Its Limits: A Critical Reading of Timothy Fitzgerald." *Method & Theory in the Study of Religion* 24/1:97–117.

Schilbrack, Kevin. 2013. "What *Isn't* Religion?" *Journal of Religion* 93/3:291–318.

Schmeiser, Peggy. 2019. "Governance and Public Policy as Critical Objects of Investigation in the Study of Religion." In *Constructing "Data" in Religious Studies: Examining the Architecture of the Academy*, edited by Leslie Dorrough Smith, 127–35. Sheffield, UK: Equinox.

Smith, Jonathan Z. 1982. *Imagining Religion: From Babylon to Jonestown*. Chicago: University of Chicago Press.

Smith, Leslie Dorrough, ed. 2019. *Constructing "Data" in Religious Studies: Examining the Architecture of the Academy*. Sheffield, UK: Equinox.

Thompson, Thomas L. 1999. *The Mythic Past: Biblical Archaeology and the Myth of Israel*. New York: Basic Books.

Tong, M Adryael. 2019. "Categorization and its Discontents." In *Constructing "Data" in Religious Studies: Examining the Architecture of the Academy*, edited by Leslie Dorrough Smith, 38–47. Sheffield, UK: Equinox.

Touna, Vaia. 2017a. *Fabrications of the Greek Past: Religion, Tradition, and the Making of Modern Identities*. Leiden: Brill.

Touna, Vaia. 2017b. "From Out of the Head of Zeus: The Context of a Lost Text." Paper presented to the Society of Biblical Literature's Greco-Roman Religions section on "Theorizing Ancient Theory of Religion." Boston, MA.

Tweed, Thomas. 2016. "Valuing the Study of Religion: Improving Difficult Dialogues Within and Beyond the AAR's 'Big Tent.'" *Journal of the American Academy of Religion* 84/2:287–322.

Whitelam, Keith W. (1996) 2001. *The Invention of Ancient Israel: The Silencing of Palestinian History*. New York: Routledge.

5 What Happens After the Deconstruction?

When I first listened to the Religious Studies Project's September 19, 2016, interview with Teemu Taira on the category religion, I was struck by how the interview was framed, i.e., "where do we go from here?" (as Taira phrases it, reminiscent of Kevin Schilbrack's own phrasing of the question [2013]).[1] For having understood that the field's primary organizing concept can itself be examined as an historical artifact and not a natural kind (as can such other categories as tradition, belief, faith, experience, myth, ritual, etc., by the way), many become rather concerned with how, in the face of such historicization, we can continue to carry out our work.

Taira's answer to the question, as illustrated by his work on, among others, Karhun Kansa (i.e., "the people of the bear," a contemporary, registered religious community in Finland), concerned scholars studying the motives and effects of groups trying to attain, or which have already attained, the status that often comes with this designation. As he puts it, we now turn our attention to studying the reasons for, and effects of, groups aiming to perform such things as ceremonies sanctioned by the nation-state (e.g., marriages and funerals), groups wishing to be included in the curricula of religious education in public schools and be eligible to receive financial support from a ministry of education, or those intent on obtaining certain social freedoms and public recognition.

In short, he proposes becoming a scholar of "religion."

As Taira says in that interview, the future of the field may be found in investigating how groups

> make use of the category religion, how they promote their own interests ..., how we are governed by the category religion .... I [therefore] tend to ask quite simple questions ..., such as: Who benefits of being a religion? Or who benefits of denying the religiosity of a group or a practice? I can also ask how are we governed, if I'm trying to look at the level of state or society more broadly ... And I think it is quite clear that people achieve something by being a religion, but that happens within the governing structures of society. So, by being a religion, you gain some but at the same time you lose some. When you get some concrete benefits you are usually molded in a way that you have to adjust yourself to the criteria that is used in an institution, in law, or wherever. And that is typical so that you have to represent your group as somehow reminding of Protestant Christianity, but at the same time you are sort of marginalized or domesticated, in a way ..., or as some people say you are depoliticized, in a way. So the idea goes that being a religions definitely guarantees some privileges of selected groups but at the same time it distances them from the so-called secular center of society the political, so-called secular power.

---

[1] This podcast interview, plus solicited responses, was published in *Implicit Religion* 20/4 (2017).

Thus, he makes clear, at least to me, that such a scholar's aim is not to define religion, debate which religion is right or which form of a religion is proper or legitimate, or then use the term to just get on with studying people (e.g., their religiosity, its history, and implications). Instead, if we understand "religion" to be nothing more or less than a folk term of relevance and thus consequence to the worlds in which many of us happen to live and work, then a scholar's goal should be examining how groups of people with specific interests (whether that group is a nation-state's leadership or a minority group within the nation) use the term in specific settings (such as law courts, perhaps) where something they value is at stake. Thus, the shift is to study how people themselves use this term, religion, in discrete settings, however they choose to define it. For, as I understand it, the presumption now is that, at least in liberal democracies, the discourse on religion—connected to the widespread discourse on the individual and the related discourses on privacy, both of which have a central place in the founding and governing documents and practices—plays a role in the day-to-day management of a group's limits and direction.

Having made this shift, the debate, as nicely outlined by Taira, is not over whether something is or isn't a religion (e.g., the once and still popular question as to whether Buddhism is a philosophy or a religion) but, instead, concerns the effects of successfully (or not) using the term—and so we become curious as to what is at stake within a society if this thing called Buddhism is a philosophy or a religion. This is a shift that I, for one, welcome, given that I've advocated such a move for quite some time.

Now, the podcast attracted not only my attention but also that of Paul Hedges, who penned a reply of his own (Hedges 2016—a version of which appeared in the issue of *Implicit Religion* already mentioned). Given that he describes himself as a scholar of inter-religious studies—defined by him in a video on his faculty website[2] as "the way people of different religions, but also no religion, meet in dynamic encounters in societies and across the world today"—it's likely fair to assume that he might disagree with Taira (as, in my reading, he does), inasmuch as *using the category*, rather that *studying its use*, is fundamental to carrying out his work (which, to my way of thinking, involves a certain sort of socially formative effort to create a world that he values). While I leave reading his response to others, what I find interesting is this question he also pursues: "what happens after deconstruction?"

While I would contest that deconstruction names the work Taira advocates (I'd happily call it historicization, to be honest, as I usually do, or the more un-

---

2 See https://www.rsis.edu.sg/profile/paul-hedges (accessed January 30, 2018).

wieldy "study of social classification systems"), what I find more curious is the assumption that a reality exists in the world that demands naming and therefore our attention—thus we apparently can't be satisfied with studying "religion" but must, at some point, get on with some new way of studying the thing we once called religion in light of, or after, the critique of "religion." That people use this word seems not to be contested in this debate, of course, but what is up for grabs is whether we, as scholars, must, sooner or later, adopt either the word ourselves or all that came with it (and, in the process, develop some synonym like faith, worldview, or tradition to name that which was once called religion), so as to then just get on with the business of describing and comparing that which was formerly known as religion, so that we can eventually either interpret or explain (to nod toward that longstanding divide in our field) the world as envisioned by those formerly known as religious devotees.

To rephrase: yes, there are consequential social realities created by the use of the word in specific institutional and historical settings—no one is questioning that. But do I, as a scholar, grant the existence of that social reality to such an extent that I then go on to develop, say, a theory of religion (not of "religion" mind you), thereby sanctioning and reinforcing some group's way of constituting their world, as if their collective efforts result in something so real and enduring as to demand my adoption and thus attention? Do I write a textbook chronicling, in great detail, the historical development and current shape of this social reality (such as the history of Christianity, as opposed to the discourse that results in the impression of this enduring this called Christianity?). And then do I study how, for instance, participation in this social reality influences, say, people's voting habits? (You'll notice that hardly any—if any at all!—theorist of religion, world religions textbook or pollster frames the issue in this manner, i.e., that they're merely studying the effects of a shared and thus presumed social reality. No, they're studying religion and thus *its* effects on people—seeing it as an independent causal force in the world.)

To press the issue, consider this analogous case: with the Religious Studies Project in mind, I think of David Robertson's work on conspiracy theories (2016). Think up a conspiracy theory that you know something about, notably one that has significant traction for some people and maybe one that has lasted for some time or one that helps people to orient themselves with regard to other institutions in their life, such as, say, the government (e.g., Kennedy's assassination? Cover-ups on the existence of UFOs? What some Trump supporters in the US now think about the FBI and the so-called deep state, let alone some of their claims about falsified COVID-19 infection rates …?): as a scholar, is your job to grant the social reality of this conspiracy theory for these people to such an extent that you carry out all of your research while working within the parameter of its assumptions, so as to, let's just say, figure out just how the mob killed Jack Kennedy, where the deep state starts and ends, and what the actual COVID-19 numbers really are? Or, instead of such descriptive work, might you study just *why* this particular viewpoint has been so persuasive for some people, thus examining the motivations for assuming it and the practical benefits for propagating it, all the while recognizing, of course, its social reality *for them* but never adopting and thereby sanctioning that reality *for yourself*, as the researcher. It's the difference between, to select but another example, tracking down specific instances of voter fraud associated with mail-in ballots and asking why Donald Trump repeatedly raises this concern.

I could name many other examples, of course, where scholars would more than likely never entertain taking others' social realities so seriously that we thought we should adopt them for ourselves, and then start using them and working within their limits; instead, in many cases, we easily recognize that our work, as scholars, ought to be focused on explaining *why* such a claim, action, or institution exists or is so successfully reproduced. Yet when it comes to some (or, again, should I say many?) people who call part of their world "a religion," or who designate something *as* sacred or *as* spiritual, as opposed to it being designated as profane or secular, well, imagining these to be efficacious discursive moves like any other is awfully difficult and represented as demeaning the people being studied.

And here the problem becomes evident: many of our colleagues, I would argue, are, to put it frankly, native informants for this particular social classifications system (thereby taking this discourse's use as necessary and inevitable, given the social world they understand themselves to inhabit), making it near impossible for them to entertain that there are only religions in the world *because many of us act like there are*. For they themselves are (understandably, of course) deeply invested in a model of the world made possible by assuming that this is religious and deep and transcendentally meaningful while that is not, because this other thing is merely shallow, contingent, or accidental—a system of distinction and value that, just as Taira argues, comes with very practical interests, costs, and benefits. And, if he's correct in his analysis (i.e., that these costs and benefits can be of great consequence to the members of groups who aim to be designated in this or that manner), then we would more than likely predict that anyone from within such societies would not give up assuming the reality of their social world without putting up a fight—scholars included.

Thus we arrive back at the "what do we do now?" question; for having historicized the concept religion, many still assume that we need to just get on with figuring out a better way to study that which we once called religion—they call it something different, sure, but they still group together the same old parts, doing so as if a stable reality lurks somewhere in the background of our naming, our acting, and our organizing. And this move, I'm arguing, is a sign of membership within, and thus care for and replication of, a social reality that some of us, instead, wish to historicize and thereby study. In fact, it's a point nicely recognized by a comment from Neil George, posted on September 22, 2016, on the Religious Studies Project's site, that directly responds to Hedges's own RSP post: "You are presuming realities that exist behind the word religion," the comment noted, "when that needs to be argued for. I don't think there are any scholars out there holding the position that 'religion' picks out something real or useful, while simultaneously refusing to use the word."[3]

So what comes after deconstruction? Well, if you had the benefit of floating outside of time and space then I guess you'd just know how things really ought to go together or be distinguished (the so-called natural joints where reality breaks into its constitutive parts). That some people put various elements of society into fixed relationships that result in their ability to identify, say, this event as a ceremony, those as artifacts, and these institutions *as* all being religious is evident and not in question—but, as far as I understand the situation in which we're in, none of us float so free of the world that we know things *ought* to go together or be divided in just that manner. So the fact that some people make just those links, fight over those divisions, and move within worlds made possible by those (dis)associations is, to my way of thinking, quite an interesting thing and deserving of some study.

So, from where I sit and, I'm guessing that, for Taira as well, there's no need to answer the opening question. For there is an after only for those who have the privileged knowledge—who just want to get on with talking about the world as it really is. That they're so confident, when others carve things up in dramatically different ways, is what some of us happen to be curious about; so watching their assembling process and tracking the devices they're using is rather fascinating to some of us and more than enough to study.

Reference List

Hedges, Paul. (2016). "The Deconstruction of Religion: So What?" *Religious Studies Project* (blog). September 22, 2016. Accessed January 20, 2018. https://www.religiousstudiesproject.com/2016/09/22/the-deconstruction-of-religion-so-what/.

---

3 George was among those later invited to contribute essays that ran in the already mentioned issue of *Implicit Religion*, in response to the Taira/Hedges exchange.

Robertson, David G. 2016. *UFOs, Conspiracy Theories and the New Age: Millennial Conspiracism.* London: Bloomsbury.

Schilbrack, Kevin. 2013. "After We Deconstruct 'Religion,' Then What? A Case for Critical Realism." *Method & Theory in the Study of Religion* 25:107–12.

Taira, Teemu. "Categorising 'Religion': From Case Studies to Methodology." *Religious Studies Project* (blog). September 19, 2016. Accessed March 15, 2000. https://www.religiousstudiesproject.com/podcast/categorising-religion-from-case-studies-to-methodology/.

Part III Institutional Implications

6 Theses on Creating Successful Religion Programs in an Anti-Humanities Age

Contrary to various attempts to defend the existence and relevance of Humanities programs in the modern research university by appealing to their intrinsic value or the inherent importance of their objects of study, an alternative and effective approach is possible—one that takes seriously the skills that we teach to our students, despite the specialties in which we each work. On our own campus, at the University of Alabama, we term this "the examples approach."

1. Despite the well-known literature on the so-called crisis in the humanities in higher education, this is a generalization that deserves some unpacking, before we proceed with offering cures.

2. Because this term, "the humanities," can stand in for many things—such as specific subject matter, a style of inquiry, or even a proposed view on "the human" or "the enduring human spirit"—we should be careful to specify just what we mean by "the humanities" or "anti-humanities," especially if we aim to diagnose problems and then offer possible solutions; for failure to accurately assess the challenges will lead to ineffective remedies.

3. There was a time during that period known as the Renaissance when the humanities might have included all higher learning not devoted to divinity or what we now know as theological studies, and then, more recently, when the now more traditional term "liberal arts" might have been considered almost coterminous with "the humanities"—as in those who might have once supported a so-called humanistic or liberalizing education for undergraduate students. Today, the term "humanities" is largely used by universities as an organizational and administrative convention to name a collection of academic disciplines or fields of study that are thought collectively to investigate the creative, expressive, personal, and thus meaning-making side of the human (from theatre, dance, art, and music to English literature, classics, modern languages, and, yes, religious studies). This is in distinction from, on the one hand, the more quantifiable studies of human beings that are grouped together as the social sciences and, on the other, the natural sciences, with their focus on either the more mechanistic and presumably impersonal and thus rule-governed aspects of human beings as well as the rest of the natural world.

4. Despite continued use by administrators and faculty in higher education, this once-common rationale for the use of the term "the humanities" no longer seems relevant, not only because of more recent intellectual approaches that now question the model of "the human" and "the individual" that reside at the center of traditional understandings of the humanities, and thereby animate

its distinction from other academic pursuits, but also due to significant structural changes in post-secondary education over the recent decades.

5. Given the steady professionalization of higher education in North America over the past generation or two—I think of my own older sisters, both in Canada and born in 1946 and 1947, respectively, who each went to what were then called Nursing College and Teacher's College, respectively, instead of a university, to train for each of those professions—it strikes me that using the term "the humanities" in the modern, professionalized university now means programs of study that seem not to prepare their students for a practical and specific career path and thus a job directly after graduation.

6. In an era when, according to a February 2019 Public Broadcasting System report, $9 billion in government funding for higher education has been cut in the past decade collectively by the states (when adjusted for inflation), thereby forcing students to pay a far greater share of their education's costs than previous generations,[1] they and their families are now more concerned than ever with what will come of their significant financial investment (much of which, as is well known, is financed each year by means of student loans; as widely reported in the summer of 2019, there were approximately 45 million people in the US who collectively held $1.5 trillion in student loan debt).

7. As a corollary to this steady cut in government funding, the reliance of many US public universities on tuition revenue to fund their operations has grown significantly during this period. A 2017 study conducted by the State Higher Education Executive Officers Association found that tuition comprised 46% of funding for US public universities, nearly twice what it was in 1990.[2] At some public universities, it can, of course, be higher—significantly so in some cases. For example, the study found that in such states as Vermont, New Hampshire, Delaware, and Pennsylvania, it was over 70% in 2017.

8. Given this context and this understanding of what we now often mean by "the humanities," responding to the challenges faced by humanities programs today therefore means that programs effectively do two things that the modern university now requires of them: (i) assist their schools to generate tuition revenue via credit hour production; and (ii) assist their students to understand the wide and practical application of what they learn in their classes—an understanding that, in part, must swim against two misperceptions: (i) that, for the most part, humanities degrees focus on ethereal, soft, and nonessential skills

---

[1] See https://www.pbs.org/newshour/education/most-americans-dont-realize-state-funding-for-higher-ed-fell-by-billions (posted February 28, 2019).

[2] See https://www.pewtrusts.org/en/research-and-analysis/blogs/stateline/2018/03/29/tuition-overtakes-state-money-as-funding-source-for-public-colleges (posted March 29, 2018).

which do not lead to careers; and (ii) that professional programs always lead to full-time employment.

9. Recognizing that our conversation about the future of the humanities today takes place in this practical context, I would therefore argue that, unless they happen to be looked upon favorably for local idiosyncratic reasons (such as the way university administrations can sometimes value music or theatre programs inasmuch as, like athletics in the case of some colleges, these can be the easily identified as the public face of the institution), successful humanities programs today will have each found their own way to address (i) what their students do with their degrees; and (ii) how their schools pay the bills.

10. For those still committed to the earlier rationale for distinguishing the humanities from other intellectual pursuits based on their supposedly unique object of study—i.e., the creative, expressive individual—the turn toward emphasizing a field's practical application and a school's budgetary needs may be seen as a crass betrayal of so-called humanistic values. For yet others, however, it may be understood as a recognition of the practical conditions in which we all inevitably carry out our work—conditions that will invariably dictate the success or failure of programs that educate students and which employ faculty.

11. At the University of Alabama—a publicly funded, R-1 university with a strong undergraduate teaching mission—we've systematically tried to address these two concerns since beginning in earnest to reinvent the department in the fall of 2001. That is to say, while working to advance goals specific to our faculty members' interests and expertise as well as their shared understanding of what the study of religion is and the direction to be taken by the department, we always did so mindful of our specific and practical context, working to address the needs of both students (whether majors or those taking just one course to satisfy a core curriculum requirement) and the wider university.

12. Key to this approach was developing a way for all faculty to contribute to, feel involved in, as well as benefit from, a shared vision for the unit, one that informs everything from new course development to hiring decisions. Although our department's initiative to identify ourselves with social theory is hardly the only way a department can do this, what is nonnegotiable is that faculty members see themselves as having offices next door to one another for a reason and not just the happenstance of past hiring decisions.

13. Related to this reason for sharing a hallway, we have found that what we now call the examples approach has been very useful, inasmuch as it recognizes that we will never "cover" all of the material. So, instead, following J. Z. Smith's model, we invite students to see each region, item, or historical period studied in a class as comparable, in some fashion, to other instances, from other classes,

inasmuch as they are all exemplary of wider, cross-cultural issues in how groups form, reproduce, and are contested over time and place.

14. The examples approach therefore prompts students not just to learn descriptive facts but to apply analytic skills acquired in one domain to another, thereby increasing (i) the likelihood of minors and either first or second majors, inasmuch as their studies in our classes can be demonstrated to have direct and practical relevance for interests that they may have in other academic fields; and (ii) the likelihood of students seeing the applicability of classroom skills to domains well outside of a university's classrooms. We therefore find that our alums, who have gone on to pursue a wide variety of careers (from working in business and education to medicine, law, and social services), consistently report the ongoing and often surprising relevance of their studies in our courses—sometimes resulting in an unsolicited blog post coming our way from an alum of our program who saw an unexpected connection between seemingly different things that helped them to better understand both.

15. The examples approach also assists faculty to develop collaborative projects among themselves—from writing and teaching projects to grant applications—by seeing the thing called "the field" not as comprised of isolated specialties but, instead, as a collective endeavor, exemplified in a variety of discrete sites but always revolving around shared inquiries into broad and common questions. Thus, a colleague's work on a region or historical period well removed from one's own can nonetheless be understood to illustrate important methods or principles of direct consequence to one's own work.

16. The examples approach is equally relevant in both lower-level introductory courses and upper-level seminars as well as in graduate school, settings that each cater to different students' specific needs but all also focused on practical relevance and wide applicability.

17. Although achieving a balance is a continual challenge (e.g., the relationship between large enrollment intro courses, who teaches them, and small, more specialized seminars), keeping students' practical futures in mind in each setting while not forgetting your own institution's larger needs can help to create conditions in which a unit in the humanities can be freed from some of the unhelpful caricatures of work carried out in the humanities. The ability to make unanticipated connections that shed new light on familiar topics is something of importance and value that will be of benefit to students, regardless the future for which our classes help to prepare them.

7 Growth, Identity, and Branding: An Interview with *Religious Studies News*

Religious Studies News: Is there a departmental identity at UA? That is, in the wider world of religion departments in the US and Canada, does the department strive to have a distinct character in its theoretical or methodological orientation or leanings or faculty makeup?

Russell McCutcheon: Our department is very conscious of defining itself—both within the national field as well as among other units on our campus that also happen to offer courses on religion. Given that we were a very small department for much of our over fifty-year history (i.e., three or four faculty members), other departments understandably own such courses as anthropology of religion, the philosophy of religion, the history of Christianity, mythology, and Roman religion, etc., so ensuring that we establish an identity and thus a domain of our own for our department—especially as we've grown over the past twenty years—has been high on our list of priorities. That we might have lost the major back in 2000, when we were not graduating enough students according to our state credentialing board, means that reinventing the department from the bottom up has kept our eye on identity issues at countless sites. And since the majority in the field seem to see theory as some sort of optional second step (hence the viewpoint that description is somehow theory-free and one therefore only uses theory as one needs it—I think here of the "I don't do theory" that we often hear in the field), our view that theory instead provides the enabling conditions for all scholarship (and, in our case, social theory) is something that we think sets us apart. So we've developed a common and explicit focus first on identity-formation (it's something our faculty members each study and teach in a wide variety of regions and eras, of course) and now on digital humanities, something that we think sets us apart from many other departments in the country—especially those still aiming to cover all the world's religions, despite the now well-established critique of that way of organizing the field. In fact, anyone paying attention to our social media or even job ads will know that there's a particular sort of thing happening in the study of religion at Alabama and, so far at least, it has been quite successful; given that success (e.g., we've added our

---

Note: My thanks to Sarah Levine, the Director of Publications for the American Academy of Religion, for kindly arranging this interview and for posing these questions. It was originally posted on March 25, 2016, and can be found at http://rsn.aarweb.org/articles/growth-identity-and-branding-department-religious-studies-university-alabama (accessed December 12, 2019). The text has been updated here.

twelfth tenure-track faculty member in August 2020), I'd hope it's a model that others would consider if they're game to rethink their own work and their departmental identity, too.

RSN: Some departments work on their public personas through events, outreach, etc. Is this something your department does, and if so, how? Is there a strategy to the way you communicate to wider publics just what it is the Department of Religious Studies does?

RM: During my job interview to be chair, back in January 2000, the newly appointed dean of the College of Arts & Sciences asked me who the various stakeholders were in the study of religion. That's a key question, I think, and any successful department, will, I assume, know who theirs are—so I'd hope all and not just some departments work on their public persona. Being a public university, ours range from the taxpayers of the state to the students and their parents, along with other colleagues (on and off our campus) as well as administrators, the general public, and even our own graduates. So while communicating effectively with them all at any one given moment is likely not possible, a strategic department (i.e., one that does not take its own existence for granted) tries to think through who this event is for or at whom that mailing is directed and for what purpose—all of which means that the department likely has a number of different personae, like each of us (e.g., sometimes I'm a professor but other times I'm a husband or a brother or a consumer or ...), and the key is knowing when and how best to operationalize which. It's likely linked to your first question as well—sure, it might sound crass to some, but among my first tasks when I became chair was to develop a motto (the result: "Studying Religion *in* Culture" [the italics matter to us]) and a logo (based on our post-Civil War gothic building and not a mash-up of world religions symbols [what we happen to study doesn't define us as a department, in other words]—my hope was that students associate us with where we were). The people who poo-poo this sort of intentional branding strike me as missing the point that the nation-state has a flag and an anthem for a reason—how many years of people's lives do they repeat the US's Pledge of Allegiance out loud and in front of each other each morning? Their publishers don't pay attention to book cover design and they themselves don't invoke the titles Dr. or Professor for no good reason. So for any social group to be successful, a host of techniques are needed—that's the social theorist in me talking—since I don't assume group identity is a naturally occurring resource. Fail to return the head nod or the text one too many times and a social bond will be damaged—sometimes irreparably. So yes, we're very mindful of our publics and trying to stay in touch with them—e.g., some events may just be for majors, for instance, hoping to benefit them intellectually, sure, but they also provide a social occasion for them to bond as a group, but we're also sure to live tweet it, probably post a picture (or several) on social media, maybe even request some financial support from the college (whether the request is successful or not, at least it knows we're doing this or that), all an effort to ensure that wider groups understand the good work we see the students and faculty to be doing.

We also learned long ago that although we try to provide programming to attract others' interest outside our department, whether from the local community or other faculty on campus, we also have to make programming choices based on our own needs and interests instead of trying to intuit what others think the study of religion ought to be. In fact, there's a relatively good chance that others will think the academic study of religion needs to be something rather different from what we actually do. So we reasoned quite some time ago that while working hard to translate what we do to wide publics (sure, we've had an annual newsletter for years but we've also had a department blog for eight years that aims at a pretty wide readership, featuring a steady stream of student and grad along with faculty posts), we also have to speak mainly to our primary public—our majors and minors, in and outside of the classroom—for they're the lifeblood of the department (at least in the state of Alabama the number of grads is the crucial measure of viability). And sooner or later, even parents who might have at first questioned their children's decision to major in REL come around once they see not only the attention their daughters and sons get but also the critically important tools they acquire in our classes. In fact, one of my favorite videos (did I say we have a Vimeo account and that we train students to make movies?) was filmed with two grads (a brother and sister) and their dad, who were all on campus for a Saturday football game. Hearing what dad thought now about what his kids studied in college (one became a public school French teacher and the other a lawyer) versus what he thought long ago when first hearing they planned to be religious studies majors was pretty gratifying.

So a strategy? Sure: use whatever is available, easily at hand, to make connections for people who aren't already experts so that they can understand the relevance of whatever seemingly esoteric topic you happen to have trained in as a scholar; sure, it takes time and energy to do, on someone's part, but it pays off in countless ways. At the end of the day, I don't think that any field is self-evidently important (e.g., our campus closed the Department of Sociology just a few years before I arrived, all the languages and even classics were rolled into one major, and the undergrad degree in physics was also non-viable and in need of reinvention) and so every communication has a pedagogical undertone, trying to bring people along who might not otherwise care as much as you about this or that. I think of Jonathan Z. Smith's work here, actually: as I read him, pretty much all of his essays are pedagogical, inasmuch as they exemplify for readers how they, too, can think more carefully about, say, doing comparison (wherever they happen to do it). I think that's the spirit of our department—we try to see much of what we do, regardless the intended audience, as having an eventual pedagogical payoff.

RSN: UA has a large undergraduate enrollment. Where and how does the department fit into UA life? Is partnering or engaging with other departments an important part of programming?

RM: In terms of courses, presumably like many departments, our main contribution is to serve what we call the core curriculum (or what others might call general education courses)—either offering lower-level core "humanities" courses for incoming students or upper-level core "writing" courses. (We offer other courses too, such as upper-level seminars mainly attended by majors/minors, but the majority of our classes carry a core designation.) As others know all too well, these so-called service courses are also the main gateway classes to the major since the vast majority of incoming students have never heard of what we do, and so few are chomping at the bit to declare REL as their major when they first arrive. And given that our campus doubled in size over the past decade (as part of a planned expansion—we were about 18,500 when I arrived in 2001, a size we'd long been and now we're at 38,000 students), we've had to be prepared to seat an always larger number of incoming undergraduate students each fall for quite some time (the expectation was 8% more incoming students each fall for about a decade). So our contributions to teaching those students was crucial—we're hardly the largest department but the core and honors seats we offer provide a real service to the university. But I'd also like to think that we fit into UA life in a variety of other ways. For example, I recall earlier in my career offering an invited lecture at UC Santa Barbara where Richard Hecht took me to lunch and we talked about the field; at one point I asked what he thought made his department so successful (he was chair at that time) and without batting an eye he replied by talking about the senior leadership role their faculty played all across campus. That stuck with me—like I said, there are far larger departments on our campus but I bet there aren't many who so consistently have their faculty step up to take on major service roles outside the department. Seating incoming students is certainly important, yes, and each faculty member's research productivity is crucial, but it takes a lot more to run a university—e.g., we help the college to administer its grants programs and a variety of other initiatives, REL faculty serve on its tenure and promotion committees (Steven Ramey is doing just this sort of heavy service lifting this year, in fact), or maybe the department reassigns faculty time to help the college cover another unit missing a department chair for a semester, perhaps supports a colleague to direct a minor for the college, or we might share yet another faculty member's time and expertise to help the college promote the use of technology in teaching. The payoff for doing this is never sure but apart from just trying to be good citizens, it comes back to Hecht's point: it never hurts a department's members to have the rest of campus see them as not only principled in the way they practice their field but also as a go-to place when things need to get done. It doesn't guarantee success, but I think success can't happen without it.

As for other departments, apart from Nathan Loewen being reassigned to A&S for nearly half his time (working on the above-mentioned technology initiative), we have one other cross-appointed faculty member (i.e., Ted Trost is appointed 25% to New College [where self-designed, interdisciplinary majors pursue their studies]), so cooperating with other units is bred into the bone, as the old saying goes. It's always a tricky exercise, of course, since the structure of the university ensures that departments are all competitors—there are only so many students to go around and there's only so much money in the budget, yet everyone wants more majors and a new tenure-track line. So intra-departmental cooperation, in my experience, happens on one level but, at another, it's not as likely. So while we chip in to help fund each other's events, maybe cross-list some courses, and surely develop a number of fast friendships, departments don't always approach things from the viewpoint that we're all pulling the same sled—since we're each preoccupied with pulling our own and we're not all necessarily going in the same direction. So while it would be nice to coordinate courses, for example, so that they all pulled together, the complexity of just setting your own unit's classes for a semester provides a disincentive to then reach out to others to find out what they're doing and when. As mentioned above, the study of religion also happens in a variety of other units on campus (and what happens when their approach undermines your own?) and so, when we redesigned our curriculum about four years ago, we built in twelve hours of electives that, with our advisor's permission, students can count toward their REL major. This revision encouraged double majors, which is great, but it was also our way to grapple with students satisfying an interest in the study of religion in units other than our own. With the number of majors, and thus grads, being the coin of the realm (along with total credit hour production), these things matter a great deal in the long run.

RSN: Are religious studies courses available to students to satisfy core curriculum requirements? If so, how do leverage that opportunity?

RM: I addressed this above, I know, but there's certainly more to say. Since having students find us often happens through satisfying their core [i.e., general education] requirements then the more lower-level core courses (or upper-level writing courses), then the better the chance they'll find us. So over the past few years faculty have been proposing new courses and identifying many as new core courses—it introduces the faculty member's area to lower-level students and, hopefully, lays a foundation for a possible repeat visit in one of their upper-level classes later. Since satisfying one of the core's writing courses is also something some of our upper-level courses do, it means that students from a wide array of majors end up enrolling to satisfy that requirement—thereby making those seminars feel a bit like an introductory course, unfortunately. Although this presents some challenges to faculty, I think we all also realize that because we can't afford prerequisites for the upper-levels (i.e., we need the enrollments), many of our upper-level courses have always had that feel to begin with. This comes back to an earlier point, actually—the pedagogical intent in many of our classes. Because we propose an alternative to how people usually talk about religion, at least as compared to what many students probably come into our classes thinking, then many of our courses must work from first principles, to make sure everyone is up to speed with the issues that need consideration if we're going to talk about this tale or that behavior in this rather than that way.

I mentioned earlier, these service courses are also gateway classes—but it's not like students, having taken a 100-level intro, immediately declare a major. Far from it; for after getting their three hours of humanities courses (six total are required by the current core curriculum—a program that's now under review on our campus), most never darken our doorstep again. That's just the way it goes—after all, they're busy getting their business degree or their nursing degree. But some do—and most who do end up doing that a year or two later. That is, we have a number of students declare their major in the junior year since they recall a good experience in an intro course with us, a couple years back, and, for a variety of reasons, they've become disillusioned with the major they declared when entering university. So in many cases the gateway has a delayed reaction.

Another thing we're sure to do with these courses is, when a faculty member agrees, to use other events in the department or on campus as extra-credit opportunities. To some faculty this might be controversial, I know, but if we take seriously that what we're doing in these core courses is introducing many of the students to university life, then maybe we all need assignments that get them going over to the library, for example. And maybe we also need some way to incentivize going to an evening lecture by a visiting scholar (Question: how many of those do we ourselves go to?)—whether or not that recruits the student to our field, it might at least help to plant the sort of seed that is needed to be curious about the world. And if nothing else, I'd hope that the university is a place premised on that sort of curiosity. So students in these courses appear at our annual undergraduate research symposium (and hear their fellow students present their own original research); they end up at our evening Grad Tales events (when we invite recent grads back to talk about their incredibly varied careers and the role they think their liberal arts training has played); or we see them at either the Day or the Aronov Lecture (our two annual, endowed lectureships). Or perhaps they attend a one credit hour, monthly evening course specifically designed for extra credit students, as a way to recruit majors and minors, to watch a movie and have a discussion—not a movie specifically about religion, mind you, or with so-called religious themes, but all sorts of films as a way to demonstrate that a scholar of religion who uses social theory has something interesting to say about all sorts of things. And, like I said, while we may never see these students again, investing this energy is, we think, among the prerequisites to hopefully finding them enrolled in another one of our courses—someday.

RSN: Let's talk more about recruitment and marketing. How do you sell your department to potential majors? What's your relationship with social media and digital media technologies?

RM: Back in 2001, when I came to Alabama, we had a pitiful website—nothing matched, it had little info, only a few pages, and all in multiple formats. So among the first tasks was reassigning my then-colleague Kurtis Schaeffer (now the longtime chair of religious studies at the University of Virginia, by the way) to build us a basic but decent site. His efforts, using a preset university template, bought the department a year or so, in which we commissioned a new design, got the logo made, etc., so that we soon after had a professional-looking site that, over the course of a few years, grew to several hundred web pages. (Like replacing the decrepit tablet chairs in one of our classrooms, the spiffy new site told students that what we did here mattered and that we took it seriously—and so, too, should they.) These were the days well before Facebook, of course, so we updated the site often and students routinely went there to get info on the department (upcoming courses, lectures, pictures/captions from a recent student event, etc.). Now, with the advent of Facebook, Twitter, Instagram, etc., not to mention our blog, the challenge is how to have a presence that reaches out to varied audiences while ensuring that the message is not necessarily the same (or redundant) but always reinforces who we are and what we do. So this is now a major service assignment in our department, with Mike Altman once taking the lead and now Richard Newton. But many hands make light work, as they say, so many of the faculty regularly tweet (or set up their own class blogs and Twitter accounts); so if you happened to be online and, for whatever reason, paying attention to our department, you might see a bunch of our faculty tweeting about, say, our annual undergraduate research event—tagging our @StudyReligion account. But the best part of all is seeing our students get into it as well and, sooner or later, people from well off campus chiming in, commenting, elaborating, seeking feedback, and, voila, something happening in a room in Tuscaloosa is relevant to someone sitting in an office who knows where around the world.

Like I said, it's all about making sure students know that what we and they do matters.

But apart from a pretty strong social media presence, we do a variety of things to get the word out. We've sometimes put what we think to be a catchy ad in the student newspaper but who knows what the return on that is; so we also book space on campus each semester for a few hours to put up the department tent that we bought years ago and to advertise upcoming classes—we get some fun buttons made, pin them to a business card with course info on it and maybe a QR code that takes you to our website, and our student association has fun giving them out to people who are on their way to the student union for lunch. These button events, as we call them, were the idea of Steven Ramey and Eleanor Finnegan (our former colleague), as I recall, and they're an opportunity for the students to bond and have fun giving out buttons that say things like "This is not a button" or there was the year they all just had pictures of clothing buttons on them. (Magritte would be proud.) We also do this at what our campus calls "Get on Board Day" at the start of each semester (a time when student clubs come out to recruit members from new incoming students). So, like I said, we hope to get the word out about us, sure, but it's also a chance for our own students to increasingly feel part of the department themselves—they're in it with us (though given that faculty hope to have whole careers here, they have a far bigger stake) and having them know this doesn't hurt us. And you'd be surprised how many return visits we get each year from people wanting this year's button.

So sure, faculty talk about upcoming courses in their classes, but we've learned that's not enough. You've got to make an appointment and go over and talk to the admissions staff and campus recruiters; you've got to talk about the department to the advisors in your college; you've got to get a flyer of upcoming classes into people's hands and posted online; you've got to invite some blogs from grads concerning what they now value about what they did way back when …. The payoff on all these investments is never really obvious but it strikes us as serving so many needs that I think we now can't imagine not doing it. So in a faculty meeting you'll hear, "When's the next button event?"

RSN: How reactive is your curriculum? How do you gauge and respond to student demand while satisfying institutional requirements and department values? And how do you gauge the success or failure of curricular changes?

RM: That's a tough one, since it often takes several years for a course or even a new faculty member to establish themselves in the curriculum. And given that we don't control many of the variables that affect things (e. g., when courses that compete with our own are scheduled), it can be a hit and a miss. But like any department, we have a variety of variable topic courses at the upper level and even our intro courses at the 100-level have a degree of adaptability so it isn't difficult to have a course on the books the very next semester if something happens that faculty feel needs to be addressed in the curriculum. And within a year it could be regularized as a course, if they're game. But given that the department sees itself as swimming against the stream a bit, and as bringing students along with us, I'm not sure the idea of student demand is necessarily how we make curricular decisions. Sure, we aim to be timely, but more than that, we aim to persuade students that studying religion as self-evidently interesting is not nearly as fascinating as paying attention to what gets called religion (or Hindu or Muslim or dominant or marginal) and how systems of designation and identification are tied to all sorts of other issues in a society—"classification is a political act" our students now tell us. And doing that seems to us to be the goal of a liberal arts degree—persuading students to become curious about their world in a new way and then seeing what they'll do with these tools.

RSN: What's your philosophy on the role higher education—and a student's chosen major—should have on career prospects?

RM: The tail end of the last answer leads here, I guess—I'm answering these questions in order but without reading ahead, so that was fortuitous. We tend to have in mind a student as an entrepreneur, but not necessarily in the business sense, of course—maybe bricoluer is a better image for some? Working with what's at hand, like I mentioned above. For while some of our graduates will enroll in further degrees in our field, many go into such a wide variety of careers that it's tough to itemize them all. From law and medicine to teaching and business, our graduates have successfully done so many different things that it reinforces our view of ourselves as using the topic of religion as a site where we teach skills (e.g., definition, classification, description, interpretation, explanation, etc.)—skills that are widely applicable, all depending on what the student wishes to do. It also fits well with the image of the liberal arts as readying a person for life—not necessarily that old Renaissance notion of the good life, whatever that is, but, instead, any old life where distinguishing and ranking and acting (and then being prepared to deal with the consequences) happens countless times a day. So while there are some programs in the modern university that are very career oriented—if you want to be a civil engineer, then you must take these classes, in this order, and then write this credentialing exam (whose contents were covered in all those courses, etc.)—the study of religion can be like that, for those who wish to enter this profession, but for most of our students it isn't. And for them we are convinced that it's the skills that we teach which will be remembered and used; for while they may or may not retain the name of this river or that god, they will more than likely remember that any two things are comparable if seen in this or that way, and that they themselves play a key role in determining how these two things are put beside each other (or not). So, while not wishing to sound too Pollyannaish, we really do think the sky's the limit for our students—so long as they make the shift and understand that their classes with us, on any number of different topics, are all e.g.s and thus places where a certain way of talking about human beings can be done in order to shed new light on a situation. Our hope is that, in the future, they'll use the method (what I guess we once called critical thinking?) but on sites in which they have investments and curiosities. What those will be, who knows? The students who "get" this really are motivated by our approach; the students who don't at least gain the descriptive information that they came for when enrolling in a course on world religions, for example. Luckily, some keep up with us (or, in the case of that particular course, Steven Ramey) and come to see that it's our very habit of calling some things world religions that we find interesting.

RSN: How do you advise students interested in pursuing an MA and/or PhD in religion?

RM: While our undergraduate advisor's role is mainly to help students through their degree, the sort of career advising you're aiming at here is something that's done one-on-one by faculty (as I'm sure it is in almost all departments) between a student and a faculty member for whom (or for whose area) the student feels some affinity. While we annually have a grad school prep evening or workshop, ideally in the spring, when students get to talk with faculty about the nuts and bolts of applying (taking the GRE in the coming summer or early fall, how to write a cover letter, what to put into a C.V., how to pick a school to which they'll apply, etc.), all throughout the year I know faculty are talking with students interested in further study. Given the variety of backgrounds in our own department (e.g., several faculty, including myself, started their careers as non-tenure track instructors), a student would have to work pretty hard to graduate without being told to think seriously about national trends in higher ed and thus the humanities job market in the US and elsewhere. While I can't speak for all of the faculty, my guess is that practical pointers are high on the list, making sure students interested in further study know that student debt should be in their mind, that gaining practical professional experience should also be there (will they get experience TAing in this or that program?), while they should also be aware of programs that likely depend too greatly on grad student labor—after all, while having some teaching experience is important once you near the end of a PhD and are ready to get on the market, having taught five or six or ten or twelve (or more) of your own courses at such an early stage might not add up to as much as you think. For the learning curve on teaching your own class is steep, but it can flatten out quickly and so while hiring departments are certainly looking for evidence of classroom success, they're also looking for plenty of other things on those C.V.s that come with applications. So while never popping the balloon of a student's excitement and hopes for the future, I think it fair to say that all of the faculty work to make sure grads see higher ed as an institution much like any other, with practical constraints and power issues that need to be taken into consideration if you wish to enter it. In my twenty years here, we've had some students go on to earn further degrees, to be sure—in fact, this very year we've had a student accepted to six or seven MA programs in the US and she's currently making some big decisions—and I'd hope they'd all agree that, though there'll inevitably be surprises, they all went in with their eyes open, ready for both the potholes and the opportunities.

RSN: Have you done any hiring lately? What's your impression of the academic job market, beyond the obvious competitiveness of the pool?

RM: We were 4.25 tenured or tenure-track faculty back in 2001 (back then I was the sole tenured faculty member) and in the fall of 2016, we'll be ten (five of whom are tenure track), so we've been quite successful in obtaining new lines and making strong hires. As I also said earlier, the university doubled in size during that time but, given that we were threatened with losing the major back in 2000, it's evident that there was no necessary reason the resources had to come our way. (I'm still thankful that our then brand-new dean decided to invest in the department by hiring an outside chair [the position I got] instead of closing us.) Unlike, say, English, which has four required English courses in the core curriculum, or history, with two of their own, there's no reason a student has to take an REL course (though they can choose to, if they like, and obtain core credit, of course). So for us to grow our faculty was a challenge to persuade the university that we were helping it to meet its goals while also meeting goals of our own (they don't always overlap, by the way). Demonstrating increases in credit hour production was the key (given that campus growth was an overarching goal), so we're now teaching about four or five times the number of students annually that we did back in 2000—some of those are online (where we usually have one off-campus person who grades courses), but the vast majority are in-person lectures and seminars (some large and some small). So yes, over the years we've had quite a few searches.

One thing that really stands out for me (and something I've written a little bit on, actually) is how unprepared I find many early-career people to be. Sure, they know much about their area of specialization but communicating to people outside of that specialty is sometimes a challenge for them—and, unless you have the luxury of interviewing in an elite department somewhere that already has five specialists on the thing you also study, what else is a faculty but a bunch of people from very different specialties? So it always seems to me that—returning to that notion of pedagogy—the whole interview is more similar to a practice teaching session than candidates realize. For all of their casual conversations and even their academic paper (should that, and a sample teaching demonstration, be part of the interview, as they are for us) are opportunities to demonstrate their ability to bridge a gap between what they know and someone who doesn't know it. But too often I meet very bright, very motivated people who haven't yet been challenged to think beyond their data domain, to be able to talk to people in very different areas but nonetheless find points of contact. It's long been apparent to me that departmental identities are built at the level of theory, not data, and so, ideally, the reason we happen to have offices next door to one another is not because we each study the same ritual but because we all see our e.g.s, as far from each other as they may happen to be, as just that, e.g.s, i.e., as illustrative of something that people do rather widely. I recall a good friend in my PhD who was in history and writing a dissertation on late-nineteenth century British identity. He and I had little in common at the level of data of course, but he's the one who got me reading E. P. Thompson and Benedict Anderson and so we had a tremendous amount in common at the level of theory.

Too few people on the market today seem to understand this.

And so when we put out an ad for, for example, social theory of religion and X (as we've recently done a couple times), specifying the approach we're looking for but leaving the area, period, topic wide open, it seems that many people overlook the ad because, I don't know, religion in America wasn't mentioned by name, or neither was Islam or Siberian shamanism, etc. (Is this also a comment on the AAR's classification system and how it steers people through the job ads?) It means to me that doctoral programs in our field are probably all still working in little world religions boxes and anyone who challenges that model, by asking why studying this or that myth is interesting or relevant, can be greeted by blank stares and repetition of the descriptive details. That we're likely among the few departments who value theory as we do means, maybe, that applicants would be wise to ignore what I'm saying, since many more hiring committees are probably looking for the descriptive specialist who will work in their own little domain. But given our successes, I'd hope others would rethink that model and challenge doctoral programs to produce more cross-cultural comparativists who are interested in answering broad questions by means of their narrow focus.

RSN: How do you think the field of religious studies is doing?

RM: Tough to say. On our campus, it's doing wonderfully though, yes, we still have a variety of challenges. But we're in the midst of proposing a new MA degree (you'd be surprised by the people who think we must have had one all along) that takes social theory of religion and the communication skills of the public and digital humanities equally seriously. (If all goes well it will start in the fall of 2017 but there are plenty of committees and hurdles to pass between now and then.)[1] So at least here at Alabama, the field is thriving—something I particularly like to say, I admit, given the negative stereotype so many in the US still have of this state. But nationally … ? I'm not so sure. I helped to organize a meeting of public university department chairs at the last AAR, in Atlanta, and about fifteen attended, from some of the big schools in the country, and it wasn't difficult to go around the room and hear tales of woe related to oversight, governance, funding, credit hour production, retention, recruiting, etc. No tale was unique, of course—it's a story told by many in the humanities. But I sometimes think that departments that are not adaptive, that are not intentional about how they are seen and how their skills relate to wider interests among their students, might be in for some big challenges in the future. But all this depends on what you mean by religious studies, of course, for if you mean by that something other than what I mean, or what we aim to have our department accomplish, then you might conclude that the field is doing really well. For instance, our main journal likely has no shortage of submissions, though from where I sit, I'm not convinced that they're all doing what I'd call the academic study of religion. So while I don't want to get into that here—my views on these topics may be well known to some—speaking as a department chair who takes seriously that not just the ability to satisfy intellectual curiosities but also the ability to have careers and to pay mortgages and raise families all depend on what we do in departments, I'd simply say that it's the long-term good of the field that our decisions today ought to be anticipating; solving a short-term issue is key, of course, but ideally we're making decisions that will leave departments in the future who will one day be hiring the undergrads we're today graduating. That I've been around long enough to now be working with colleagues who earned their own undergrad degrees, though at other schools, during just my time here at Alabama, makes this evident to me all the time.

RSN: The recession had an incredible impact on public universities and colleges. How was your department affected? Is there a "new normal" when it comes to higher ed funding?

---

[1] This interview predated the establishment of the department's MA degree, in its fourth year in 2020–21, now with seven graduates (three of whom are pursuing their PhD in the study of religion) and fifteen students currently in either their first or second year.

RM: Given the planned campus growth, begun around 2004 (by a new president who arrived in 2003 with a mandate from our Board of Trustees) with the goal of doubling enrollment in a decade (or sooner, as it turned out), we've had resources on our campus and, in many ways, didn't really feel the 2008 collapse all that much. Sure, we didn't have raises some years but the rate at which we've been hiring new positions stayed steady or even increased. We've not doubled the size of the faculty across campus, of course, but our total faculty number is significantly larger now than it was fifteen years ago. So our growth plan put us in a good position to weather what other public universities, that still largely rely on state appropriations, could not. While this doesn't mean that we're somehow awash in money, it does mean that the administration has been able to address historically low salaries here, as compared to the Southern University Group (those against whom we measure ourselves when it comes to things like salaries), and that new positions have indeed been given to departments that can demonstrate they're helping the college and the university to meet their goals.

RSN: What's something you've learned as chair that you didn't know as a regular faculty member?

RM: Hearkening back to something I wrote earlier, about job candidates: I think many faculty also are trained to focus on their data domain and subject area (the silo model), whether in their research or teaching. I recall an experience with someone once presuming that we'd of course get a replacement position for an Asianist (a vacancy made when Kurtis left for UVA)—it's Asia, after all, I was told, and we all know just how important it is to study Asia, right? Now, while not disagreeing over that particular importance (and our campus indeed has too few Asianists), I recall answering by saying that this importance would likely not necessarily be among the reasons for us getting the position—if we were lucky enough to get it, that is. For every department probably had self-evident importances that had to be addressed. I'm sure the Shakespearian scholars in the Department of English longed to return to a day when they had who knows how many in their ranks and who knows how many climate change specialists we ought to be employing across the sciences, let alone all the mathematicians needed to teach all those students from other colleges whose majors require math courses. No, these were decisions that would probably be made using other scales of values—credit hour production, graduation rates, student-to-professor ratios, research productivity, grant success rates and external funding budgets, and, as mentioned above on a few occasions, whether the desired position helped the university to achieve its goals, were all invoked, in varying measure, as the criteria to determine if we get that new line. Case in point: we have a brand-new president and a new strategic plan is being devised, and, anticipating it, we've all just put in new position requests and chairs were specifically asked to talk about each request in light of how it would address very specific campus-wide goals.

My point? Not unlike my earlier comments on the job market, thinking well outside one's own data domain is a necessary skill for anyone interested in helping a department (a.k.a. helping one's students and colleagues) to succeed today. And this is maybe not all that apparent to some faculty members. It doesn't mean leaving your research interests behind but, instead, learning how one's own focus is somehow interrelated with other things that others think are no less important. That's one of the key things that I've learned as a chair; a field-wide interest is something I came to the job with—in fact, that's what prompted me to apply in the first place. (I still remember talking to Julie Ingersoll, back in our Springfield, Missouri, days, about whether I should apply.) But an institution-wide awareness, well beyond your own field, let alone own research, is what you need to be able to anticipate opportunities and see overlaps that advance your unit's interests. And those "other things" are not just the work of your peers or the curiosities of your students but goals other departments are working toward, the aims of administrators further up the chain, as well as the goals your department might have in some imagined future that you're working toward.

8 Reinventing the Study of Religion in Alabama: An Overview

At 7 p.m. on Monday, November 4, 2002, Professor Martin Jaffee, of the University of Washington, delivered a public lecture at the University of Alabama. Hosted by the members of the Department of Religious Studies and funded by the department's Aaron Aronov Endowment for Judaic Studies, his lecture was the first in what has now become our annual "Aronov Lecture."[1] Next door to my office is the seminar room that the department uses and there hang all of the framed flyers that advertised each of these annual events. Thinking back on that first evening provides an opportunity to pause and consider where we, as a department and a field, have been and where we're going.

Although we were an small, average-sized department when I arrived in 2001 from what was then called Southwest Missouri State University to become the department chair at the University of Alabama, what sets us apart—or, better put, what makes us an example worth considering—is that we have gone from only one of those faculty members (myself) being tenured back in 2001, a time when the department's future was in question, to growing the faculty dramatically and starting a new MA degree. Due to the long predicted demographic shift among the professoriate hired to teach the first waves of baby boomers arriving on college campuses some decades ago, no one currently serving in the department was here prior to the arrival, as a tenure-track assistant professor, straight out of his degree at Harvard, of our colleague Ted Trost, back in August 1998.[2] So, despite being of average size, we were rather different from the portrait found in the American Academy of Religion's *Census* from some years back, in which I recall the tenured to tenure-track ratio for the average department

---

[1] As I revise this chapter for inclusion in this volume, the lecture series has now hosted seventeen guests with the eighteenth, in the spring of the 2019–20 school year—Annette Yoshiko Reed—rescheduled for the following year due to the impact of COVID-19 on classes and academic programming.

[2] Careful readers will ask how long the department's staff members have served. As is often the case, the institutional memory resides primarily among the staff, without whom the day-to-day running of the unit (everything from ordering supplies to putting together a class schedule, admitting students into courses, and bringing people onto the payroll) would be an utter impossibility. With that having been said, Ms. Betty Dickey, the department's administrative secretary, served the department for thirty-two years prior to her retirement on April 1, 2020. She was succeeded then by Ms. LeCretia Crumpton, whose transition into the department coincided with the university's COVID-19-inspired move to limited operations—which presented a host of challenges that she admirably tackled, helping to keep the department upright.

being about 3:1. For when I arrived in 2001, our ratio was 0.2:1 but, with a successful tenure track search last year for a specialist in the digital humanities (adding Jeri Wieringa to our faculty), the ratio is now 2:1, with those once tenure-track faculty now holding the rank of professor and long serving on our tenure and promotion committee. How things have changed over the past twenty years.

With this dramatic change in faculty rank in mind, the question that lies in the background of our main lectures series is: How does one reinvent a department of religious studies in the early twenty-first century? For, although not stated explicitly, the establishment of this series, let alone the prominent place for its framed flyers (along with the forty-or-so framed flyers for our more informal "Religion *in* Culture" lecture series that also line a wall in the seminar room, not to mention all those lunchtime discussions and "tech talks" [which, for the time being, are online videoconference sessions] that we've hosted where our students met visitors as well as professors from across campus) is evidence of a set of self-consciously developed strategies to revive a small department in a major public university. But to know this story fully, we need a little more background: when I first arrived, the unit had just been judged "non-viable" by the statewide accrediting body (more on that below), a new dean of the College of Arts & Sciences had just been hired, the previous year's search for a new chair had ended in a failed search, and the state of Alabama was in yet another "proration" year, in which various sectors of state government (such as education—both K to 12 and higher ed) were constitutionally mandated to return significant portions of their already committed operating budgets—conditions that might cause one to be somewhat pessimistic about the future of this small department filled with non-tenured faculty. But the fact that our dean had, in his first year on the job (2000 – 1), committed once again to hire an outside chair (the position into which I was then hired, as of August 2001) had already made clear that our challenge was to reinvent the study of religion—in the eyes of the accreditors, yes, but also in the eyes of university administrators, colleagues, as well as students who might see majoring in the study of religion as something worth doing.

As with many North American programs in the academic study of religion, the University of Alabama's—by my accounting, still the only publicly funded department of religious studies granting a BA major in the state and one that is unambiguously devoted to the academic study of religion—dates to the mid-1960s (it is tough to pin down an actual date; only someone spinning an origins tales, such as this, could possibly conjure up a definitive date since the current department developed from various antecedents that don't much resemble what we today call comparative religion, the history of religions, or simply religious studies).³ Prior to that, the university certainly offered courses on religious topics, but —as with so many other programs in the US and Canada at that time—they were taught on a volunteer basis by a variety of religious functionaries who were already involved in various forms of campus ministry. As described frankly in the university's 1965 proposal to the Danforth Foundation, requesting financial support to institute a new department of religious studies:

> These courses have been limited to two hours credit, and students have been permitted to count no more than eight hours in the Department toward graduation. The ministers have received no pay for their teaching. Courses have been devised and offered according to the interests of the individual campus ministers with little thought given to the general curriculum in religion or to its relation to the over-all University curriculum. As one might expect, the quality of the courses has been mixed. (A Proposal by the University of Alabama to the Danforth Foundation for a Grant to Assist in the Establishment of a Department of Religion [July 12, 1965]:1–2)⁴

According to an October 1964 document which is included with this proposal, between the fall 1960 and the fall 1964 semesters, a total of eighty-one courses were taught (with an average of nine courses per semester), with a total of 3,253 students attending these courses, averaging forty students per class and 365 students per semester—simply put, there was quite an operation up and running despite no department actually being present, at least as we today understand

---

3 I should add that we did indeed do just that: celebrated our fiftieth anniversary in 2016–17, based on that being the fiftieth year in which not only PhDs, rather than campus ministers, were listed in the undergraduate catalogue as comprising the faculty of the department but also a description of the department that would be recognizable to us today. Settling on this date was the result of a discussion among the faculty the year before, to identify a rationale to determine an origin that was of significance (and thus use) to us, at the time, thereby nicely exemplifying our own approach to understanding origins as being about the teller, and not the subject, of the tale. See this August 8, 2016, blog post for more details regarding this decision: https://religion.ua.edu/blog/2016/08/08/celebrating-merrily-their-happy-anniversary/ (accessed June 15, 2020).

4 During the mid- to late-1960s, it was common for the private Danforth Foundation to fund a department chair's salary for a newly instituted department of religious studies, under the condition that the institution would continue to budget for the position after the foundation's initial three-year funding period ended. (My thanks to the late Charlie Reynolds, of the University of Tennessee [and my first department chair when I was an instructor there (1993–6)], for his anecdotal comments on the role played by the Danforth in helping to create our field.) The Alabama proposal requested funds for faculty salaries and library purchases, totaling between $17,124 and $28,750 between the years 1966–7 and 1969–70. According to a September 28, 2003, correspondence with Diane Moleski, then the office manager for the Danforth Foundation, in 1966 a three-year program was indeed funded (for $16,500) "to aid in establishing a Department of Religion" at the University of Alabama.

the composition and mission of a department of religious studies. Given the voluntary nature of the instructors staffing these courses, these are truly impressive numbers; but, for such reasons as early-1960s US Supreme Court judgments banning prayer in public schools as unconstitutional, the increasing interest in "the East" that was occasioned first by the war in Korea and then in Vietnam, as well as the counter-culture movement of this period, studying religion as a religious vocation was, by the time of the mid-1960s, starting to give way to a professionalization of the field.

Although the voluntary, "potluck" nature of the curriculum at that time was definitely a "good buy" for that day's administration (given that its instructors were all voluntary), for a public university these classes were rather troublesome, for their topics (let alone the manner in which they were more than likely taught), were (as with much of the field then—and, regrettably, some of it today) exclusively drawn from a Protestant seminary model, including such old standards as: Old Testament, New Testament, Faith and Reason, Life and Teaching of Jesus, Christian Ethics, and the perennial Contemporary Religious Thought. Whatever the quality of these courses, the rationale that drove them was exploring the foundations of the faith, and that faith was a specific form of Protestant Christianity. Of course there were also those more specialized classes that simply narrowed the focus (as, lamentably, happens so often when one moves through a curriculum—the same skills are taught at all levels but the focus intensifies, from studying the New Testament in a survey course to instead writing a dissertation on but one verse), such as entire courses on such figures from early Christian history as Peter, John, or Paul; although likely not peculiar to our state, there was even an entire course, offered once every semester, on the Ten Commandments (as one of the department's standard classes, it seated a total of 549 students in the early 1960s). What's more, I would hazard a guess that, much like the earlier course in archeology, its Hebrew language course (offered in the fall of 1960 and which attracted only five students), the course significantly entitled Old Testament (offered every semester and seating 456 students in total—a course title finally changed to Hebrew Bible only during the time of our colleague and one-time holder of the Aronov Chair, Steve Jacobs),[5] along with the course on Judaism (offered only three times and seating a total of thirty-eight students) were

---

[5] Regrettably, we changed the title back not too long ago, at Steve's recommendation, inasmuch as he had concluded that students seemed not to understand what a course on Hebrew Bible was all about, despite the course description making this clear. In our experience, with modern universities relying on online registration and a series of online aides to registration, all many students ever see is a course title, with some focusing exclusively on the class's meeting days and times, as they aim to build a schedule that suits their needs.

more than likely all efforts to find new significance in "other" people's textual artifacts—artifacts that, importantly, were assumed not just to predate but, as this old theological model presupposed, prepare the way for the eventual Good News (what was once, following a work by the fourth-century Christian apologist Eusebius, called in Latin, *praeparatio evangelica*).

In the nearly forty years between the Danforth proposal and that first Aronov Lecture, a lot happened to ensure that the department move away from its overt theological motives and, instead, work toward training students in what we might term an anthropocentric approach, studying religion cross culturally and in a descriptive and comparative manner. Among the most evident of the changes was the arrival (and, eventually, the retirement) of faculty who had earned PhDs in what was then the newly forming field of religious studies. The first chair of the restructured department was Joseph Bettis (PhD Drew University), who stayed only several years after his arrival in 1964 and who eventually retired an emeritus professor at Western Washington University; the late Leon Weinberger (PhD Brandeis) came to Tuscaloosa in 1964 as the director of the local chapter of the Hillel Foundation but was hired full time by the department soon after (and then retired in 1999); the late Patrick Green (PhD Drew University), the longtime chair of the department and into whose faculty line I was eventually hired, was first hired in 1970 and retired in 2000 (though we often saw him around teaching a course here and there since then); and the late William Doty (PhD Drew University), who first came to the department in 1981, retired in 2001, but, like Patrick, continued teaching on campus for different units. (Those working in myth studies will surely know Doty's name from his various publications.) Luckily, the College of Arts & Sciences had the foresight to fill these open lines with tenure-track hires; although it might be an error to suggest that the department thrived during the 1970s, 80s, and 90s, (for, in 2001, it is was not too much larger, in terms of faculty positions, than it had been in the 1970s), it did survive, which is no small feat, as already intimated, in the budgetary environment public education sometimes experienced here in Alabama, where those institutions that are dependent on our largely sales-tax-driven state budget can sometimes be hit hard by economic slowdowns. Most recently, however, I think that the word "thrive" aptly captures what has happened here in Tuscaloosa, linked to such factors as the department:

- Sharing two cross-appointments with New College as of 1998 (Catherine Roach and Ted Trost; Roach's position went exclusively to New College in 2006)
- Gaining a targeted affirmative action hire back in 2005 (when Maha Marouan was hired, who later left for Penn State's Women's, Gender, and Sexuality Studies program)—a line into which the department was then able to hire

- Merinda Simmons in 2010 (who served as our inaugural grad director and who has been promoted to the rank of professor)
- Sharing, as of the fall 2013 semester, a new cross-appointment with the Department of History (75% REL and 25% HY), devoted to the study of Islam (held by our onetime colleague, Eleanor Finnegan), which was followed a few years after Eleanor's departure by the hire of Edith Szanto, who also works in the study of Islam and is fully appointed to REL
- Being fortunate to attract Nathan Loewen to the department (who also works on technology projects for the College of Arts & Sciences) as well as Mike Altman (who first came as a one-year instructor and who is now the PI for "American Examples," a major Luce Foundation grant)
- Having good fortune in being awarded a new line in Asian religions back in the late 1990s (first held by Reiko Ohnuma [now of Dartmouth], then by Kurtis Schaeffer [now the longtime department chair at the University of Virginia], and then by Steven Ramey [our current graduate director and who also co-edits, with Aaron Hughes, *Method & Theory in the Study of Religion*])
- Receiving, despite tight state budgets, a replacement position when William Doty retired (his line was held Tim Murphy, until his own retirement, and then untimely death, in 2013)
- Having the ability to hire Vaia Touna, out of her PhD at the University of Alberta, to work on social theory of ancient religions and then also Richard Newton, previously holding a position at Elizabethtown College
- Enjoying, most importantly perhaps, the good fortune that comes with dedicated resources, such as a student scholarship fund kindly established by the late Dr. Joseph Silverstein, as well as the Aaron Aronov Endowment in Judaic Studies, the latter of which enabled Richard Cohen to be hired in 1989 as the first person to hold the department's endowed chair in the study of Judaism

Since 2003, the Silverstein award has been given out over 130 times, helping students to pay for their education, while, over the past twenty-five years, the Aronov Endowed Chair has been held by several people (either as professors, visiting professors, or postdoctoral fellows). Between January 2001 and August 2019, it was held by Steve Jacobs, a specialist in Holocaust and genocide studies, who has been succeeded now by Daniel Levine, cross-appointed to REL from the Department of Political Science.

And it was with funds from this endowment that the department brought Professor Jaffee to campus so long ago, to speak not specifically about the data that falls within the admittedly wide area known as Judaic studies but, instead, to speak as a scholar of religion involved in debates of relevance not just to our department but to all of our peers in the university. Very early on in our reinvention, the department decided that what made us unique was *not* that our object of study was special—as so many scholars of religion yet presume, seeing in it a deeply meaningful experience or item that is somehow set apart from all others—but that although we studied religion it was simply a word that we used to name a specific subset of mundane but no less interesting human beliefs, behavior, and institutions, along with the various things that past actions left behind. (The theme for our 2012–13 public lectures, "The Relevance of the Humanities and Social Sciences in the 21st Century University," was but an example of this attempt to persuade students and colleagues from across the university that we are all in the same boat and can therefore benefit from each other's insights.) But instituting a lecture series to feature national speakers able to translate their work for a wider audience was just part of our reinvention plan—an effort to ensure that people understood that although we were small, our reach through teaching, research, and service was surprisingly wide. For if a department such as ours was to reestablish itself successfully, it meant rebuilding from the ground up:

- Designing a new curriculum driven not by personalities that happened to work here and the data-domains that come and go with every departure of a faculty member, but by the common set of skills we hope our students will gain, regardless the material on which they work (e.g., defining, describing, comparing, interpreting, explaining)
- Designing new and engaging online courses to replace the sadly dated distance education booklets that were then being mailed to a small number of distance learners taking courses in the department
- Rewriting and then regularly updating long-outdated tenure and promotion documents (which now recognize the importance of digital projects)
- Developing PR materials to distribute throughout the state's public and private secondary schools
- Contacting graduates and developing mailing lists and annual newsletters
- Rewriting job descriptions among the staff, developing a host of procedures, and routinizing the ways in which student workers assisted the department in its work (hiring our own undergraduate students to work in the main office and assist in some of our classes has been one of our most successful, though low-key, mentoring programs to date)
- Setting up a rationale for awarding student scholarships and a way to publicize it every year come what we call Honors Day (banners bearing every recipient's name now annually fill our second-floor balcony railings)
- Investing energy in reinvigorating our student associations (something most recently accomplished by Merinda Simmons)

- Tackling the work necessary to give the department's physical space an overall face-lift—everything from obtaining new classroom furniture to address the unfortunate *Welcome Back Kotter* feel of the classrooms back in the late 1990s to creating a student lounge (a fridge and a microwave are tremendously useful and thus important—not to mention a snack bar)
- Creating an informative, content-rich website, a blog, a motto ("Studying Religion *in* Culture"), and a logo designed by our campus's branding office; yes, we also have mugs and t-shirts. It's tough to ignore us—and that was the goal

At the end of the day, all this effort was aimed at establishing rewarding work conditions for the faculty and staff with the hope that this too would bring students our way. For reinventing a department also meant meeting some practical and necessary criteria established by the already mentioned Alabama Commission on Higher Education (ACHE). Comprised of commissioners appointed by the governor, ACHE set the bar at 7.5 BA graduates per year (based on a rolling three-year average; MA and PhD degree-awarding programs have their own, somewhat lower, minimum numbers, of course). Failing to meet this minimum meant that a degree program was deemed "non-viable," a status that risked the loss of the major—a loss that would turn our department into a "service unit" delivering only what we call core curriculum courses (i.e., general education classes) to students from other departments. Our department's most recent average, when I arrived in 2001, was 6.6 graduating majors per year (up considerably from what it had been when ACHE first came knocking at our doors in the late 1990s), which meant that a detailed waiver application had to be submitted to the commission as soon as I arrived, outlining the specific reasons why the status of "viable" ought to be granted, which it eventually was (in the fall of 2002; that our dean had invested in a new, outside department chair likely went some distance to help persuade ACHE that the University of Alabama was serious about this reinvention). Regardless of one's opinion of the role played by such state regulating bodies, the "bottom line" reality that such commissions and state legislatures inject into our lives provides a practical rationale for investing serious energy into reinventing the material conditions that make our own profession and careers possible. Since the department had most recently seen itself mainly as a service department (with students wishing to specialize in the study of religion often taking independent study courses to fulfill the requirements of the major), meeting the 7.5 bar required collective ingenuity and effort. And, with the successful proposal to add an MA—focused on the intersection between social theory and digital humanities in the study of religion—we are now four years into a new degree, with new ACHE viability numbers to focus on and new students to train and inspire. How to reinvent graduate education during these trying times in the humanities is thus one of our current challenges.

But of all these separate sites of social formation, the one that underlies them all involves constituting a shared imaginary among the faculty, staff, and our students. Despite their own individual accomplishments and expertise, 2001's small group of energetic, tenure-track scholars had yet to figure out precisely how and why—apart from sheer happenstance—they comprised an academic collectivity. While we had adjacent offices and a classroom, it was not all that clear to me when I first arrived and Betty handed me a master key that there was a department here. For it surely takes more than just having adjacent space to form a department. To rephrase: the sort of intellectual and institutional space in which current faculty and students think and act themselves into an identity had, when the Aronov Lecture series began, yet to be formed, making the narrative briefly outlined above, of our department's successful changes, not something that we could have easily imagined back then. Inviting Professor Jaffee to set the table with his inaugural Aronov Lecture—an invitation extended because of the way in which he theorized his classroom experience and own sense of identity in his 1997 essay, "Fessing up in Theory: On *Professing* and *Confessing* in the Religious Studies Classroom" (originally published in *Method & Theory in the Study of Religion* 9/4 [1997]:325–37)—provided the faculty with a common starting point that allowed them to pursue a year-long meditation on issues of methodology, theory, the history of the field, the history and context of our particular department, the place of self-disclosure and identity in our work, the sorts of students we teach, the goal of our curriculum, and the rationale behind our own teaching styles—all topics at the heart of an active and engaged department's work. That this conversation continues, exemplified early on by the publication of a set of our faculty's responses to Jaffee's lecture (published in what was then known as *Bulletin of the Council of Societies for the Study of Religion* [2004]—a publication that has since been sold to Equinox Publishing, renamed, and which now calls the department its editorial home, run by Newton and involving a variety of MA students), is the evidence of just how fruitful our collective labors have been—efforts that have results in a number of collaborative projects, not least of which is the American Examples grant that is among the faculty's current shared projects.[6] As briefly mentioned above, an ac-

---

[6] This already-mentioned four-year grant, for which Altman is the PI, also involves six other members of our faculty as workshop mentors and a group of about nine early-career participants each year (who also join in on subsequent years' workshops), all devoted to rethinking how studying and teaching about religion in America can be done.

tive department blog now exists where the relevance of the humanities is discussed by faculty, students, alums, and invited guests, an initiative that inspired a lecture series in the College of Arts & Sciences, and over the past twenty years some pretty thoughtful and motivated students have made us their home while figuring what they wanted to do with their lives—today some of them are in grad school, but many more are teachers, small business owners, lawyers, social workers, and medical doctors.

We were indeed small at one time, but not anymore; in fact, when measured pound-for-pound (i.e., per capita), our faculty are among the most productive units in our field in the US—making evident to anyone wishing to judge a department in Alabama that big ideas and impressive accomplishment come to fruition in all sorts of places. For I couldn't have imagined a series that would eventually include the likes of Jonathan Z. Smith, Amy-Jill Levine, Arjun Appadurai, Tomoko Masuzawa, Bruce Lincoln, Eddie Glaude, Linell Cady, Laura Levitt, and Aaron Hughes back when I was listening to Professor Jaffee's talk that evening, which makes it rather exciting to wonder what the future holds for this department, its faculty, staff, and students. Of course, many challenges have also come with the successes that resulted from all of this change—how to ensure that we maintain the sort of direct and personal contact with our students that they so value is one of them, despite inventing large enrollment lower-level classes (that seat from 120 to 150 people) and designing online courses that sometimes have on-campus students enrolled in them, all in an effort to help a growing university meet its enrollment needs (in 2001, we had about 18,000 students at the University of Alabama and now we have about 38,000). We often have a renewable, fulltime instructor now working in the department—a position we aim to use as a mentoring experience for those hired into it (usually for up to a three-year appointment), instead of seeing them as a "hired gun" brought in to generate credit hours to subsidize the department—and now, with the MA program, we have a variety of graduate students working as teaching assistants, requiring mentoring of their own. And while not having control over the larger structural conditions that have led to such things as declining public financial support for higher education and thus increasing tuition, the department does control a number of factors that can make larger courses engaging and intellectually provocative, limit the footprint that the impersonal online environment has in the lives of local students eager for a face-to-face exchange with a passionate professor, and ensure that early-career people eager for tenure-track work can gain valuable experience in a supportive, small department. Our long-term well-being depends upon successfully managing all of this, along with making sure that we have a good supply of department mugs on hand.

9 Learning to Code: Digital Pebbles and Institutional Ripples

> Well I started out
> down a dirty road
> Started out
> all alone ...
>
> – "Learning to Fly" (Tom Petty and Jeff Lynne [1991])

9.1 Knowing Enough to Make You Dangerous

Yes, I know enough about Dreamweaver 3, released in 1999, to make me dangerous; for while I didn't really know how to do all that much with it, even once I attained my own level of mastery (i.e., I just knew what I needed to know), upon writing the first draft of this chapter, in the summer of 2017, I saw that version 17 was available—that's right, 17. So I'm a little behind the curve. But given that I was trying to build a department website while learning it on my own, back in the very early 2000s—consulting "how to" books and scrounging off of the knowledge that a very few friends had already accumulated for themselves, while also doing the various other things that a new department chair might do in a struggling department—I'd like to think that I was actually ahead of the curve. For some of us were doing what we now call digital humanities well before it was considered a distinguishable thing that deserved a name of its own.

But this story is not simply about a department website, of course; as I learned from the late Jonathan Z. Smith's writings, the things that scholars discuss are best understood as an e.g. of some larger topic, and so focusing too closely on any single example may trick us into thinking that it somehow stands on its own, moves of its own steam, and is therefore inherently interesting or obviously valuable. So, while none of us should trust our own memory (let alone those of our research subjects), I do recall that all along the new department website that I was building on evenings and weekends wasn't simply about having a decent site; instead, it was but a node in a concerted effort to revive an entire department—one that, back in 2000, was on the brink of losing its major and either becoming what we call a service department or, perhaps, closing entirely.[1]

---

[1] As described in previous chapters, this was due to its inadequate number of majors and thus BA graduates—the latter being the coin of our particular corner of the higher-ed realm.

So that investment of time and energy (and, yes, some department resources as well—but far less than you might think, so long as one has the goodwill and energy of a committed faculty) into building a content-rich website was just the first of many interconnected digital initiatives tackled over the years by the members of our department; and although each project was motivated by a specific need, they all eventually pulled the same wagon: reinventing a humanities department at a time when they were (and continue to be) under considerable attack.

Of course such a reinvention is never complete; as any good social theorist would likely tell you, groups are always on the brink of demise.[2] But despite being ongoing, even to this day, these interconnected digital projects have been quite successful, inasmuch as they have not only played a prominent role in people across the US and around the world taking an interest in this thing called the Department of Religious Studies at the University of Alabama but, more importantly, those same people trying on for size some of the things that we've successfully been doing in Tuscaloosa—and then having successes of their own.[3]

In fact, that I was invited to contribute to Christopher Cantwell and Kristian Petersen's *Introduction to Digital Humanities: Research Methods in the Study of Religion* strikes me as persuasive evidence that something that we did in Tuscaloosa worked. While my own research is hardly characterized by the forms that one might reasonably imagine the digital humanities might take in our field today, the collective digital work carried out in our department, by a variety of actors (from faculty and staff to guests, students, grads, and especially our various undergraduate student workers), strikes me as a fitting example of how assorted digital tools affect more than just an individual faculty member's research and teaching.

So the goal of this chapter, much like our reinvention itself, is both modest and ambitious. Initially, it is merely to outline just what we did do over the past

---

[2] Because their ranks are in a constant state of flux, members are always in need of injecting new energy and new resources into them (e.g., to recruit and initiate new members), making what the late Gary Lease (1994) once characterized as a social formation's emergent phase a constant, inasmuch as any group's so-called dominant phase is just the result of a continual state of successful reinvention.

[3] While I wouldn't want to overestimate our effect, a casual look at other departments' presence online makes evident, at least to me, that people have been paying attention (such as the time the American Academy of Religion's head office contacted us for advice on the video equipment it needed to begin a new initiative of their own). My hope is that this chapter provides further incentive for those who understand their own department's identity and existence not to be on autopilot—a view held by a surprisingly large number of faculty who seem to take the units in which they do their work for granted.

twenty years, making evident not only why web-based/digital projects suited what was originally a very small and regionally marginal BA-granting unit, but—thinking back to its more ambitious goals—also how they helped us not just to save a department but to position it to triple the size of its tenure-track/tenured faculty and, in the fall of 2017, launch a new MA in which *these very digital tools figure prominently.* So this chapter's aim turns out to be rather more aspiring than simply a list of projects; instead, in the midst of doing that, it also makes an argument for why a faculty member who sees their "serious" research and teaching to lie elsewhere might also learn to code, or at least learn enough about Dreamweaver (let alone Fireworks, Photoshop, Final Cut Pro, some FTP programs, GarageBand, WordPress, Python, etc.) to be just a little dangerous. For although we all earned a PhD by focusing on mastering a narrow specialty, and some of us think that being a professor entails each of us diving even deeper into our own particular rabbit hole, many of us have likely found that our professional success—along with the success of the institutions that employ us and in which we teach our students—also hinges on acquiring some rather unexpected and collaborative skills along the way.

9.2 The Digital Pebbles

As already indicated, the first thing on our list was a new website—one of what I'll simply characterize as the various pebbles that, over the past two decades, we've successively tossed in the water in our effort to get this department back on its feet. Although 2001 was certainly not the earliest years of the web, it was well before Facebook, let alone the very term "social media"—in fact, Facebook's precursor, FaceMash, wasn't created by then Harvard sophomore Mark Zuckerberg until the fall of 2003 and it wasn't until 2006 that Facebook opened its membership ranks to almost anyone (instead of just those with a .edu email address). But even though we were still using hardcopy phonebooks and printed course catalogs, the almost limitless footprint of the online world was already pretty apparent.

So we reasoned that if we were trying to recruit students (whether as majors or just to enroll them in our lower-level core courses—enrollments that so dominate most religious studies departments' credit hour production that they can't be ignored), let alone assure the administration (which included a brand new dean of the College of Arts & Sciences—a college with many departments far larger and thus more consequential than our own) that it had made a wise decision hiring an outside chair instead of just closing the department, reclaiming its space, and distributing its tenure-track faculty and staff to other units, then, in relatively short order, we needed something that someone in another building, either next door or far across campus, could see and which would help to provide them with evidence that their investment was already paying off. (I have in mind, here, other faculty and department chairs, the dean, and the provost/vice president for academic affairs, not to mention our faculty themselves, since finding a faculty member's page is more than likely the first place someone will start when looking for information on them or while trying to contact them.) So while assessing the state of our physical facilities, reviewing faculty productivity reports from the year before, becoming familiar with the budget, learning to work with the staff, deciding what department procedures needed to be invented, meeting and advising students, etc., it was obvious to this incoming chair that the website needed attention. The few pages that it then had relied on so many different styles and fonts and image sizes, not to mention resolution, that inconsistency painted an unflattering picture of a unit that was trying to instill a rather different image in people's minds.

So step one was a short-term fix: reassigning a faculty member—Kurtis Schaeffer, in fact, who was then in just his second year as an assistant professor but who went on to become the longtime chair of the Department of Religious Studies at the University of Virginia—from one semester's regular courses; he was someone who, despite being a specialist in medieval Tibetan Buddhism, was also willing to learn enough about creating a website to take a stab at adapting a basic university template to our needs and then populating it with consistent and thus professional content. Step two was then commissioning people on campus who did this for a living to come up with a design that might set our department apart, which included a logo (but what our campus's recently established branding office now tells us we need to call "a graphic element"). The site they came up with—a stark black and white design that we felt would age well, and which included a stylized version of the late-nineteenth century building in which we were located (an image that intentionally avoided the collection of diverse religious symbols that so many departments in our field opt for when devising an identifying emblem of some sort)—lasted for many years and was only redesigned in 2017–18; in fact, it was a redesign that prompted us to reconsider the work now done by a website, since our former site, inasmuch as it predated social media, had to serve far more purposes than do sites today. For example, now we just put up a blog post instead of making a new html page filled with photos from the most recent student event or public lecture—but I'm getting ahead of myself.[4]

---

4 See McCutcheon 2018 for more background on the choice of a scholar to blog—a venue seen by some as either passé or beneath the dignity of a serious scholar.

Although the website was our only online presence for many years, because it predated the arrival of Learning Management Systems (LMS) on campus, we were able to gain some of that eventual functionality by having a password-protected folder created on the site, thereby allowing us to move reserved readings online as PDFs. (At that time they were retained as hard copies in the main library, which students would photocopy on their own). Actually, we did this several years prior to the rest of the institution catching up. (Moral of the story: there's a nimbleness to the digital world, if you're willing to take advantage of it.) So although our site's "secure" folder (filled with each class's photocopied articles/readings) and our "PDF" folder (filled with public-facing syllabi or flyers) have now been replaced by centralized technologies at the university (aside: what we gain from IT centralization comes at the price of what we inevitably lose from that very centralization), back then they introduced an ease into at least one aspect of our jobs and also into the lives of students. For although few were then using laptops in classes and iPads and smartphones had yet to be invented, and thus no one was relying exclusively on digital readings, the department was able to take a significant step away from expensive textbooks and their continual (and sometimes suspect) replacement by new editions.[5]

Then, in early 2009, the department created a page on Facebook; I'd joined back in the summer of 2005, mainly to stay in touch with family back in Canada. In fact, I can still see the August 5, 2005, post from one of our majors at the time: "You, Dr. M, are the first of my many professors past and present to venture out into the previously uncharted territory known to modern man as thefacebook.com; I salute your bravery, sir." But social media hadn't taken off all that much until a few years after that and it was only then that we realized that this was also a place for the department to have a presence, to more effectively communicate with our own students and also with our graduates. (Seeing Facebook as a place to convey an image of the department to people beyond our campus wasn't something we initially thought much about, to be honest. But now we do, of course.) Not long after that, our undergraduate student association established its own Facebook presence. We didn't start up a Twitter account for the department (which happened in May 2014) until Michael Altman joined the faculty in 2013–14 and persuaded us that we needed to think of the different

---

5 In fact, at the close of the semester when I first drafted this chapter, as I reviewed student evaluations for all of our classes, comments from an undergraduate seminar relying completely on PDF readings posted online stood out, with a student thanking us for not making them pay for "a $200 textbook" (as the student phrased it).

audiences that each social media site helped us to reach. (He also organized a contest for students to name my Twitter account, since he also convinced me to join.) What's interesting to note, however, is that the student association had been tweeting, based on our students' own initiative, since July 2011—but we obviously hadn't paid the proper attention to the signals that they had sent us by joining up on their own.[6] So this marked the first time that we started thinking far more intentionally about social media, especially reaching audiences beyond those who already felt some affinity for us (such as current students and our grads).

This had long been apparent at the website, of course, which by then had grown to something like 400 pages (making them became a bit of an after-hours hobby—the sort of work that we never really tend to track *as* work), many of which provided substantive information on the field and which were aimed at people far from Alabama (as well as providing our faculty with plenty of resources, such as searchable online catalogs for the department's library and fairly large video/DVD collection). But we had not yet really thought through social media as a complement (or replacement?) to the department's site—a site which, being so large, had by then admittedly become a bit of a task to manage and keep up to date. So, we did some thinking about what to name the new Twitter handle; we were surprised to learn that @studyreligion (notably in the imperative) had not been taken; it was not only nicely in keeping with a motto we'd come up with over a decade before, Studying Religion *in* Culture,[7] but it also made a strong statement that the Alabama experiment might have implications in other departments. After all, ours was hardly the only one in the country in which major/graduate numbers had been declining. But, as we looked around, it seemed we were among a rather small number that were taking an entrepreneurial, and intentionally department-wide, approach to social media as a way to do something about it. And so @studyreligion was born and in October 2015 it made its first appearance on Instagram as well.

The story so far: a complete website redesign and revision, accomplished initially by faculty as service to the department, led to enhanced features that im-

---

6 Students continue to send signals, such as the current generation's migration away from Facebook, which challenges us to continue to be relevant on social media platforms while recognizing that older alums are still on such sites as Facebook.
7 The italics were meant to convey the distinctive approach we were then hoping to develop at Alabama, in contrast to the, in my view, problematic Tillichian model associated with the more common nomenclature of religion *and* culture.

pacted our teaching, and which was later complemented by Facebook (2009), Twitter (2014), and Instagram (2015).[8]

At this point, we also need to take into account the May 2012 launch of our department's blog, during Ted Trost's tenure as department chair (2009–13). Set up and first managed by our colleague Steven Ramey, its initial aim was to provide a place for conversation about the theme of that year's lecture series: the relevance of the humanities.[9] But it soon grew beyond that as more faculty, and then students, grads, and even invited guests began posting pieces that they'd written especially for this venue, on a wide variety of topics, either briefly summarizing current faculty research or applying class content to understand day-to-day life, politics, and pop culture.[10] This was how WordPress first came into our orbit—a software used in our college's technology office (called etech, and distinguished from the university's central Office for Information Technology). With their assistance to customize the theme and provide just a little more functionality, we added an active blog to our social media presence, making even more evident that the days of a website handling all of our online duties had passed; for, as noted above, adding a quick WordPress blog post immediately following an event, containing photos and captions, maybe even an embedded video, and which then automatically hits Facebook and Twitter, was far simpler than html coding in Dreamweaver.

And then, the same three faculty members (Steven Ramey, Merinda Simmons, and myself) joined up with colleagues elsewhere (Craig Martin, Monica Miller [who later left the group], Leslie Dorrough Smith, and Vaia Touna) to

---

[8] Side note: the University of Alabama's Twitter account is eager for content that promotes the campus, so not long after our Twitter account was launched it became clear that they'd happily retweet posts, especially interesting photos of campus. Given that the department had long ago gotten into the habit of regularly changing the cover pictures on our Facebook accounts—after all, not just content posts and links communicate activity on a page—it wasn't much effort to start tweeting pictures periodically at the university and appending the #TodayatUA hashtag. The result? While it's unclear exactly what it is worth to a unit, the university and its followers certainly know that this one department exists.

[9] The first post on the site, from May 7, 2012, was by Ramey and entitled "What is the Purpose of Education?"; see https://religion.ua.edu/blog/2012/05/07/what-is-the-purpose-of-education/ (accessed June 14, 2019).

[10] The blog (https://religion.ua.edu/blog/) has had well over 150,000 hits since then, with over 1,000 posts on the site, one garnering 2,000 hits in a single day, and another over 3,000 visits in total. We find that it has been an excellent vehicle for continuing to engage students after they've graduated, either by how faculty and current student posts solicit their comments on social media or their willingness to write guests posts.

form a research collaborative that we named Culture on the Edge. With the help of funding from Trost, who was chair at that time, a working meeting at the University of Alabama took place, a common book project was launched, and the group set to work trying to think through the application of Jean-François Bayart's work on identity formation (notably his *The Illusion of Cultural Identity* [2005]) to the study of religion. The reasoning was that if, as all of us agreed we ought to, we dropped the pretension that religion is an autonomous and privileged domain and, instead, presumed it to be but one more mundane social site, then what might the work of a scholar of religion look like? A year later, in May 2013, the group launched a blog of its own (hosted by the University of Alabama) and, for the next three years, amassed a pretty intensive series of pithy but intellectually thick posts, written for a wide audience, in which the group's approach was exemplified and explored.[11] Although, strictly speaking, not a department initiative, Touna eventually joined our faculty (in the fall of 2015), bringing the UA contingent of the group to four, by which time the move from studying identity as a stable quality to studying (as Bayart phrases it) "acts of identification," had made headway throughout other parts of the department—both in our teaching and our writing. "Classification is a political act" some of our undergraduate students then started responding, on social media, to news stories they'd find and post online, tagging the department, influenced by what they were learning in our classes. And while those classes certainly drew on detailed historical or rich ethnographic information, this material was seen not as self-evidently interesting but, instead, used as a pedagogical means to another end, i.e., as noted in the opening of this chapter, as an e.g. of some wider process in which social actors, embedded in contexts not of their making, made moves and engaged in contests. Coming as it did just over a decade after our reinvention began and resulting from initial conversations between Simmons, Ramey, and myself—three colleagues, all at different career stages—concerning things we had in common despite the different areas in which we did our work, Culture on the Edge nicely exemplifies where I'm going in this chapter, for the form our work takes in the online world has had substantive and long-lasting effect on the content of our research and our teaching.[12] And the fact

---

11 The blog (https://edge.ua.edu/), which all along had a pedagogical tone (hoping to reach newcomers at whatever level), is still active but, as the group expanded, has been reinvented as a peer-review blog working with early-career scholars who find the group's approach useful.
12 The Culture on the Edge site, now with 1,000 posts, has had 277,000 hits since going online in May 2013, with the single most visited post receiving 1,900 hits in one day and the all-time most popular one chalking up a total of 10,500 visits; see the preface to Touna 2018 for more on that site.

that a variety of thematically related posts from the group's blog turned into a series of small books, aimed at the classroom (each with an original introduction and substantive afterword by the volume editor), makes the benefits of cross-pollinating from the digital world evident once again.[13]

But again, I'm getting ahead of myself.

Returning to the various digital pebbles that we've tossed out there, there's also Vimeo. In the summer of 2012, to kick off the new semester, we posted our first "welcome back" video to that new account, borrowing the recording equipment from a student media lab on campus. The aim was to surprise returning students, a little, or at least a little more than just putting up different bulletin board content in anticipation of their arrival in August—not realizing that, as with the other digital initiatives, our intended audience would, eventually, reach far beyond our campus. I drove a student worker (Andie Alexander, now working on her own PhD at Emory) around town, with her leaning out the passenger side window, filming local landmarks, and she then learned enough about iMovie to edit it, give it an older sepia look, and pair it with John Sebastian's old theme from *Welcome Back Kotter* (on TV from 1975 to 1979 and John Travolta's big break). Faculty names were listed as if we were co-stars and the dean's name appeared in the credits as the executive producer. Eventually, the department purchased its own camera, tripods, and mics (a Zoom mic and a lapel mic), started regularly filming our guests' public lectures, doing some interviews with them, and creating a variety of short series featuring our students and faculty (looking around almost any prof's office, there's likely an interesting story associated with each trinket on their book shelves …). Each summer we also make a new welcome back video—usually featuring any new faculty member we've hired. And, as with previous social media ventures, we again learned that the success of any one venture is linked to how a coherent, collective wagon can be pulled by them all, e. g., a new video is embedded in a blog post and it then hits Facebook and Twitter.

Now, as I briefly noted earlier, Altman has moved us into the latest social media direction with the Study Religion podcast (hosted at SoundCloud and also available for download on iTunes).[14] With the fifteenth episode recently pro-

---

[13] Two of the volumes were edited by myself and one by Steven Ramey; the books appear in Vaia Touna's book series, "Working with Culture on the Edge" (published by Equinox of the UK) and are entitled *Fabricating Origins, Fabricating Identity,* and *Fabricating Difference.*

[14] Although also available on other platforms, you can find the podcast at https://soundcloud.com/studyreligion; the seven extended, unedited interviews for the J. Z. Smith episode were then used in a book I co-edited with a former instructor on our faculty, entitled *Remembering J. Z. Smith: A Career and its Consequence* (Crews and McCutcheon 2020).

duced (the seventh, of which we were quite proud, focused on a variety of scholars' memories of Jonathan Z. Smith [1938–2017]), we have high hopes for the site inasmuch as it makes a statement about the department but in the context of the field at large (both in the US and beyond). Although the work of students and faculty are certainly featured, guests to campus appear as well, along with conversations on topics that range widely and which take place far from our home in Presidents Hall—again, making evident, we hope, that the approach we've developed here at the University of Alabama pays off when applied elsewhere, inasmuch as we might learn something new about seemingly mundane, culture-wide processes of social formation if we approach our topic in just this or that manner.

There are still many challenges ahead of us, of course, so I don't want to get lost in the list of digital initiatives that I've just put before readers. To name but one such challenge: the faculty involved in these initiatives—more or less involving everyone in the department, in varying ways, but with Richard Newton (who joined us in August 2018) now taking the lead, especially on producing short, engaging videos for social media that promote our courses and which are aimed at incoming students—have active research and publishing programs of their own, not to mention their teaching and supervision of students. Even recognizing the self-beneficial role played by carrying out department service, one still must take into account that the management of these social media sites takes time and effort (especially throughout the summer when faculty normally are not engaged in performing all that much service). How to ensure that does not get out of hand and that the payoff is in proportion to the work invested is something of which we're certainly aware. Another issue (already mentioned) is how each of these complements the others, rather than repeats (or even undermines) them. While some posts and projects are better suited to certain sorts of content, others attract a distinct audience; so, while a shotgun approach to social media seems inevitable (for one never knows which post will stick with which reader), ensuring that one's efforts are well invested means trying to make sure all facets of this initiative play their own role while also contributing to an overall impression of what we're up to in the Department of Religious Studies at the University of Alabama. This is an impression no longer simply in the minds of administrators who were once asked to question whether the unit had a future and students unsure whether to do their major with us but now also in the minds of graduate students and faculty around the country and around the world, who have found us only because we've taken our presence online seriously. After all, there are many departments in the country, let alone elsewhere in the world, yet people somehow know that we exist and are interested in what we're up to in Tuscaloosa. Hopefully, we have the substance in our individual work to back up the presence that we have online, so that the tweet, the post, the picture, the video, or the audio file are not just digitally accessible but intellectually useful and provocative of thought.

But enough with the list of what we've tackled; what about their effects?

9.3 Institutional Ripples

These various pebbles certainly produced ripples. The challenge was in trying to get them all going in the same direction and reinforcing each other—either that or, as if often the case, figuring out whether (and if so, then how) to follow the direction in which they were moving us. While certainly not wanting to portray our work as omnisciently managing all of the above moving parts, reflecting with the benefit of hindsight on the past couple of decades, it seems possible to discern a variety of beneficial effects that our assorted digital experiments have had—whether alone or, as has increasingly become apparent over time, in concert.

First off, early on our department became known on campus (which, given that we were possibly due to be closed just a couple years earlier, is an accomplishment on its own) for web-based projects—to such an extent that, within a couple years of arriving, I was asked to chair a three-person committee that made sweeping recommendations for overhauling how technology was managed and utilized throughout the College of Arts & Sciences. By that time I'd also served on an A&S committee working to establish new relationships with the College of Continuing Studies, which built and managed all online courses (though departments provided the content and the instructors). Like many others in higher education, our department was wary of moving to the online environment, especially because such courses competed with our regular lecture classes and no matter how well designed, they couldn't match standing in front of a student and answering their question. We already had several old and poorly delivered distance learning courses (i.e., the once-common model of a textbook and a booklet arriving for the student in the mail), but because distance learning plays an important role in some students' education, we at least saw this as an opportunity to revamp these courses and turn them into respectable and engaging pedagogical experiences for students far from campus—thus a good that we achieved through this relationship.[15]

---

[15] For a while, departments on our campus lost the right to limit these courses to distance learning (DL) students, thereby allowing all students to enroll and, possibly, bypass a lecture course. That right, however, was eventually reinstated and so our small number of online courses (with limited seating) continue to play an important role in our teaching mission while serv-

So, ripple #1: the department quickly developed an identity with the college, helping the college to achieve some of its aims while also working to benefit the department and its own goals in the process. (Aside: anyone familiar with working in large institutions will recognize that not every unit's goals completely overlap or complement the institution's other units; making this happen, or at least minimizing the effects of goals that run counter to one another, sometimes takes craft and effort.)

This first effect was crucial, since achieving our primary goal—increasing demand for classes and increasing the number of majors and graduates (i.e., recruitment)—was a slow process, sometimes with only incremental gains that took years to accomplish. So, while working diligently to accomplish those necessary goals (or what we're now told to call outcomes), through a wide variety of strategies, the more instantaneous effect of paying attention to the web helped to secure the confidence of an administration that took a chance protecting what was then our little (and, at least back then, very exposed) department. It demonstrated ingenuity and actually helped move the College of Arts & Sciences in its own new direction. (While the payoff of such work is never guaranteed, I have learned over the years that, despite possible disagreements, it is never a bad idea to build up a small store of good karma with others in your institutional setting.)

A second effect concerned what we all now refer to as retention, i.e., the small number of majors we already had, plus any newly acquired majors, needed a reason to stay with us. Given our small size then and for many years prior to that (i.e., the department had been just three faculty for decades, was 4.25 faculty when I arrived in 2001 [we had two cross-appointments], though now we're twelve with a full-time instructor as well), we exerted little control over our own subject domain; a variety of courses from across our campus therefore focused on the topic of religion, offered by a variety of departments (units that, to this day, still exert territorial control over some classes that other departments of religious studies might reasonably see as their own).[16] So students could satisfy an interest in studying such things as the history of Christianity (Department of History), the study of myths and rituals (Department of Anthropology), or religion in ancient Rome (Department of Modern Language & Classics) by taking courses in

---

ing as an opportunity for a small set of off-campus instructors to earn some extra money and continue to be involved in university instruction.

16 We see here a common (and for me, problematic) model of religion, inasmuch as it is presumed to be an inner, pan-human experience, only secondarily expressed, and thereby something that virtually anyone—inasmuch as they are human themselves—can talk about authoritatively.

other departments, and, perhaps, enrolling in other majors. Again, given that this was long before social networks were something that we talked about, the new department webpage, with regular and timely updates, candid pictures from student events, temporary (and sometimes fun) fake homepages announcing events or new courses, and substantive pages on just what the study of religion was (and wasn't) functioned to unify our current students, in an almost Durkheimian fashion, by prominently featuring the logo that we settled on (which was also displayed around the department as well), making plain who we were, who they were, and where you were when you landed on our page. (Given the standardized web template that units on campus must now use, thanks to those who work to brand the university and not just its various departments, we have strived to ensure that the newly designed page continues to reflect this hard-won identity.) The engaging nature of our classes and personable style of our faculty played a significant role in this, of course, as did the fact that we quickly established a department lounge, but I think that it would be shortsighted to downplay the role that the website played in providing these students with a virtual home.

Ripple #2, then? The establishment of an effective virtual identifier of considerable reach.[17]

The third effect was also focused on students, for despite an early course release for a faculty member to create an initial website, and even though I made a number of the pages on the site myself (actually, before publishing an intro book in the field, I even created an online version that was on the web for years, for free), it was undergraduate student workers who played a key role in building and maintaining the site. For the ability to engage a work-study student was soon followed by hiring one and sometimes two part-time students in the main office, often doing so with one throughout the summer as well—they tackled a wide variety of projects, of course, as any student working in a department's main office will, from running errands on campus to making photocopies, sorting the mail and answering phones. But learning Dreamweaver for web design, using FTP (file transfer protocol) software and Fireworks for handling images soon became a requirement for students who were working in the department. Now, Photoshop has replaced Fireworks and WordPress has almost completely replaced Dreamweaver, but since we now make movies, that means Final

---

17 In fact, it was so effective that, upon learning a couple years ago that our longtime site was being replaced, a group of alums (some of whom graduated over a decade ago and many of whom had worked on our site under my direction) quickly started an initiative to petition the dean to let us keep the site. The result was that the new site tipped its hat enough to the look of the old site that everyone ended up being happy with the change.

Cut Pro has also become a required software. And Altman's initial experiments in podcasting have even involved students as well (from reading and recording their own work to doing the intro and credits), meaning that learning to use GarageBand and other audio software will also be required. Inevitably the students we hired would learn far more about each software once we had taught them the basics about html coding and so, in some cases, they'd graduate and put those same skills to work in other degrees, with other departments, or even in jobs. In fact, I recall one major and former main office student worker whose first job after graduation was working in a real estate office and her ability to make and manage their webpage played a role in her getting that job. While I wouldn't want to overplay this hand, realizing that students were not just helping us maintain our site but were acquiring and using these digital skills on their own has played an important role in how we most recently charted the future course of the department.

So, ripple #3: the digital emphasis provided practical, transferable skills for our students.

Recognizing this third effect—an effect that was not initially apparent of course, since our minds were then just on the task of getting it done and not on the longer-term effects of students learning how to get it done ("teach a man to fish ... " and all that)—marks a shift in the role that our various digital initiatives have played in the department; for, at the outset, students were just the target audience for our various initiatives—we wanted them to know what courses were being offered, to see the events taking place, to learn more about each faculty member's research, so as to consider taking our classes or even entertain becoming a major. But, slowly, we realized that we were transitioning to students, always under the faculty's direction, becoming not only the readers but also the providers of the content and the producers of the sites—a shift that quickly puts their skills in focus (both for writing online to reach wide audiences and for learning the software necessary to distribute the material online). In part this was out of necessity—after all, we needed assistance to manage these sites—but in part it was also a conscious effort on our part to, for example, refashion campus-wide initiatives (e. g., the now national trend toward emphasizing undergraduate research as a way to retain students and improve graduation rates), to help us to make plain, by making public, what had been going on in our classes all along. (In our experience, this is also the key to the nationwide assessment initiative: determine how to effectively publicize the work we're already doing rather than inventing things to satisfy credentialing agencies.) Although we're known among those in our classes for emphasizing writing, the student blog makes that clear to a far wider audience, helping us to showcase our students' research and writing and doing so by student workers preparing and posting their peer's work. And although it has detracted from the site's "cool factor," with moms and dads now on Facebook, we regularly reach them as well—and families are not an unimportant audience. (In our case, a few families have so welcomed our work with their children that very kind endowments have resulted.) The video initiative might be an even better example, inasmuch as no faculty member has ever learned the ins and outs of Final Cut Pro but, instead, a student worker, with some assistance from a media lab in our main library, learned it on her own, after transitioning from iMovie; then, because she overlapped with her successor, she passed the skills on to him. And he passed them along to another. And now, we have the fourth and fifth students in this successive tradition of student workers who pass along their video production skills—working under a faculty supervisor, to be sure, but more as a producer of a film might work not only with a director but also a cinematographer, sound engineer, and editor (all roles our student workers play). The skills now largely operate well apart from faculty. So while I wouldn't claim that the department's current emphasis on what others might characterize as skills-based education is wholly due to our digital emphases—for, from the start, focusing not simply on mastery of data domains but also on learning how to define, describe, compare, interpret, and explain was something that we emphasized across our classes (e.g., see McCutcheon 2001, chapter 13 for my early attempt to discuss integrating the skills that, in my reading, Jonathan Z. Smith had long advocated)—seeing the practical effects of undergraduate students having learned these digital skills certainly reinforced our sense that a methodological focus would be beneficial to their educations and, hopefully, careers and lives.

Ripple #4? The shift from delivering information *to* students to being collaborators *with* them.

And this brings me to the last, but perhaps the most significant and lasting, effect; for combining much of the above—e.g., grappling with nation-wide criticisms of the humanities' relevance, our department's emphasis on skills, the role students played in assisting our various digital initiatives, the shift many faculty came to share by studying situated acts of identification rather than identities that are simply expressed, and the practical benefits we witnessed these skills having for our students—we began seriously discussing (back in 2013–14) developing a new MA degree program that explicitly integrates much of what we had learned over the past decade or so. For while it could certainly be questioned whether the world needed another graduate degree in the study of religion (due to declining academic job opportunities and the increased expense of tuition), it has not yet been established whether scholars of religion are incapable of using their skills to train students in social analysis that's accessible to wide audiences—which implicitly makes the case for what we, in the humanities, have to contribute. So, after several years of planning, led by Merinda Simmons (who chaired the committee, joined by Ramey and Altman), our new MA was approved by the University of Alabama Board of Trustees and also by the Alabama Commission on Higher Education—the latter being the very group that, back in the late 1990s, had come to the conclusion that our department was "non-viable," due to a severe shortage of majors and thus graduates, and that we should therefore lose our undergraduate major. The degree that they approved, and which was launched in the fall of 2017 with an incoming class of three students (two of whom were our own BA grads), involves two required foundations courses in the first semester, one focusing on social theory and the other on the digital skills necessary to make a contribution to the public humanities (designed and then taught, in alternating years, by Altman and Nathan Loewen—who, in 2019, began his own "big data" research project, working with one of our BA majors—and again we see the effect of working with students).[18] While learning of the scholarly literature and debates around such categories as agency, authorship, intension, race, gender, class, identity, etc., in the social theory class (categories of analysis that we expect our students to use in the eventual thesis they produce in their second year—a course Ramey, Simmons and Newton share), the public humanities foundation course ensures that, by the time they complete it, students have not only acquired skills to create and manage a variety of digital projects—from, yes, tackling geographic information system (GIS) projects and big data to producing a podcast or obtaining a domain name and making a website of their own—but will also have developed an entrepreneurial attitude toward mastering new technologies and incorporating them in their own research, whether in data gathering, analysis, or presentation. (For the software they'll work with in the course, all of which are widely available to the students, are hardly the only digital tools they could use to get the job done.) Also, their MA thesis can either be a traditional piece of writing (ideally, we've decided, a more practical article-length piece of original work that can be submitted to a journal) or an original and substantial digital project (one that, though presenting their findings in a novel manner, still requires the same sort of research that

---

[18] After learning of the JSTOR Data for Research (DfR) site (https://www.jstor.org/dfr/), Loewen (half of whose teaching time is loaned to the college for technology projects) developed a project using this tool to analyze the contents of entire journals in the philosophy of religion (his specialty area). The June 4, 2019, post on our department blog has a description of his project and a narrative of how it developed/how he acquired the skills necessary to carry it out. See https://religion.ua.edu/blog/2019/06/04/reading-writing-and-r-how-i-began-to-study-the-philosophy-of-religion-with-digital-tools/ (accessed July 2, 2019).

scholars have done for ages). Given that so many of our undergraduate majors have not gone into the study of religion for a career but yet continue to report to us how important the skills were that they learned in our classes, we've reasoned that, for it to succeed, this MA should be of interest both to students hoping to pursue a PhD in the study of religion immediately after as well as to those who wish to work in any number of other fields where critical thinking and creative but effective communication skills are valued.[19] This makes clear how, in a way that was surely unplanned, our early and ongoing digital initiatives have fed back into the degree programs of the department itself, not just helping to rejuvenate it but transforming it in the process, opening a variety of futures we'd not anticipated whatsoever but which we're now pursuing. Five MA students enrolled in the fall of 2018, four more in fall 2019, and nine in 2020 (with all but one of the enrollees in the most recent class coming from outside the department).

And so we come to ripple #5: The unforeseen feedback loop whereby what started as a variety of discrete digital initiatives coalesced into a refined identity for the department and a new graduate degree program that further sets us apart in the field today and thereby continues to model for others possible futures for the academic study of religion. In fact, it's now so central to who we see ourselves to be that contributing to what we're calling our public and digital humanities initiative has done more than shaped a request for a new tenure-track line in the department and impacted a hiring decision for a new instructor (to which we were very pleased to hire Jeri Wieringa, for the former, and Lauren Horn Griffin, for the latter, both with significant digital humanities expertise and both joining us as of August 2020). It has also inspired Altman to propose a new BA crash course on digital tools for undergrads (offered for the first time in fall 2019—the only such course on campus, as far as we can tell). It's also put one of our current MA students in the position of being an appealing summer hire to work full time in one of our campus's tech offices and helped another find an internship with *Alabama Heritage* magazine while also working with a local museum in northeast Alabama for the summer. Add to this that one of three annual early-career workshops, to be offered over the coming four years to four different groups of applicants, will be modeled after our MA degree's course on digital tools as part of a $350,000 Luce Foundation grant that the department received in the summer of 2019 (with Altman as the PI but with six of

---

[19] At present, we have graduated three MA students, with one enrolling in a PhD in religious studies at the University of North Carolina, one working full time in a museum, and the last entering architecture school.

our faculty acting as workshop mentors).[20] It should be obvious that a set of specific digital tools initially used to help reinvent the department's online presence has turned out to be the major theme driving that reinvention's success all across the unit—a success that includes an enhanced entrepreneurial attitude among the faculty as well, evidenced in the increasingly novel and bold research projects that they're tackling as well as their pedagogical experiments in the classroom, with or without the use of technology.[21]

9.4 Still Learning to Fly

And so we return to the epigraph, which, by now, hopefully makes a little more sense to readers; for what has become a series of interrelated and collective initiatives that help to keep our department central to discussions of how to renew the study of religion in the current higher ed environment (i.e., moving away from a descriptive, world religions model and, instead, investigating so-called religion-making, and even identity-making, processes and strategies) first started out as a variety of isolated digital experiments, usually linked to a discrete need and a lone professor with time on his or her hands. Whether the eventual overlaps between these projects were planned or (as was sometimes the case) sheer happenstance, we've tried to put our own social theory to good use in understanding the conditions of our own institution—conditions that, as with any social group, change and which sometimes present unanticipated opportunities to the social actor who is paying attention. And these are the skills that we've tried to convey to undergraduates for the past 20 years and which we hope to refine with the graduate students who now decide to join us in Presidents Hall—with an emphasis on the qualifications implied by "tried to" and "hope to," since the experiment that we call the Department of Religious Studies at the University of Alabama is ongoing and we're still learning much.

---

20 The workshop, initially piloted with a small group of participants in spring 2019 (with matching funding from the college and the department), is entitled American Examples. Learn more at https://blogs.religion.ua.edu/ae/. See the June 2019 Luce announcement at https://www.hluce.org/news/articles/luce-foundation-awards-14-million-new-grants/.
21 My thanks to Mike Altman for this final observation, as part of his comments after reading an earlier draft of this chapter.

Reference List

Bayart, Jean-François. 2005. *The Illusion of Cultural Identity*, trans. Steven Rendall et al. Chicago: University of Chicago Press.

Crews, Emily D., and Russell T. McCutcheon, eds. 2020. *Remembering J. Z. Smith: A Career and its Consequence*. Sheffield, UK: Equinox Publishers.

Lease, Gary. 1994. "The History of 'Religious' Consciousness and the Diffusion of Culture: Strategies for Surviving Dissolution." *Historical Reflections/Reflexions Historique* 20:453–79.

McCutcheon, Russell T. 2001. *Critics Not Caretakers: Redescribing the Public Study of Religion*. Albany, NY: State University of New York Press.

McCutcheon, Russell T. 2018. "Why I Blog." In *"Religion" in Theory and in Practice: Demystifying the Field for Burgeoning Academics*, 133–54. Sheffield, UK: Equinox Publishing.

Touna, Vaia. 2018. "Preface." In *Strategic Acts in the Study of Identity: Towards a Dynamic Theory of People and Place: Towards a Dynamic Theory of People and Place*, ix–xvii. Sheffield, UK: Equinox Publishing.

10 On Making a Shift in the Study of Religion

'Cause I know you're no good for me
but you've become a part of me ...

– "Nowhere to Run," as sung by Martha and the Vandellas (1965)

Influenced early on by, among others, Tim Fitzgerald's critique of the world religions concept (Fitzgerald 1990) and sharing much with the basic premise of his critique of, as he once phrased it, the modern myth of religion (2000, 31), this chapter reflects on how a critical project in the academic study of religion can be institutionalized, based on the experience of reinventing of the study of religion at the University of Alabama (a publicly funded R-1 research university in the US, one which also places a heavy emphasis on the importance of undergraduate education). Although more nuanced and genealogical studies of the idea of literature, offered by literary critical (i.e., lit crit) scholars in the 1970s and 1980s, did not lead to the end of departments of English literature, adopting an analogous approach to studying the modern practice of designating certain things in our daily world *as* religious (and thereby studying the practical implications of this discourse) struck many in the 1990s as sounding a death knell for departments of religious studies (as it is usually known, at least in North America, but also elsewhere). As it might be phrased by those whose work is critiqued via what I'm calling a shift in approach, how can one not only study something presumed to be illusory, nonexistent, or a mere discursive construct but how can an entire curriculum be organized around and an "it" in quotation marks (i.e., one that is apparently not even really there)?[1] Instead of defining religion

---

Note: My thanks to Mike Altman, Nathan Loewen, Richard Newton, Steven Ramey, Merinda Simmons, Edith Szanto, and Vaia Touna—some of my colleagues at the University of Alabama, along with Emily Crews, our former colleague—for their helpful comments on an earlier version of this chapter.

1 The so-called social constructionist approach—such as the position generally adopted by those who study religion as a discourse that enables social actors to distinguish and rank actions and organizations, some as sacred and others as profane, to the benefit of just some segments of society—is often greeted by its critics as advocating for a non-realist position, one which, in a suitably Dr. Johnson-like response, is often greeted by its foes with much stone-kicking to demonstrate just how real the real world is. (In other words, merely repeating, orally or in text, how *real* things are is somehow seen as sufficient evidence of their actual reality, instead of being understood as but more claims people are making.) A recent example can be found in Krech (2019, 2): "Exaggerated deconstructivism overlooks the fact that religious traditions—although socially constructed—are nonetheless observed (i.e., distinguished) as distinct entities

in the usual substantive or functionalist manner—regardless which of those definitional strategies one adopts—and then studying both its manifestations (i.e., the world's various religions and the specifically religious actions of their so-called devotees) and its constitutive components (experiences, myths, rituals, symbols, doctrines, etc.), the University of Alabama's Department of Religious Studies, indebted to the work of Fitzgerald and others, went down a rather different path over the past twenty years, not by taking religion seriously (to reference how phenomenologists of religion once phrased their position, in contrast to the so-called reductionist with whom they disagreed) but, rather, by taking "religion" seriously and studying it as one of the rhetorical and organizational tools that has helped to establish and reproduce the modern world. Despite each of them being trained in very different specialties, both within and outside of the traditional academic study of religion, our gradual realization of the faculty's common focus on social theory directed toward studying the formative effects of interconnected and closely policed classification systems (e.g., sacred/profane, private/public, citizen/foreigner, etc.—disputes over which are often at the center of the modern legal system.), coupled with their shared attention to inviting incoming students to become curious about how their own taken-for-granted social worlds are created, reproduced, and even contested, has helped the department to succeed by a wide number of measures, doing so at a time when other humanities programs have felt challenged or even under threat.[2] But, contrary to those who think that this alternative approach jeopardizes the future of the field, our department's ironic relationship to what is usually termed religion—a term that, as my epigraph should have already indicated, we likely can't live without in this modern world of ours, but one whose often unnoticed effects nonetheless deserves our critical attention—has resulted in a revived undergraduate major, a new graduate program, and a faculty who are among the most productive scholars of religion in the US today.[3]

---

in practice and thus have effects in a pragmatic sense." On this rather poor, at best, and caricatured, at worst, understanding of the social constructivist approach as it has developed in our field, see Martin 2019. (My thanks to Teemu Taira for bringing Krech's article to my attention.)

2 I feel that the current "humanities in crisis" literature is great enough and sufficiently well-known that I do not have to document here the actual or at least perceived threat to what was once called the liberal arts by the so-called professionalization of the modern research university.

3 The last claim is based on data presented by Academic Analytics, a company that measures and reports on faculty productivity (publications, citations, grants, awards, etc.) in the US, providing services to which many university administrations subscribe (including the University of Alabama). While there have certainly been critiques of the accuracy of their data as well as rank-

To understand the gains made by this one department when it adopted a critical approach to the study of religion (to borrow a phrase from my Alabama colleague, Steve Ramey [2005])[4] and to therefore see how its successes provide a possible model for others who are interested in opting for a critical approach to the study of religion, some background on the department and the turn toward theory, over the previous decades (and its early impact on the religious studies classroom), is required.

10.1 Background: The Department

As I've already discussed in the previous chapter, the department into which I was hired as an outside chair, back in 2001, had, just a couple years before, been classified as "non-viable" by the Alabama Commission on Higher Education (ACHE)—the governing body for post-secondary education in the state of Alabama.[5] This judgment, based on the insufficient number of majors graduated annually by the department,[6] resulted in it being threatened either with losing its undergraduate major (but retaining its existence as a so-called service department)[7] or closure altogether (with the faculty and staff, hopefully, reassigned

---

ings based on quantified productivity (at the expense of judging quality), measures such as those of Academic Analytics play an increasingly significant role in administrative decisions within universities, suggesting that department chairs and faculty alike should be well versed in such systems and their use. Visit https://academicanalytics.com/ to learn more.

4 See McCutcheon 2018a, 95–120 for a further discussion of the varied uses of the term "critical" in the field today, including so-called critical realist approaches, which should be clearly distinguished from the sort of critical project associated with Fitzgerald's work (e. g., the essays collected together in Fitzgerald 2007).

5 With the members of the commission appointed by the governor of the state, ACHE is but one of many examples of such bodies across the US, where education is generally a matter left to the states. Such government commissions are, of course, to be distinguished from (at least here in the US) the six non-governmental accrediting bodies (such as our own region's Southern Association of Colleges and Schools Commission on Colleges) that also play a role in assessing and credentialing higher ed throughout the US.

6 ACHE standards, then and now, require a program to produce a minimum of 7.5 BA graduates per year (measured on a rolling three-year average), 3.75 MA graduates, and 1.25 PhD graduates. When I arrived in August 2001, programs in the state had already been scrutinized by ACHE for about two years and our department had been able to increase its three-year graduation average to 6.67, making it the second strongest of a wide number of programs at UA that were deemed non-viable.

7 A service department, for those not acquainted with this terminology, "serves" the needs of other majors on campus by offering such things as the core or general education courses that

to other units on campus). Given that I was hired to be the department chair by a brand new dean of the College of Arts & Sciences (who was well aware of the unit's challenges), at a time when a wide variety of other programs across campus and across the state were also addressing their own ACHE viability issues, the university was interested in having the department submit a request to the commission, asking that they waive the minimum graduates number, for a short period of time, while the department reorganized, so as to increase its students' graduation rates, thereby bringing it into compliance. By August 2001, when I arrived, a draft of the waiver request had already been written by the then-interim chair (who was himself about the retire, which was the third such retirement in recent years—a large turnover for a department of only 4.25 faculty members);[8] but because of what I read as its disciplining tone, the waiver needed to be rewritten from scratch. (Failing to understand that priorities and interests representative of those who are outside of academia often determine the practical conditions in which our work and careers [at least in public universities which exist as one arm of state government] take place, I find that many scholars react poorly to external governance, as if legislatures and credentialing associations will finally leave us alone once they fully appreciate the self-evident or inherent worth of our intellectual pursuit.) Steering well clear of criticizing the commission for interfering in our work as faculty (as some might characterize governmental oversight), and avoiding schooling them in the importance of the humanities (as yet others might do on such an occasion), the new waiver request instead brought to the commission's attention the university's recent investment (in 2000) in a brand new tenure-track line (for an Asianist), as well

---

most undergraduate degrees in the US require of students, such that all graduates with a bachelor's degree have at least taken a small number of so-called breadth requirements, such as some English lit courses, some math courses, a science course with a lab, a language course or two, etc. Our department, like many others in religious studies, offers humanities as well as writing core credits (as do many other departments on our campus), helping undergraduate students (who will likely take no classes with us beyond these) to satisfy a requirement for at least two lower-level courses from the humanities and two upper-level courses that emphasize writing skills.

8 Two faculty, hired into tenure-track assistant professor positions in the fall of 1998, each held cross-appointments to another unit on campus, such that a department that, for many decades, had had no more than three or four faculty members, was, in the late 1990s, comprised of three full-time senior tenured positions (that would all retired by the fall of 2001) plus two new cross-appointed tenure-track positions; together, the latter two lines added only 1.25 of a faculty position in our department. Of note is that, when I arrived in 2001, and once the interim chair retired two months later, I was the sole tenured faculty member in the department with all of the others being tenure track (making their continued employment potentially vulnerable, given ACHE's judgments about the department's viability).

as hiring an outside department chair (myself, in 2001, after a failed outside search the previous year), and the practical plans already being implemented. All of this aimed to ensure that the department increased its number of majors by helping its current students through their degrees more promptly (by faculty members agreeing to offer independent study courses tailored to these students' interests and needs [courses which were unpaid overloads for the faculty members who taught them]) while also instituting new recruiting strategies to attract more incoming majors (e.g., offering, for the first time, large-enrollment courses).[9] As the revised waiver concluded: "[w]e are encouraged by the fact that ... we have maintained a steady graduate rate very close to the ACHE guidelines. This having been said, we wish to stress that we are not content with these past numbers."[10]

As a result, the commission was persuaded and granted our waiver request; within a couple of years, our graduation numbers met ACHE's minimum and, although our students will more than likely never rival the very large numbers of majors in such departments as criminal justice and crimonology, English, biology, or history, we have never slipped below it since then.

I position this chapter in the (too briefly stated, I realize) context of this departmnet's late 1990s and very early 2000s history so as to convey how this one unit was not just ripe for a new vision but to make clear that, not so very long ago, its continued existence was entirely in doubt and that a reinvention, from top to bottom, was the only way that the university's administration and the state's higher ed commission would continue to support its existence. That there may have been any number of other ways to reimagine the study of religion

---

9 As elaborated upon elsewhere in this chapter, the US system's focus on general education requirements in an undergraduate degree, coupled with the near-universal lack of classes on religion or world religions in American public schools, leads to a situation where the intro course in the study of religion both recruits incoming majors (few of whom have ever heard of the field before, or assume it to be akin to their private/parochial school religion classes in some high schools) while also generating tuition revenue for the school and credit hours for the department (by serving the needs of students enrolled in other degrees across campus). Though the pedagogical challenges to teaching large lecture classes is well known (and by large I mean up to 150 or 200 students), the larger format does increase credit hour production (thereby helping to strengthen a department's productivity in the eyes of the administration) along with increasing the likelihood of finding those few students who may be interested in majoring in the study of religion. As such, instituting such large lecture classes, which continue to this day in the department, was a strategic decision at the time.

10 Quoted from the March 2002 version of the Request for Waiver for non-Viable Program, University of Alabama/Tuscaloosa, College of Arts & Sciences; BA major and minor and Judaic Studies minor in Department of Religious Studies, CIP 38.0201.

at the University of Alabama should be acknowledged, of course—reiventions that may have had just as much positive effect as the one that the department tackled.[11] But that its faculty elected to support a vision in which the department entertained that it was not so much religion as the discourse on religion that would occupy our collective attention as teachers, and, increasingly, as researchers, is the thing that ought to attract our interest. For, in hindsight, it turns out to have been a strategically beneficial decision.

10.2 Background: The Field

For anyone who lived through the 1980's so-called theory wars in departments of English literature (or, usually, just called departments of English)—in which traditionalists who carefully read and interpreted texts for their timeless meaning (the "what did Shakespeare mean ...?" model of the field)[12] were challenged by scholars trained in a variety of subfields, all intent on challenging the literary canon as well as the very idea of a canon and even a text, along with the methods used to study both—the following may be relatively uninteresting or even insufficient; for how to capture in a few paragraphs the hotly contested disputes that were then taking place, let alone the stakes and implications of these disagreements? But for anyone who came along later, such as undergraduate students today, a few decades after the dust has settled, it may be tempting to just assume that today's wide array of Norton Anthologies has always existed (in which we find far more considered as literature than just Beowulf, Shakespeare, and the poetry of Thomas Gray) or to think that everyone had always just been acquainted with the implications of Jacques Derrida's work on the boundless nature of text or Roland Barthes's even earlier thoughts on how read-

---

11 In the opening chapter I discussed in detail problems that I see to be associated with the religious literacy model which a number of departments in North America have now adopted as their *raison d'être*.

12 I've repeatedly referred to our work as comprising a field, and, notably, not a discipline—the latter term having more currency today in Europe than in North America. Although the term "field" is often associated with assumptions that religion is multifaceted and therefore comprised of what the late Ninian Smart famously called dimensions, thereby requiring for its adequate study a variety of methods drawn from other disciplines, I do not share this rationale for using the term, given how an essentialist understanding can easily animate the dimensions approach (with each dimension seen as an "expression" of the supposed kernel of religion). Instead, I merely mean to distinguish my understanding of our collective work from assumptions that a distinct phenomenon is the focus of our studies, one which requires a distinct method—a common, though somewhat traditional, understanding of an academic discipline.

ers and scriptors alike conjure authors into existence. But these, among other sources, blew the literary doors wide open back then, one might say, by drawing attention to the manner in which the very idea of literature had long been quite effectively policed (via the idea of an author's own meaning [i.e., intention] governing how we were allowed to approach a text, along with such a loaded pairing as high and low culture, for example—with corollaries in the older distinction between high and low church and the manner in which the wide variety of dialects within the English language itself had long been distinguished and ranked [i.e., the queen's English distinguished from slang]). This resulted in a world in which some things (or, better put, the products of just some people) were considered to be obviously worth reading, knowing, remembering, and quoting, while others were, well, just a little humdrum and beneath a person of culture and thus standing. But, if there was no obviously high culture that was of great importance and if there was no pristine and timeless authorial intention floating around in a text, awaiting careful hermeneuts to read it in just the right way and thereby unlock it and re-experience it for themselves (as what a so-called formalist might have maintained), then there was no longer a single, authoritative, or correct answer to the "what did Shakespeare mean when he wrote ...?" question. For *now* there were only readers offering readings (of all sorts of new and different things) and giving answers (all in the newly potent plural) of their own to such queries—readings and answers that were up to far more than was previously assumed (implying that so-called reader response criticism, with its origins dating to the early twentieth century, had only identified the tip of the iceberg).[13] That thing previously known as the text now turned out to be something onto which readers projected their own hopes and dreams, as well as their fears and insecurities—making readers themselves an integral part of the now virtually boundless text, using their readings to establish or legitimize not just their sense of self and the groups of which they were members but also the far wider, impersonal structures in which they were themselves

---

13 Reader response theory or reader response criticism names an earlier school of thought in which the role of the reader in determining the meaning of a text was greatly expanded. Although his concern was for how people misread a text, its early years could be traced to, for example, the English literary scholar I. A. Richards (1893–1979), who famously deprived Cambridge undergraduate students with contextual clues and information (e.g., who the author was) and then asked them to read and interpret thirteen poems, some, it turns out, by famous poets (see Richards 1929). A contemporary example would be Stanley Fish and his work on the linguistic competence of readers, based not just on their supposedly personal experiences but on the interpretive communities of which they happen to be members (see Fish 1982).

(knowingly or not) situated, from class, gender, and racial systems, for example, to the economy and even the idea of the nation itself.

Seated back then as a graduate student in the nearby field of religious studies, it was not difficult to peer over the hedge and hear the disputes as analogues for what was going on in our own yard. There was an uncanny familiarity to the differences between, on the one hand, those traditionalist English professors who thought literature operated in an autonomous symbolic realm all its own, and, on the other, those who saw literature as an effect/product/evidence of other human situations as well as those in their ranks who questioned why certain definitions of literature prevailed while others were dismissed. For, as readers likely know, not a few scholars of religion advocated for the irreducibly religious nature of religion (the circularity seemed never to bother them all that much, by the way) by asserting that religious things had to be studied in their own unique way and thereby interpreted properly, having their camouflaged and deeply symbolic meaning not just decoded correctly but re-experienced and realized in the life of scholars themselves. (I imply here the once much read work of the late Mircea Eliade, of course, but, as I have argued on previous occasions, I see his work as an example of a wide consensus in the field, then and now, making it more representative than influential.) And, on the other side, there had by then already been a long-established tradition of those who saw in religion a mere secondary or derivative component and thus an effect of prior, structural factors or far greater interest, such as the classic trinity of Karl Marx, Emile Durkheim, and Sigmund Freud, all intent on studying religion to get at yet other mechanisms that helped to make possible such things as economies and political orders, social life, and the psyche itself, respectively. In fact, the analogy of literary studies went even further for, along with those questioning just why we privileged some texts *as* literature, or as worth having in the canon, it was also possible to stop talking about religion altogether and to begin talking, in its place, about why certain sorts of claims, actions, and organizations were routinely collected together and treated *as* religion—whether to exalt these varied collections of human doings or to demean them. Although one could add to the external influences a variety of influences internal to the field, such as Wilfred Cantwell Smith's *The Meaning and End of Religion* (1963)—though its analysis is directed toward recovering the essential and authoritative personal core [i.e., faith] to those things commonly called religious—or, better yet, Jonathan Z. Smith's now (in)famous aside in the opening pages to *Imagining Religion* (1982)—concerning there being no data for religion, since, as Smith claimed there, scholars invented it—work from within the study of religion on the effects of the category religion only started to be done in earnest by the mid- to late 1990s, with Tim Fitzgerald's and my own counting among the earlier books,[14] to which we can also add the early works by such scholars as Richard King, Tomoko Masuzawa, Malory Nye, and now others, such as Naomi Goldenberg, Suzanne Owen, Teemu Taira, and Brent Nongbri.[15]

That such work was greeted, early on, by traditionalists in the study of religion—those who, at the time, might have termed themselves historians of religion(s)[16]—as portending the end of the field goes without saying, perhaps.[17] For it was—and for many still is—unimaginable how to study religion (in the singular) if one did not first begin with studying in detail the descriptive ins and outs of each of the world's many religions (in the plural), only to then focus more closely (as described earlier) on each of their shared components, such as their myths, their rituals, their symbols, etc. Whether one follows the example of the classic phenomenologists in the field or not, the analytic they employed to break religions down into their presumably common elements was (and is) the

---

14 Our approaches, while overlapping in some regards, differ in other ways, such as what I've read as Fitzgerald's early interest to call those things designated as religion by a better name (e. g., soteriological ritual complexes)—a critique animated, in my reading, by what he understood as the inappropriately theological (and Christian) engine driving the world religions discourse. My own interest in the constitutive function of the discourse on religion steered me clear of trying to develop better names for religions while it also highlighted for me the need to problematize the notion that theology was a genre unto itself. Also, while Fitzgerald's *The Ideology of Religious Studies* had yet to be published by the time of my own first book, four of his works were cited there, ranging from a 1990 essay to two of his pieces that were forthcoming at that time. Only Fitzgerald 1990 was cited in the dissertation, the earlier version of what later became McCutcheon 1997, written largely in the early 1990s and defended in January 1995.

15 The influences from lit crit disputes, briefly summarized above, certainly characterize my own introduction to the critical moves that later allowed me to develop my own approach to "religion;" there are, of course, other genealogical roots to the shifts in our field, with literary theory being just one among them. For instance, I've always thought of anthropology and political theory as more important to Fitzgerald's early work than was literary theory.

16 The singular or plural religion/religions is significant to those who make this distinction, inasmuch as the former signifies a species-wide tendency while the latter points only to one or more of the many traditions that can be studied empirically.

17 Readers may have realized that I have opted for the term field rather than discipline when discussing the study of religion. While I realize that there's much riding on the distinction, at least in Europe, where we miss the authority of the university's disciplinary structure if we call our pursuit anything but a discipline (minimally implying a unified datum and a shared method for its study), in North America we often opt to call it a field, inasmuch as it is assumed to be a cross-disciplinary pursuit, requiring a variety of methods, given that the object of study is often presumed to be so complex or deeply meaningful as to defy the scope of any one method. While I certainly do not share this latter rationale, I also distance myself from the idea that the study of religion comprises a discipline in the traditional sense of the term (though favoring the more Foucaultian reading of the term as applied to the governing role of the discourse on religion; see McCutcheon 2003]).

model used across the field. Following this template, we still find broadly generalist survey courses at the start of one's undergraduate degree that later lead to more specialized courses, such as a survey of the New Testament at the 100 level followed by 200-, 300-, and finally 400-level courses that increasingly limit their focus, steadily moving from studying but one gospel to an examination of just one verse—with doctoral dissertations then writing on but a textual fragment or the root of an ancient Greek word. Given the prominence of this curricular and career structure and the way in which it presupposes a specific conception of religion (i.e., as intangible yet having dimensions, expressions, manifestations, or facets, as described earlier), it is understandable that its advocates were, and remain, suspicious of anything that possibly calls it into question (i.e., by reducing or redescribing it). That I've had reported back to me, by a variety of colleagues with whom I've worked over the years, that friends elsewhere in the country have queried them on what it was like to work with me, as their chair, when it's apparently widely known that, or so I've been told, "McCutcheon is out to destroy the field" should be evidence enough that anything that even vaguely smells of a critical approach is seen by many as a threat to the field.

That it may indeed be a threat *to a certain version of the field*, one that is no doubt widely adopted today, ought to be noted, of course, though—which should also be observed—this is hardly the only way to go about studying religion in a university classroom. For, unless I'm mistaken, I'm not sure I've ever called for the field to be demolished. Changed? Yes. Significantly so, in the judgment of at least some? Yes again. But demolished? Never. So, as Peggy Schmeiser has wisely concluded, "acknowledging that there is no 'it' called religion to locate and mine for data need not signal an end to our discipline" (2019, 129). After all, following Schmeiser, the shift to studying the discourse on religion modeled by Fitzgerald and others—what Daniel Dubuisson has most recently called "a veritable scientific revolution" (2019, 1)—means that there are still plenty of "government documents, consultation transcripts, court submissions and rulings to understand what is obscured and at play when the category of religion is invoked in public contexts" (Schmeiser 2019, 131).

10.3 Background: The Classroom

Despite my own early attraction to carrying out research not on religions or even religion but on the implications of classifying something *as* religious,[18] in the

---

[18] To be fair, my early work mainly constituted a critique of the notion of religious as unique

classroom back then one was hard pressed to do anything but teach courses on either religions and their texts or such things as myths and rituals. To rephrase: given that credit hour production, recruiting majors, and, as already indicated, the overall numbers of graduates are the coins of the realm, the gap between such critical scholarly interests and what goes on in the classroom can sometimes be great. Add to that the complete nonexistence of resources to use in the class that did anything but implement the then-dominant model and you arrive at a situation where it was rather difficult to do anything but teach world religions. So the challenge, as I discovered early in my own career, was how to bridge that gap by introducing these more technical, possibly counterintuitive interests into the classroom in such a way that did not frighten colleagues (most of whom held a superior rank, making them authorized gatekeepers to the profession and thus one's own career development) or scare away students (who generally arrived in class with a specific sort of folk knowledge or common sense about what religion was and what it did or didn't do for people). For, once assigned to teach the world religions class—a so-called bread and butter course whose enrollment often helps to justify a department's existence—how to go about calling into question the very basis for how we organize and package the information in the course itself? This was a challenge from the outset in my own career, begun in 1993 at as a full-time instructor at the University of Tennessee. Asked that first semester to teach a section of world religions, a section of the alternate, thematic introductory course, as well as a then-popular upper-level undergraduate course whose professor had recently retired, entitled, "Myth, Symbol, Ritual," all while finalizing the last chapters in my dissertation,[19] presented a number of challenges, not least of which was developing classroom goals and material that were not directly contradictory of the work that I was then doing in my research. (Aside: my early aim to develop and publish resources of for others to use in their classes—from topical anthologies and a co-edited handbook eventually to an intro book of my own—was directly linked to the

---

and socio-politically autonomous (i.e., *sui generis*). Only a few years later did my interest in "religion" extend to any use of the category, including that of so-called reductionists and naturalists let alone governments and legal documents (e.g., constitutions).

[19] Moving to Knoxville, Tennessee, in the summer of 1993, my dissertation was then about two-thirds complete, with some new writing to be done and a variety of revisions yet to be made over the coming eighteen months or so. (I defended, at the University of Toronto, in January 1995.) It was in Knoxville, for instance, that I conceptualized and then wrote chapter 6, "The Imperial Dynamic and the Discourse on Sui Generis Religion," using the intentionally provocative e.g. of Thich Quang Duc's June 11, 1963, self-immolation in Saigon, as well as the new final chapter for the published version.

dearth of such resources back then.) So although the course on myths and rituals soon developed into a class on *theories of* myths and *theories of* rituals (relying, in large part, on Lessa and Vogt's once well-known anthology, *Reader in Comparative Religion* [1979]), for the first few years of my career the world religions course was, despite my attraction to an early version of Fitzgerald's critique of it (1990), simply a version of the world religions course for which I was one of the teaching assistants at the University of Toronto (team taught in the early 1990s by the late Willard Oxtoby and Joseph O'Connell).[20] In other words, my course was a pretty standard descriptive survey of beliefs and rituals among the world's larger or better-known religions, with me writing copious, detailed notes the night before each lecture that I would mostly just read to students, supplemented with selections I chose from both Ninian Smart and Richard Hecht's co-edited *Sacred Texts of the World: A Universal Anthology* (1982) and Harold Coward, Eva Dargyay, and Ron Neufeldt's *Readings in Eastern Religions* (1988).[21] But as my writing career developed, so did my frustration with the way this course not only presented the material but with the material itself, i.e., the way it asked students to think about the people doing things, as if outward action were but a poorly phrased/poorly interpreted expression of some prior, pristine, universal inner sentiment (which is none other than the dominant model of the field, in which—or so Cantwell Smith, like so many others, would have argued, an inner faith motivates and thereby grounds outward tradition).

Although I would certainly not want to trust my memory today, nor assume that the path from that early course, over 25 years ago, to the version of the introductory course that I still regularly teach today was smooth and continual, from my point of view these two very different courses are actually the same course, but it is one which has continually developed and, flashing forward to today, one that now has nothing whatsoever to do with a standard world religions class. As is evident in the 2008 book that I wrote to support the course (for the second edition, see McCutcheon 2018b), the entire course focuses only on the act of defining something *as* religion, along with the inevitably practical implications of any classificatory system. So from an early attempt to get my students thinking critically about the world religions material by at least having them discuss, for a week or so, various classic definitions of religion while asking if our textbook author was even using a definition—and then, by extension, soon

---

20 The course served as the jumping-off point for a still-in-print, two-volume world religions textbook edited by Oxtoby and published by Oxford University Press.
21 See McCutcheon 2016 for further thoughts on the choices that we make in approaching how we teach in the introductory classroom—along with helpful replies from several earlier-career scholars.

after inviting them also to think about what makes something Christian or Buddhist, to eventually get to the point of realizing that there are varieties of each, with internal contests, with much policing and authenticating, and with, much like those nested Russian dolls, with often unseen and even deeper insides to the supposed insides, etc.—a different course slowly but surely developed. Semester by semester, the self-evident descriptive or phenomenological data slowly moved from center stage. Instead, we examined the moves that people (scholars included, sure, but everyone makes some truly fascinating moves in day-to-day life) make to create the impression that some domain—any domain, in fact—is set apart and privileged (with a generous nod to Durkheim, not to mention Mary Douglas, of course, to whose memory the second edition of my intro book is dedicated). Although it was a gradual shift (over a period of eight years when I was either an instructor on an annual contract, in Tennessee, or as a tenure-track assistant professor, in Missouri, who lacked the protections of tenure), the change was steady, sometimes intentional and planned yet at other times happenstance and in response to either unforeseen current events or changeable and idiosyncratic student interests. For instance, as an example of the latter, I clearly recall learning the news of the Heaven's Gate suicides, on March 26, 1997 (on the news on a TV in a laundromat, as I remember it), and the media coverage that followed over the coming few days, as more information became known, all of which long served as an example in my intro classes of the challenges of talking about "others" who were different from oneself, not to mention the death of Princess Diana in car wreck in Paris, on August 31, 1997 (reported here in the early evening), which allowed students, near the very start of their semester, to witness and track, over the coming weeks, a veritable mythology arising in real time.

What this steady shift from religion(s) to "religion" allowed those of us who adopted it to accomplish was a move away from seeing our objects of study as unique to seeing the things commonly (and sometimes uncommonly) designated *as* religion as being exemplary of far wider tendencies that attend virtually any classificatory act—tendencies that could be studied almost anywhere that people called something by a certain name (i.e., definition and distinction) and then positioned it in a specific relationship with other things that were not considered to be the same as it (classification, organization, comparison)—which, as became apparent over time, are really just interrelated moments in forming an identity. Now, as broadly interested as someone might be in studying what Jean-François Bayart would later call operational acts of identification (2005), sooner or later we all need a place to illustrate what we consider to be the general principles of identity formation, what J. Z. Smith would have just called an e.g.—as in how the relationship between varieties of early Christianity, on the one hand,

and other Greco-Roman religions were, for him, but a detailed *exempli gratia* that was useful in illustrating how past scholars went about (and how current scholars might instead go about) using the comparative method, something made evident in his 1988 Jordan Lectures in Comparative Religion, published as *Drudgery Divine* (1990).[22] But this is evident, I should add, only for the careful reader for, in many cases, readers may come away with the impression that his book is written by a specialist in Christian origins for readers who share that same specialty. While there is, of course, a tremendous amount of nuanced detail in the book that only specialists will likely understand or appreciate (and which will undoubtedly be of interest to them alone), the shift named above allows a far wider array of readers to understand that the descriptive details Smith included in such a book, mainly concerning how previous generations set about placing early Christianity into an historical context (that still somehow privileged it despite seeming to contextualize and thereby historicize it), are necessary *not because they ought to be known, due to their self-evident value* but merely *to get his own comparative enterprise off the ground*. The book, therefore, is of generalist tone, inasmuch as it is all about the comparative method. While one still needs to know the languages and the histories and the texts, etc., to do the work at that particular site, the work is in common with others who labor far afield at yet other sites, who therefore know different details, from other texts, written in other languages. For now the details can be understood to be in support of a general human practice—how we identify ourselves as members of groups, in distinction from yet others, for example—placing them in the service of a scholarly interest that, ideally, plenty of others well outside your specialty also share.

And that's the shift that I think the lit crit disputes helped us, in the study of religion, to make, and one that I've worked to develop in my own career, with the help of a wide number of influences—from seeing our object(s) of study, whatever it/they may be, as unique, set apart, and thus obviously and irreducibly religious, to instead seeing it/them as exemplary and thus illustrative of more general human practices, leading to scholars with other training learning something applicable to their own field by reading us writing about issues in our own. Thus the cross-disciplinarity of the field, as I've come to see it, is not premised (as it once was for so many) on the varied dimensions of a difficult-to-define datum that inevitably eludes each method but, instead, on our common focus on people doing things or on the items they left behind (for these two are really what

---

[22] The University of London's School of Oriental and African Studies hosts this annual lecture series, established in 1951 in memory of the Canadian scholar Louis Henry Jordan (1855–1923), author of, among other works, *Comparative Religion: Its Genesis and Growth* (1905; see also 1908).

most of us study, no?), though coming at that common item from a host of vantage points, one of which has something to do with the way that people authorize their doings by representing them to be eternal, necessary, and self-evidently important.

And thus the study of religion ends up being about something far bigger, or at least other, than religion—whatever one may define that as being. For now, the study of "religion" is but one component in the far-larger study of signification and identification—indicating that we, in the study of religion, have all sorts of conversation partners, in all sorts of other fields of study. What's more, working in a US context where the introductory course is largely comprised of students from all across the university (from engineering, business, nursing, etc.), each enrolled to earn humanities credits to satisfy their degree's general education requirements, this ability to demonstrate wide applicability came in quite handy.

10.4 The Result

Taking the three above contexts into account—our specific setting in Alabama, developments in adjacent academic fields, and how those developments could be implemented in courses to make them relevant to our students—one can see how a small, seemingly marginal and non-viable department could, over the coming years, adopt a self-understanding that not only helped its members and students to weave their diverse interests and work into that which was already being done in far larger and better established departments on its campus but also provided a framework for a group of people, all trained in different specialties and who joined the faculty at a variety of times and in a variety of ways, to understand themselves as sharing something more than happenstance in common.[23] Having grown over these years from just 4.25 faculty members to thirteen today (only one of whom is an instructor [full-time renewable]; all others are either tenured or tenure track), such a framework was needed if a shared identity among the faculty was to develop.

---

23 Although some might think that departments grow their faculty in an intentional and planned manner, obtaining faculty lines can be a surprisingly uneven process, with opportunities for hires presented at unexpected times or in areas newly prioritized by the administration and thus not something the department had previously considered adding to its strengths. Given this, a framework such as the one being discussed, in which the differences at the level of data were, to whatever extent, resolved at the level of theory, provided an ideal setting in which diverse faculty, let alone student, interests could still contribute to a uniform departmental mission.

While there are those in other departments on our campus, like about just any other, who still think that the study of religion is but an elaboration on "Sunday school" expertise that almost everyone somehow just possesses (including themselves, leading to our challenge of having a variety of faculty outside our department who see themselves as qualified to teach courses on religion—an occupational hazard we have all more than likely experienced), the consistent manner in which the faculty's teaching and research illustrates that their expertise provides but a handy place to examine culture-wide processes that we see in plenty of other places as well—notably in the areas where our other departmental colleagues carry out their work, in history, anthropology, gender and race studies, English lit, classics, etc.—has persuaded quite a few colleagues and students alike that the study of "religion" is something entirely different than they had at first thought. The shift that has been so important to the reinvention that we've carried out is realized in most of our courses—where the students' attention is, sooner or later, turned to just why we even call something a world religion in the first place or which of the many definitions of myth or ritual a certain writer was using and for what practical purposes (putting on their table a series of questions and examples they had never thought possible to study in our classes).[24] It's also realized in much of the scholarship that the faculty themselves produce and publish, from an international research collaborative in which several participate, Culture on the Edge,[25] to the book series that several of them edit, and the articles and books that they each write and edit, not to mention a new grant-funded initiative for early-career scholars that attracted the interest of the philanthropic Luce Foundation and which will initiate a new generation into what we're now calling the examples approach.[26] Finally,

---

24 To name but two quick examples, as some may already know that in my introductory course, I've often used an 1893 US Supreme Court case (Nix. v. Hedden) in which the question of whether a tomato was a fruit or vegetable was posed (to settle an import tax issue), and, in upper-level seminars, I've sometimes played well-known rock songs only to have students later read and study the lyrics, to be shocked by what they actually say, in order to illustrate the general principle that meaning is a product of structure—a point that we then examine in more detail by reading the late Frits Staal's once well-known essay "The Meaninglessness of Ritual" (1979).
25 Established in 2012, it now involves sixteen scholars of religion, all at a variety of career stages; visit edge.ua.edu to learn more about both the active blog produced by the group (with posts all devoted to the process of identification, studied at diverse sites, and written for a wide readership) and the two-book series supported by the group.
26 American Examples, a four-year workshop, with my colleague Mike Altman as the PI, brings each year's nine participants to the University of Alabama for three workshops (on research, teaching, and digital humanities), and invites participants to see their objects of study as illustrative of wider, cross-cultural trends or principles, ideally so that their work becomes appealing

the shift is also reflected in a new MA degree, directed by Merinda Simmons and begun in August 2017, which takes seriously that preparation for an eventual (and hoped for) PhD degree is not the only reason why someone might wish to enroll in a master's degree in the study of religion.[27] In each of these cases the data is important, of course, but it is always seen as a place that provides an opportunity to employ skills that will also be handy elsewhere, sometimes in unexpected places.[28]

The manner in which what I'm just calling a shift (from religion to "religion") has provided a wide, shared framework, uniting students in their classes to faculty in their research, to investigate culture-wide processes, but always starting with a particular, sometimes familiar item but then, eventually moving to unexpected analogues. I tend to think that this careful movement from the familiar to the unfamiliar or the unexpected has been among the reasons that some of our students have stuck with us, because it provides them with a way of forming new knowledge that goes in directions of relevance to each of them—and that's the thing that higher education really ought to be about, I'd argue: preparing students to leave our classrooms and do something with what we've taught them. And it is equally important to the context in which faculty do their teaching and writing, for while allowing them to overlap and reinforce what their peers are teaching and working on, it also enables each person to showcase and refine their own specialized training, of which others inevitably have very little knowl-

---

for non-specialists outside their Americanist field to read. Learn more about this new initiative at https://americanexamples.ua.edu/.

[27] Although it does aim to prepare students for further graduate studies, should they wish, the examples approach, as it informs this degree, also helps students to be proactive in finding analogues and application sites, possibly far afield from where their interests first took them, all as preparation (for those not aiming to apply to a PhD somewhere) for the practical application of their degree in a career of their choosing. Although the program is still in its early years, we have so far placed three of its graduates in a PhD, while another has entered architecture school and a third was the manager for guest experiences at a history center and another a freelance archivist. And current students are carrying out internships in a variety of local sites (e.g., the University of Alabama Press and the quarterly *Alabama Heritage* magazine), where they regularly apply the skills learned in our classes—which include a focus on social theory and the digital humanities.

[28] I think here of a recent graduate of our MA who, now in a PhD degree, found herself as the teaching assistant in a subject area far removed from her own expertise. Instead of reinventing herself, she reports being able to see the data of the new and largely alien domain as being just as illustrative of the very same identity formation techniques she was accustomed to studying in her own research area. She reflected on her experience here: https://religion.ua.edu/blog/2019/10/14/how-not-to-reinvent-yourself/.

edge, but doing so in a manner that allows their colleagues to read and interact with their work. For if:
- Steven Ramey writes a blog on something to do with current Indian politics or maybe the Nones
- Vaia Touna has students read an ancient Greek tragedy
- Richard Newton examines Alex Haley's once widely read novel *Roots*
- Ted Trost takes a look at some contemporary pop song lyrics
- Nathan Loewen reconsiders how philosophers of religion go about their work
- Merinda Simmons asks a few questions about post-Blackness
- Steve Jacobs studies genocides around the world
- Edith Szanto teaches a course on modern representations of Islam
- Daniel Levine is interested in how cultivated fear drives politics
- Mike Altman supervises an MA student who poses some questions about how belief and tolerance were intertwined in early America
- Our newest colleague, Jeri Wieringa, uses computational analysis to examine large archival databases

... well, in all of these cases, I know that each place where they focus their work requires their expertise. But I also know that it's an instance of something general and typical, something that, more than likely, I've come across somewhere else in my own work, which means that we can all talk with one another, share ideas, read and comment on drafts of each other's work, and guide our students along as they take discrete courses on discrete topics with different faculty, but all of which reinforce and drive each other in ways not initially apparent when you're just browsing a lone syllabus.

Of course, doing this successfully relied (and still continues to rely) on a host of interconnected strategies implemented at a wide variety of sites—from revamping the curriculum and degree requirements to focusing effort on empowering students to organize and meet outside class time (coffee breaks, movie nights, reading groups, and events to promote awareness of the department among yet other students, etc.) and even assisting the larger units of which the department is a member (i.e., the College of Arts & Sciences as well as the university itself) to pursue and achieve goals of their own—the latter recognizes that a department's goals are not necessarily or always the same as the university's. None of this was done overnight, of course, but knowing the undesired result of failing to succeed at this reinvention, coupled with a department mission and identity closely linked to a model that allowed all faculty members to contribute and to see that their teaching and research were a relevant part of the larger project, created conditions in which faculty correctly understood that they and their hopes for long and productive careers were the direct beneficiaries of the so-called professional service of which other faculty members complain, as if it takes them away from what really matters.

So defining the department's work not by each of our seemingly unique and self-important objects of study—whether that means in the classroom or in our research and publication—but, instead, by larger questions about human behavior and organization that we all asked and wished to have answered, was probably the key move that, looking back now, enabled all of our successes. While there was likely a fair amount of dumb luck as well can't be overlooked, of course, such as a new university president, in the early 2000s, setting the goal of doubling the undergraduate population within a decade (a goal achieved ahead of schedule). This increased tuition revenue across campus meant more resources were available, certainly, but there was no necessary reason that our then-little department should have received any of them, what with being just a couple years out from having been declared non-viable. But we did receive resources—our tripling in the size of our tenure-track and tenured faculty since 2000 should make that obvious. It means that the administration of the college and the university saw us as a good investment, both because of how we worked to help them achieve their goals and how we turned around this unit in a relatively short period of time. Credit hour production quadrupled across the department, the number of majors increased, and, as mentioned from the outset, when measured against our peers across the country, our faculty research productivity (whether measured collectively or on an individual basis, regardless career stage) has consistently been enviably strong. Our successes were therefore the college's and the university's successes and, though, like any department, we don't always receive what we request, those successes have put us on the local map and have helped us to succeed at a variety of other things. Case in point: as I first write these lines, we have just announced an ad for yet another new tenure-track position in the department, to begin in the fall of 2020 and to teach and do research in an area central to both our MA and BA degrees: the digital humanities. The research specialty, as other colleagues might call it, is open, of course, for we merely ask that their work on a specific time, region, or topic enhance the department by bringing something new to us that we don't already happen to cover (and, since the world's a big place, there's lots we don't already cover). But it's not mainly about coverage, of course, for what is not open to debate is a desire for a colleague who agrees that the items on which they happen to work, for all sorts of curious reasons, are useful e.g.s where they can investigate some of the big questions that we're already tackling, such as how it is that we come to see ourselves as members of groups that sometimes seem to last forever despite continually reinventing themselves (not unlike what we did here in Alabama).

10.5 Conclusion

The argument that I've been developing is that it's not so much that religion is always in the room, as Liz Kineke's recent talk at the University of Vermont was entitled,[29] but that "religion" is always in the room—not just as a modern regulatory device that, once enshrined in law (notably in liberal democracies), is intimately tied to other no less effective governing techniques, such as the distinctions of private and public (i.e., self and other), but also that the wider issue of classification itself, and the fallout that invariably attends each effort to distinguish and rank our world, is always right under our nose, being at the root of many of the issues and clashes that define society today. (It's something that we may critique, by the way, but it's also something that, again as per my epigraph, we can't help but live with, even by means of, given that it's how we arrange the world, in order to know something about it.) In fact, #classificationmatters has caught on a bit on social media as the punch line to a variety of posts on various news stories and political contests. And many of our students started saying, in unison several years ago, "classification is a political act," in response to a variety of the classes they were then taking in our department—classes not intentionally coordinating shared data but rather investigating, at different regional, ethnographic, or historical sites to be sure, a common human process for making our environments meaningful and habitable. By means of this focus on classification systems, of which "religion" is but one example, and also a focus on the practical implications linked to transgressing the order established by their authorized use, we all come to think and act like, for example, religion is everywhere, that we ought to have one or, just as possible, that we ought to rebel against having one by asserting yet other, no less private beliefs and sentiments that we think are ultimately important to us, as principled individuals. Should this be the approach to religion—or, as I keep repeating, this approach to "religion"—be appealing, in that it is one that adopts an ironic stance that requires a critical distance from its common, day-to-day use, not to mention the wider systems that help that use to seem so natural, then estab-

---

[29] Kineke, a journalist and producer/director, spoke as part of their Religious Literacy Week on October 28, 2019, and is also an executive producer with CBS television's Religion and Culture team. Learn more at https://www.cbsnews.com/religion-and-culture/ (accessed September 21, 2019).

lishing such a field of study in the modern university is not only possible but it can also be a site where faculty and students with diverse interests and skills thrive. For if semiotics as a field is possible—the scholarly pursuit of how signification itself works—then the critical study of "religion" is possible as well; though, just like semioticians who are themselves making meaning in the midst of studying how it's done, scholars of "religion" are no less situated at the conjunction of seemingly commonsense belief/practice binaries, for they too see themselves to be citizens and individuals who presumably have intentions and experiences of their own. But as products of the shift described throughout the paper (one that has roots outside our field but also inside it, in the writings of Fitzgerald, among others), they, just like students in our introductory classes, may come to see their own taken-for-granted knowledge as but one more example in need of analysis, for not just charity but also critical thinking begins at home—a home that can indeed be made within the institutions where many of us work and study.

Reference List

Bayart, Jean-François. 2005. *The Illusion of Cultural Identity*, trans. Steven Randall et al. Chicago: University of Chicago Press.

Coward, Harold, Eva Dargyay, and Ron Neufeldt, eds. 1988. *Readings in Eastern Religions*. Waterloo, ON: Wilfrid Laurier University Press.

Dubuisson, Daniel. 2019. *The Invention of Religions*, trans. Martha Cunningham. Sheffield, UK: Equinox Publishers.

Fish, Stanley. 1982. *Is There a Text in this Class? The Authority of Interpretive Communities*. Cambridge, MA: Harvard University Press.

Fitzgerald, Timothy. 1990. "Hinduism and the World Religions Fallacy." *Religion* 20:101–18.

Fitzgerald, Timothy. 2000. *The Ideology of Religious Studies*. New York: Oxford University Press.

Fitzgerald, Timothy, ed. 2007. *Religion and the Secular: Historical and Colonial Formations*. Sheffield, UK: Equinox Publishers.

Jordan, Louis Henry. 1905. *Comparative Religion: Its Genesis and Growth*. Edinburgh: T. & T. Clark.

Jordan, Louis Henry. 1908. "Comparative Religion: Its Method and Scope: A Paper Read (in part) at the Third International Congress of the History of Religions, Oxford, September 17, 1908." London: Oxford University Press.

Krech, Volkhard. 2020. "Relational Religion: Manifesto for a Synthesis in the Study of Religion." *Religion* 50/1:97–105.

Lessa, William A., and Evon Z. Vogt, eds. 1979. *Reader in Comparative Religion: An Anthropological Approach* 4th ed. New York: HarperCollins.

Martin Craig. 2019. "'The Thing Itself Always Steals Away': Scholars and the Constitution of Their Objects." In *Constructing "Data" in Religious Studies: The Architecture of the Academy*, edited by Leslie Dorrough Smith, 151–74. Sheffield, UK: Equinox Publishers.

McCutcheon, Russell T. 1997. *Manufacturing Religion: The Discourse on Sui Generis Religion and the Politics of Nostalgia.* New York: Oxford University Press.

McCutcheon, Russell T. 2003. *The Discipline of Religion: Structure, Meaning, Rhetoric.* New York: Routledge.

McCutcheon, Russell T. 2016. "A Baker's Dozen of Choices in the Introductory Class." Forum: Crafting the Introductory Course in Religious Studies (plus four responses). *Teaching Theology & Religion* 19/1:80–9.

McCutcheon, Russell T. 2018a. *Fabricating Religion: Fanfare for the Common e.g.* Berlin: Walter de Gruyter.

McCutcheon, Russell T. 2018b. *Studying Religion: An Introduction.* 2nd ed. New York: Routledge.

Ramey, Steven W., ed. 2015. *Writing Religion: The Case for the Critical Study of Religion.* Tuscaloosa, AL: University of Alabama Press.

Richards, I. A. 1929. *Practical Criticism: A Study of Literary Judgment.* New York: Harcourt Brace & Co.

Schmeiser, Peggy. 2019. "Governance and Public Policy as Critical Objects of Investigation in the Study of Religion." In *Constructing "Data" in Religious Studies: Examining the Architecture of the Academy*, edited by Leslie Dorrough Smith, 127–35. Sheffield, UK: Equinox Publishers.

Smart, Ninian, and Richard Hecht. 1982. *Sacred Texts of the World: A Universal Anthology.* New York: Crossroad.

Smith, Jonathan Z. 1982. *Imagining Religion: From Babylon to Jonestown.* Chicago: University of Chicago Press.

Smith, Jonathan Z. 1990. *Drudgery Divine: On the Comparison of Carly Christianities and the Religions of Late Antiquity.* Chicago: University of Chicago Press.

Smith, Wilfred Cantwell. 1963. *The Meaning and End of Religion: A New Approach to the Religious Traditions of Mankind.* New York: Macmillan.

Staal, Frits. 1979. "The Meaninglessness of Ritual," *Numen* 26/1:2–22.

Afterword: Five Examples

Anyone familiar with our department at the University of Alabama may know that we have a pretty active social media presence, among which is a Facebook group devoted to our current students and graduates of our program. Apart from putting a variety of department announcements there, such as recent posts from our blog (on everything from student writing to updates on how we're handling the fall 2020 semester, which awaits us as I write this), I occasionally put a few news item there, sometimes with #inthenews as the tag, to suggest to our students that there's considerable application of the skills that they're learning in our classes—such as understanding groups via the way that their members classify, rank, and thereby organize themselves. That the alums who stay current with the group sometimes send us guest blog posts of their own, illustrating this very point—despite each of them working in pretty diverse careers today—confirms for me that opting for such a focus in a department of religious studies was a wise choice.

Just the other morning, for example, I posted an item from the July 8, 2020, *New York Times* concerning a just-released US Supreme Court decision that will allow employers to opt out of what had previously been federally mandated health insurance requirements—opting out based on religious grounds.[1] As the article's opening lines phrased it:

> The Supreme Court on Wednesday upheld a Trump administration regulation that lets employers with religious or moral objections limit women's access to birth control coverage under the Affordable Care Act. As a consequence of the ruling, about 70,000 to 126,000 women could lose contraceptive coverage from their employers, according to government estimates.

As for the text that I wrote to accompany the post? "Need another reason why it's a good idea to have someone studying the practical effects of classifying some things, claims, or people *as* religious?" I open this afterword with yet another example to reinforce a simple but, I think, far-reaching point that sometimes seems to elude those who say that they're tired of work that focuses on the category religion. (It's a weariness that surprises me, I admit, given that people are still turning out plenty of dissertations on Augustine, St. Paul, or Jonathan Edwards, so just a couple decades' worth of focus on "religion" itself hardly seems to have exhausted everything that there is to say about it—indicating that claims of tedi-

---

[1] See https://www.nytimes.com/2020/07/08/us/supreme-court-birth-control-obamacare.html (accessed July 13, 2020).

um are but a handy way to dismiss what is increasingly becoming a focus of people's work in the field.) For the ease of assuming that "religion" innocently and properly names an obviously distinct and self-organized set of items in the world is something that we need to work against should our interests be more aligned with studying how groups of people signify, navigate, and, yes, contest their worlds. So any opportunity to provide our peers or our students with a manageable thought experiment, where the impact of the designation itself can be considered or seen to be working in real time, isn't something to pass up. And that Supreme Court decision—as with a host of legal rulings over the years in liberal democracies, all of which focus on the extent to which exemptions can be granted as a way to manage social discord—struck me as yet another moment where designating something *as* religious could be seen to have a practical effect of real consequence to people's lives.

Whatever else this thing some now call critical religion may be, it at least strikes me as an agreement that this shift—from studying religion or religions to studying why we even call anything religious in the first place—helps us to produce new knowledge about the way our modern lives work, the way our spaces are managed, and the way that identities are created and reproduced within them. Contrary to those who study religion or religions, then, I have no interest in normalizing let alone using any given understanding of the term, something that inevitably occurs, I'd argue, when we just get on with studying religion, as some call us to do. So, with another recent but rather more international news story in mind,[2] the goal of such work is not to decide whether the Hagia Sophia in Istanbul really ought to be understood and used as a museum (as it has been for eighty years) or, as the Turkish government today wishes, a mosque, and, should its religious identity be successfully asserted, neither is it to do a careful ethnography of what some call religion on the ground at this location. Instead, it's the classificatory contest itself that can attract our attention, as a way into studying—in this case—the role of populism in politics today let alone a long history of conflict between two modern nation-states that draws on pre-national allegiances and disputes, along with the manner in which these disagreements have (or have not been) been managed by that artful designation of "museum." For the issue is not whether the building *really is* a Greek Orthodox cathedral or a Muslim mosque but, instead, is whether we can better understand how the compromise of designating it as a museum worked and why it now fails to negotiate

---

[2] See https://www.nytimes.com/2020/07/10/world/europe/hagia-sophia-erdogan.html (accessed July 12, 2020).

not just these differing significations but the larger sociopolitical structures of which each designation is but the visible sign.

So the shift that I am recommending throughout this volume, and which an increasing number in the field are now exploring, opens us to working with those across disciplines who are equally interested in such pressing issues as how identities are formed, reproduced, and contested—whether those identities are local, national, or trans-national. And, along with that, it draws us into studying the structures, whether political, economic, gendered, racial, etc., in which identification and, to put it more broadly, signification takes place. It thus invites us to take our Durkheim all the more seriously, for now we will indeed be examining those unified systems of beliefs and practices that, insomuch as we participate in and thereby perpetuate them, establish a social world in which significance can be established and experienced or historicized and questioned.

Long ago I lamented the strategy adopted by previous generations of religion scholars, insomuch as they sought to build an autonomous field based on the presumably unique and set apart nature of their object of study—and, along with it, the distinct methods needed for its study and the departments that housed those doing such work. I thought that while it did indeed help to create the modern field, such an approach inevitably marginalized it as well, given that such scholars lost their voice and their relevance when it came to studying anything but the supposedly ethereal and elusive thing that was once called the sacred. (By asserting that the sacred animated everything, Eliade thought that he could reinstate the field's preeminence via what he called the New Humanism, by the way—a claim that I certainly resist.) I thought that shifting the field to studying classification, and the sociopolitical worlds made possible by designating things either in this or that fashion (such as sacred/secular, religious/political, private/public, religion/cult, myth/legend, or ritual/habit, etc.), would not only make good use of our skills but would also demonstrate to those outside our field—whether on or off our campus, in or outside of our classrooms—that we had something to contribute to understanding this thing that so many others also study: people, what they do and what they leave behind once they're gone. Sure, we might each study it in a rather specific and different site— those places we known as modern India, the Afro-Caribbean, popular culture, or maybe ancient Greece—but our work is animated by a shared set of questions which we're not the only ones asking.

And it's that shift to broader questions, explored at discrete sites (made possible by an interest in what contestable systems of designation tell us about groups of people) that, to my way of thinking, demonstrates the relevance of our work—something apparent to me last week when a grad of our undergraduate program, who has been out working in her career for 14 years, unexpectedly contacted me asking about some of the books that we had read in a course long ago, since she was aiming to re-read some of them. Why? Well, she and her sister-in-law were discussing US monuments commemorating the Civil War, what they meant, to whom they meant it, and whether they should remain in place or just come down—at least here in the US, racism and how we signify the past are among the most prominent current issues demanding our attention. While I'm not sure what conclusions they'll reach, what seems to have been clear to that onetime student was that the sort of scholar of religion that I've been discussing in the previous chapters, and which was modeled for her long ago in our department, has a surprising amount to contribute to helping others make sense of how and why we talk about the past as we do, how we manage the many possible pasts that are all competing for our attention today, and the sorts of people that we will see ourselves and others to be by adopting this versus that way of signifying a statue.

But the essays collected in this volume, written mostly over the past couple of years, likely present a view of the field that some may today judge as inadequate, given that they do not directly engage political action in the service of remaking society—an alternative view of the field that's long been popular among a certain segment of its members. While I have written on this topic on a variety of past occasions, disagreeing that such socially formative work is within the scope of the scholar of religion *qua* scholar (that we all inhabit a variety of other social roles and personae should go without saying, however), I feel that there's no better way to end a collection that advocates for a new but also relevant mode for the academic study of religion than to tackle head-on a series of (at least when finishing this book) timely events taking place here in the US, where I have lived and worked for nearly thirty years and where, as a Canadian, I became a citizen in the summer of 2019. For if what we did in the classroom a decade and a half ago strikes one of our former students as having continuing relevance for understanding disputes over Civil War monuments today, then perhaps the shift that I'm advocating, and which we've explored here in our department, has more relevance than we might at first think.

So I would argue that the reimagined field being outlined in some detail in the previous chapters can make rather effective interventions in a variety of situations and moments—should we agree, that is, that our collective aim, *as* scholars and *as* teachers, is to help our readers and our students to understand *how we understand things to work*, leaving to them the inevitable and no doubt difficult challenge of coming up with how they wish society *ought to* work instead. Part of the rethinking that I recommend for the field means inviting students and readers to take seriously the sheer happenstance *as well as* the interest-laden way in which things now happen to work, before they go charging forward with designs of their own. Armed with the critical tools of analysis and redescription that they can gain from our writings and in our classes, I'd like to hope that they will be better equipped first to understand their current situation but then also to make the inevitable choices that attend being a member of any of the groups in which they find themselves, often through no choice of our own—from families to the nation-state.

That graduates of our department, those who have taken courses that employ the approach recommended in the previous chapters, often report on the ongoing relevance of those classes, long after leaving our program and moving on to lives in any number of careers—careers that, for the most part, are far from the rather narrow number of fields for which some might think the study of religion prepares its students (such as social work, counseling, ministry, the sorts of professions often listed on the nationally produced and distributed advising resources on which universities often rely)—confirms for me that the model for which I've been advocating throughout this book has direct relevance and continuing value. For that most recent message I received on social media is hardly unique. And so I draw it to a close with five brief but interconnected examples, each from discreet moments and some that certainly will read as being of more consequence than others, in hopes of priming the reader's pump, as it were, to consider adopting the examples approach for themselves, since each illustrates, at a discrete, analogical site, something of more general importance to understanding much the bigger and more complex topics that eventually attract our attention as scholars and teachers—for, I'd argue, there's no way to change anything without first understanding how, why, and even for whom things now happen to work as they do.

I Plan and Accident

I was putting some clean dishes away the other morning—a mundane activity if ever there was one—and got to thinking about issues of structure and agency, about how chance relationships can, under the right conditions, become taken-for-granted, normative patterns—and the choices that we purposefully make, but doing so within parameters that we never intended and might not even understand to exist.

You see, our kitchen has a small piece of countertop above the microwave, adjacent to all the fridge. With an electrical outlet centered on the wall, just above the counter, it seemed like the ideal place to put the coffeemaker when we first moved into this house, a few years ago. Since outlets usually come in pairs (and just what is the history of that?!), it soon turned into our recharging area too, with a handy iPhone cord now always plugged in there. And since the coffeemaker is there, the jar of coffee should be too and—yes, you guessed it—the cupboard above makes the logical place to store all of the mugs (as well as the various plastic water bottles that are so necessary for those Alabama summer days working outside in the yard). Oh, and there's a mug in the back of the counter where the dead batteries go, for later recycling, along with random receipts that first start out in my wallet and which end up being strewn across that small countertop, eventually making their way to that year's income tax file upstairs. As for the glass jar that's also back there, by the mug? That's where the loose change goes at the end of the day. And, of course, there are a few invitations and notices posted on the side of the fridge with a magnet or two.

Apart from the pretty obvious decision for where the fridge would have to go in the new kitchen, who knows how the architect who drew up the house plans intended this little space to be used, such as the narrow drawer below the low-mounted microwave, beneath the countertop, as well as that deep cupboard up above the fridge, neither of which we've really yet figured out how to use. But that's what we've done with the space—little by little, adding each of these elements and layers one at a time, until we periodically decide that it's "gotten too messy" and then we reset it back to some near-to-original state, with the receipts filed and the old batteries moved to the bigger bag elsewhere; but, inevitably, with new accumulations that start all over again, it just ends up getting messy once again. And again. And then again. In fact, this ebb and flow of what we see as order and disarray has been so successful that this is not just the only place where the coffeemaker and the mugs can be but, should we move that recharging cord for some reason then, sooner or later, it'll just have to be returned to this specific outlet. Why? Well ... , because "that's where it belongs." After all, we can't be charging things near to where the fresh fruit now always sits in baskets, elsewhere on the kitchen's countertop, near to where the blender and the mixer always sit.

It might be a pretty ordinary example, sure, but it does capture how much sheer happenstance is combined, in unanticipated ways, with prior but isolated decisions, all of which were made by a variety of actors at different times and for different reasons—such as the day we thought, "Sure, that painting could go on the wall, over by the coffeemaker," as if its arbitrary placement on that small stretch of countertop was now an anchor against which we could judge the placement of other things around it. All of this gets mixed together to produce what we take to be a structured, even sensible setting, one that we now just take for granted as the way it ought to be. That a number of other examples can quickly come to mind, where this curious mix of agency and structure are also evident, but only if we only look in the right way, should be easy to see—dare I mention those seemingly more consequential things that scholars of religion commonly designate as canonical texts, just for starters? For placing them on our countertop, alongside the coffeemaker and the receipts, will help us to shift the conversation from studying those collections of texts that we call scriptures as special repositories of deep and timeless meaning, in need of nuanced interpretation and maybe even appreciation, to seeing them as but another curious site where we can see how people grapple with the meeting of plan and accident.

II "Violence is Never the Answer"

If you were watching CNN midday on May 30, 2020, as I just happened to be while I ate my lunch (working at home during our university's move to limited business operations, to deal with the fallout of COVID-19), then you might have heard the interview with the journalist LZ Granderson, commenting on the ongoing nationwide protests in the US (and, in fact, throughout the world) that resulted from yet another African American man dying at the hands of the police—this time it was George Floyd, in Minneapolis on May 25, 2020. What Granderson said caught my ear, for it's just the sort of thing that I'd hope that the students trained in our department would not just understand but be able to use in understanding not just the moment in which we now find ourselves but also how we got here.

For, on the heels of CNN's broadcast that day of New York Governor Andrew Cuomo's daily COVID-19 press conference, during which, with regard to the fires, looting, and damage associated with some of the early protests, he commented that violence is never the answer, Granderson observed that:

> You know, I was really stunned by Gov. Cuomo's statement that violence is not the answer, and I was stuck there not because I don't agree with it but because I always hear it in relationship to people protesting, well sometimes rioters, following an act of violence. I never really hear "violence is not the answer" before that; I don't hear it directed toward the police department, I don't hear it directed towards law enforcement, security guards, I only hear it in response after violence is committed. Black people are told violence is not the answer; Black people are told you're supposed turn the other cheek. Black people are told you're supposed to be better than this. But you don't hear a great deal of people being told this in the direction of, from an official, to the police department or to the larger white community as a whole.[3]

---

[3] Although I watched this interview live, the transcript was created from the clip later posted by CNN on his CNN Replay Facebook page: https://www.facebook.com/watch/?v=175708797210828 (accessed June 5, 2020).

As he rightly notes, such a caution is never spoken in response to the original act of violence itself, in this case the actions (and, yes, even the inactions) of the four police officers in Minneapolis that so many of us saw on video for ourselves, three of them holding a handcuffed man face down on the street, one with his knee on his neck, for almost nine minutes and until he died. Instead, these words, as Granderson points out, are always spoken with regard to the angry reaction that follows such events.

What his observation should make evident is that this term "violence" is hardly an innocent descriptor of some obvious state of being; after all, when it comes to law enforcement in the US, the official word that is used is not "violence" but "force," such as employing the term "use of force" to name the varying degrees of physical coercion that, according to official policies, an officer may use, in differing circumstances, to compel a person to do as they say—and among those options is, of course, so-called deadly or lethal force. Come to think of it, that very term "law enforcement," that I used just above, the one that many of us unthinkingly and routinely use, now takes on new meaning, much as the longtime habit (going back several centuries, in fact) of talking about such things as "the police force" or "a military force"—terms that likely strike many of us today as simply or neutrally naming such units or groups rather than reading them as adjectives that modify a specific mode of exercising coercive action—or, in a word, violence.

Digging a little deeper into Granderson's point, we might argue that many would probably not even think to caution that violence is never the answer in response to these initial police actions because, by definition, some would not even see them as being a form of violence but, instead, a "necessary" or even "reasonable use of force," as some might phrase it—a term that effectively authorizes just some actions by helping many to see them as legitimate, called for, unavoidable, etc. But if you were on the receiving end of some of the police "use of force" that I saw in news coverage from various protests across the country that week—not to mention the lamentably long list of African Americans who have died at the hands of police in the US for what most of us would surely see as either trivial or even nonexistent offenses—then my guess is that you'd likely not have any trouble identifying the rhetorical work being done when we choose which and whose actions count as violence.

And this is what students trained in our department hopefully understand; for they come to see that our faculty members use instances from the study of religion as an opportunity to delve into one specific area of human culture and history, sure, but in order to also investigate the different ways in which people have organized and identified themselves, and the different ways of authorizing each of those organizations and identifications.

So, I'm hopeful that our students and our graduates come to all of this with critical tools to make sense of their current historical moment. For, as Granderson so nicely recognizes, words are about so much more than mere vocabulary—something more than evident in how quickly those on the political right in the US jumped at the opportunity to represent calls to "defund the police" as radical efforts that would lead to lawlessness. Instead, words, and the actions that come with them, are all about how social groups represent, naturalize, and entrench their interests and their limits, along with the institutions that support them—and how they can sometimes get critiqued and re-imagined.

III "Guys Like Us"

If you're of a certain generation, then you likely recall the opening theme song to *All in the Family*, a once-popular TV show that aired in the US for nine seasons, all throughout the 1970s. Sung before a live audience by Carroll O'Connor and Jean Stapleton, the actors who starred as the leads of the show, "Those Were the Days" spoke of a nostalgia for the good old days—a past constantly in tension with the present of the series.[4] The shorter version, that started each episode, reads as follows:

> Boy the way Glenn Miller played
> Songs that made the Hit Parade.
> Guys like us we had it made,
> Those were the days.
>
> And you knew who you were then,
> Girls were girls and men were men,
> Mister we could use a man
> Like Herbert Hoover again.
>
> Didn't need no welfare state,
> Everybody pulled his weight.
> Gee our old LaSalle ran great.
> Those were the days ….

In early 2019, the show was recreated for a special, one-time live broadcast of a recreated episode, this time with Woody Harrelson and Marisa Tomei in the lead roles of Archie and Edith Bunker—the latter the eternally optimistic and long-suffering wife of the grumpy (and yes, openly racist and sexist) patriarch

---

[4] The song was written for the series by Lee Adams (lyrics) and Charles Strouse (lyrics).

of the family. That Archie and his painfully outdated views were often the butt of each episode's joke—while somehow always working to recover something endearing in his missteps, somewhat akin to the character of Michael Scott, played by Steve Carell, in the equally successful US half-hour series *The Office*, decades later—was among the things that made the series so popular for so many, for it was broadcast at a time when race, gender, class, and even generational relationships in the US were very much under the microscope and ripe for reimagining. So it's not difficult to read that theme song as rather ironic, given the way this sort of nostalgia for the good old days was regularly lampooned throughout the series—notably by the blunt reactions of the Bunkers' various neighbors, not to mention the regular criticisms of Archie's views that came from his grown daughter and her husband (the one Archie regularly referred to as Meathead).

But it's that line near the opening of the song, the one about "guys like us, we had it made," that makes the song particularly useful, I think—notably with the earlier comments on studying how groups entrench and naturalize themselves and their picture of the world; for the song explicitly states, right up front, that nostalgia is not really about the past but about, in this case, the singer and a present that feels that it has lost something in an idealized yesterday. So, nostalgia is not about just any old present but a rather specific one that's occupied by the person doing the reminiscing. And, in this case, it's—yes, you called it—a middle-aged, working class white, heterosexual male saying that "those were the days," making the song all about guys like Archie. For, despite her joining him in a duet, it's sung from his point of view and not Edith's—a character whose appeal was based in the fact that she wasn't nearly as naïve and pliant as she might have seemed.

So if you're trying to mull over how discourses on the past, not to mention discourses on origins, are artfully coded attempts to speak of a specific subject's understanding of their current situation (whether to authorize it or undermine it), then thinking a little about that old TV show's theme song could be a pretty good starting point. For if we can understand how nostalgia works in this one, seemingly simple instance, then we might be able to generalize our findings from there to all sorts of other sites where people also talk of a golden age before the fall—some of which may strike people as so deeply significant and dare I say sacred that they would likely never assume that their tales of the good old days have anything to do with Archie and Edith singing at the piano. But they'd be wrong.

IV Symbolic Conflicts

There are certainly those scholars of religion who will study the June 1, 2020, episode in Washington, DC—when a large number of peaceful protestors in Lafayette Square, just north of the White House, were dispersed by police and the national guard, uniformed in riot gear and shields and using smoke canisters, tear gas (technically, as was later reported, no CN or CS gas was reported to have been used, though pepper balls and pepper spray were employed as "riot control agents"[5]), batons, and flash-bang canisters (otherwise known as stun grenades), about a half-hour before a curfew went into effect, so that President Donald J. Trump, along with some of his senior advisors, could walk the short distance to St. John's Episcopal Church, just across the street from the park, to pose with a Bible as part of a seventeen-minute photo-op[6]—as an episode in the misuse of a holy object.

It's a common enough way of studying religion, after all, such as those who study what they term as radical Islam or political Buddhism in an effort to explain why each differs from their orthodox and quietist majorities—which entails examining how they mistakenly interpret their texts and misuse their traditions. This approach was captured nicely in how the Episcopal bishop for Washington, DC, and parts of Maryland commented, for *The New York Times*, on Trump's photo; Bishop Budde denounced the way the president held up a Bible during his visit, a move she interpreted as a political prop. "The Bible is not an American document," she said. "It's not an expression of our country. It's an expression of the human struggle to serve and love and know God."[7] As she later elaborated for ABC News, "He is not entitled to use the spiritual symbolism of our sacred spaces and our sacred texts to promote or to justify a completely, an entirely different message."[8] But there are also those scholars of religion who will approach this episode in a rather different fashion, leaving to the various theological insiders, not all of whom occupy the same position on the interpretive spectrum, the debate over what counts as the proper use or essential meaning of their own symbols and texts.

---

[5] On this clarification, see https://www.vox.com/2020/6/5/21281604/lafayette-square-white-house-tear-gas-protest (accessed June 5, 2020).
[6] See video of the photo-op at https://www.youtube.com/watch?v=OoRQF68psdY (accessed June 5, 2020).
[7] The quote comes from a *New York Times* article: https://www.nytimes.com/2020/06/01/us/politics/trump-st-johns-church-bible.html (accessed June 5, 2020).
[8] Find the full interview at https://www.goodmorningamerica.com/news/video/bishop-overseeing-st-john-episcopal-church-reacts-trumps-71015163 (accessed June 5, 2020).

The scholars whom I have in mind will instead assume that signifiers work at the level of form just as much as at the level of content—in other words, you don't have to read a Bible to "get" its meaning, thereby leaving to others the proper way to interpret the text and to decide how and how often it ought to be read. The sense of making this shift should be obvious to anyone familiar with people displaying "a family Bible" prominently in their houses, for its very presence "says" something to family and guests alike, regardless of turning its pages and reading its text. This is something that President Ronald Reagan's re-election team seems to have understood when, as is often reported, they tried to use Bruce Springsteen's hit song *Born in the USA* as their campaign anthem—a song whose memorable but simple chorus, nicely following the rules of pop music, might easily distract listeners from what's going on in the verses. After all, who really thinks much about the lyrics sometimes?

So, not unlike the authorizing clerical collar and vestment worn by the bishop in her interviews after the event, which convey meaning to many even if their finer liturgical details are not known, and not unlike the significance effectively conveyed by the style and black color of the riot gear worn by the police and national guard as they advanced on protestors that evening, simply posing with a Bible outside a boarded-up church *functions* and is therefore *effective* for many viewers, which Trump's team more than understood when planning this photo-op before the press corp. "My mother started crying," Benjamin Horbowy, in Tallahassee, Florida, later reported to *The Guardian*. "She comes from Pentecostal background," he continued, referencing how she saw the event, "and she started speaking in tongues. I haven't heard her speak in tongues in years …. I thought, look at my president! He's establishing the Lord's kingdom in the world."[9]

The trouble is, of course, that, like any symbol and any act, it has *many* effects; for, as literary theorists told us long ago, its many viewers are all reading it in different ways, each from a different position. So the question is: which of these effects, which of these meanings, will come to be most closely associated, or associated by the majority or the powerful, with that event at St. John's Episcopal Church? Surely, the White House hoped that their supporters saw in this, as Trump himself phrased it, "a law and order" president defending the faith (which, we surely can't overlook, means a certain form of Christianity, of course). But it's not tough to imagine what others saw in the same episode—such as all those who were tear gassed and forcibly cleared out of the way for the staged

---

9 See the British newspaper article, "'He wears the armor of God': Evangelicals Hail Trump's Church Photo Op," at https://www.theguardian.com/us-news/2020/jun/03/donald-trump-church-photo-op-evangelicals (accessed June 5, 2020).

photo to be taken. In fact, that the mayor of Washington, DC, Muriel Bowser, just four days later (on June 5, 2020), had the street from which those peaceful protestors were cleared renamed Black Lives Matter Plaza—complete with street-sized yellow lettering saying as much down the length of it, leading to the church, the square, and, eventually, the White House itself—makes painfully obvious that there's a contest going on here in the symbolically displaced terrain where physical and social conflicts often play out.

V *Caveat Auditor*

There are times—often unexpected and sometimes rather rare—when a situation arises that happens to provide, for those paying attention, a nicely paired example that enables a comparison that makes profoundly evident how groups represent the world to their members in a manner that supports their interests. Such a moment made the rounds on social media during the US protests that followed news of George Floyd's death at the hands of police in Minneapolis. I have in mind video of when then US Secretary of Defense, Donald Rumsfeld, spoke at an April 11, 2003, press conference on what was, at the time, the early stages of what turned out to be the long war in Iraq.

> Reporter: Television pictures are showing looting and other signs of lawlessness. Are you concerned that what's being reported from the region as anarchy in Baghdad and other cities might wash away the goodwill the United States has built? And are US troops capable of or inclined to be police forces in Iraq?
>
> Donald Rumsfeld: Well, I think the way to think about that is that is that if you go from a repressive regime that has … , it's a police state, where people are murdered and imprisoned by the tens of thousands, umm, and then you go to something other than that, a liberated Iraq, that you go through a transition period. And in every country, in my adult lifetime, that's had the wonderful opportunity to do that, to move from a repressed dictatorial regime to something that's freer, we've seen in that transition period there is untidiness. And there's no question but that that's not anyone's choice. On the other hand, if you think of those pictures, very often the pictures are pictures of people going into the symbols of the regime—into the palaces, into the boats, and into the Baath Party headquarters, and into the places that have been part of that repression. And while no one condones looting, uhh, on the other hand, one can understand the pent-up feelings that may result from decades of repression, and people who have had members of their family killed by that regime, for them to be taking their feelings out on that regime.[10]

---

[10] See the video of this April 11, 2003, press conference (especially beginning at the 6:55 point) at https://www.c-span.org/video/?176134-1/defense-department-briefing (accessed June 2, 2020); also, see a portion of the transcript published the next day by *The New York Times*, at https://

The context for reposting this old clip on social media was the manner in which then-current protests against racialized police violence all across the US had been represented by some in the media and by some politicians as "riots" that were said to be indicative of "lawlessness" and "looting" by, as President Donald Trump himself tweeted early on May 29, 2002, "thugs." Regardless who carried out some of the acts that these designations named (such as smashing windows, ransacking stores, and burning buildings—not insignificantly, the political right and the administration as well quickly blamed antifascist protestors), the manner in which Rumsfeld's much earlier comments explained such actions away in the case of Iraqi citizens is somewhat remarkable, especially if we consider the way some conservative politicians and media outlets today are unwilling to extend the same sort of interpretive generosity regarding motives, despair, and frustration to contemporary US citizens taking things out on what some might equally refer to as "symbols of the regime."

It has long struck me as a cornerstone of scholarship that scholars rely on the same methods for studying *all* situations, regardless our sympathies or antipathies for the circumstance under examination—our goal, after all, is to try to figure out how things work and not to determine the workings of only those things with which we agree, dismissing the rest; but the ease with which civil unrest that "we" start, in which "we" participate, or from which "we" may benefit is anything but rioting and looting, makes pretty plain that Rumsfeld's comments were anything but scholarly. Instead, much like attempts to dismiss protestors as thugs, let alone the still easily found effort to explain systemic racial bias as the result of "a few bad apples," they were part of a proactive effort to manage public perception of a situation that didn't go the way everyone had been told it would—such as, early in the buildup to that war, when the American public was told by then Deputy Defense Secretary Paul Wolfowitz in a message that was then repeated by Vice President Dick Cheney that the Iraqis would greet us as liberators. (This a statement that the former made as part of his testimony during a defense department budget hearing on February 27, 2003, and which the latter made on March 16, 2003, on NBC's weekly politics show *Meet the Press*.)[11]

The lesson here is a hardly a new one, but perhaps it is one that's always worth repeating: those watching coverage of such events, and those listening

---

www.nytimes.com/2003/04/12/world/a-nation-at-war-rumsfeld-s-words-on-iraq-there-is-untidi ness.html (accessed June 5, 2020).

11 For the former, see the video clip posted at https://www.c-span.org/video/?c4501032/user-clip-wolfowitz-iraqis-greet-liberators; for the latter, see the transcript posted at http://www.nbcnews.com/id/3080244/ns/meet_the_press/t/transcript-sept/ (accessed June 5, 2020).

to everyone from pundits to politicians reflecting on their significance, must always consider the source when considering the representation. For, as scholars have long known, description is anything but disinterested; after all, carefully itemizing the features of something called a cult has already implicated both the scholar and the list of traits in a strategic (though usually undisclosed and sometimes unrecognized) way to normalize just some groups and just some actions while marginalizing alternatives.

So our motto, as scholars, ought always to be *caveat auditor:* Let the listener beware.

* * *

Why did I end the book with these five somewhat interrelated yet discrete examples? My initial hope is that they capture, one last time, some of what can be gained from studying whatever it is that we define as religion as a *mundane* (but nonetheless interesting, for any number of good reasons) aspect of *everyday* culture and history—an approach that resists the urge to reserve a special, undefined something that eludes our critical examination. But also, I hope that they inspire readers to do a little comparative work of their own, looking initially for a few manageable and familiar instances, as exemplified above, that, after a little digging and some creative thinking, can be shown to contain features also found in the claims, practices, or institutions that are regularly found in the seemingly set apart things that usually make their way into the scholar of religion's writings and classes.

For, as my previous collection, *Fabricating Religion*—a book whose argument is closely linked with the current volume—argued, and as the chapters in this book have tried to demonstrate in some practical ways at a wide variety of sites, there's success to be found in seeing the field as mundane and comparable, leaving to others to study religion as unique and incomparable.[12]

---

12 The opening of this afterword was originally written for The Critical Religion blog; the five examples each derive from earlier and shorter blog posts that I each wrote at the time of the events being narrated and analyzed; their sources are, in their order of appearance here: https://edge.ua.edu/russell-mccutcheon/the-way-it-ought-to-be/; https://religion.ua.edu/blog/2020/05/30/violence-is-never-the-answer/; https://edge.ua.edu/russell-mccutcheon/guys-like-us/; https://religion.ua.edu/blog/2020/06/02/the-uses-of-symbolism/; and https://edge.ua.edu/russell-mccutcheon/caveat-auditor/ (accessed June 5, 2020).

Index

Academic Analytics   168
Adams, Douglas   67
advocacy   18
agency   39, 69
– passive voice   69
agnosticism   48
Alabama Commission on Higher Education (ACHE)
– waiver   170–1
– viability   125, 139, 145, 163, 169, 170
Alles, Greg   28
Altman, Michael   34, 129, 143, 146, 153, 156, 161, 163, 164, 165, 182, 184
American Academy of Religion (AAR)   11, 18, 21, 22, 23, 48, 63, 97, 123, 134, 135, 149
– big tent   11
– Religious Literacy Guidelines   36
American Examples   34, 143, 146, 164, 165, 182
American Religions Sound Project   23
anachronism   20, 96, 97, 102
analogy   5
Anderson, Benedict   134
Armstrong, Karen   39
Andresen, Jensine   78
Appadurai, Arjun   147
Arnal, William   17, 31
Arthur Vining Davis Foundation   21
Asprem, Egil   18, 40
atheism   14, 48
authenticity   34, 36, 37, 90, 102, 105
authority
– authorizing mechanisms   69

Baldwin, Matthew   21, 35, 96, 97
Barthes, Roland   12, 68, 172
Barton, Carlin   100f.
Bateson, Gregory   93
Bayart, Jean-François   37, 44, 155, 179
belief   38, 44, 40, 66, 67, 94, 111
– as agonistic affirmation   50
– discourse on   36, 50

– disembodied   36
– unbelief   37, 47, 48
Berger, Peter   29
Bettis, Joe   142
binary   65
– rhetorical utility   44
blogging   3, 31, 34, 35, 125, 129, 145, 147, 152, 154, 155, 161, 184, 189
Bond, Sara   92
Borges, Jorge Luis   12
Boyarin, Daniel   100f.
bricoleur   131
Brown, Wendy   89

Cady, Linell   147
Campbell, Joseph   39
Cantwell, Christopher   149
Carp, Richard   35, 37
Casanova, José   43
chaos, rhetoric of   98
Chicago School   27
church and state
– wall of separation   70
civility   21, 23, 26, 29
– as rhetorical term   24
claims   36, 44, 50, 69, 84
classification   16, 31, 113, 131, 186, 191
– at the joints   65
– practical consequences   65, 73
– politics of   64
– socially invested   17
cognitive science of religion   50
– embodied cognition
Cohen, Richard   143
cold war   11
colonialism   66
compartmentalization   18
Cotter, Christopher   25, 48, 68
COVID-19   6, 113, 138, 195
Coward, Harold   178
creationism   34, 41
Crews, Emily   20, 21, 34, 156
Crumpton, LeCretia   138

culture 74
- high vs. low 173
- material 35
Culture on the Edge 34, 155, 182
Cuthbertson, Ian 20

Danforth Foundation 140
Dargyay, Eva 178
data
- as self-evidently interesting 4
decontextualize 41
defamiliarize 99
definition (of religion) 11, 86, 112, 131, 144, 162, 167-8, 178
- as constitutive 98
- family resemblance 34
- know it when I see it 65
- lack of in US law 46
- of scholarship 19
dehistoricize 42
department 3, 123
- affirmative action hires 142
- assessment 161
- effects of recession on 135-6
- fiftieth anniversary 140
- identity 134, 159
- logo 124, 129, 151, 160
- marketing 129, 130, 144
- matching funding to establish 140
- motto 124, 145, 153
- original seminary model 140f.
- outcomes (goals) 159
- physical space 145
- service department 145, 148, 169
- website 145, 148f.
deprivatization 43
deracination 17
Derrida, Jacques 37, 172
Desjarlais, Robert 82
Deusen, Nancy van 33
Dickey, Betty 138, 146
distinction 81
Doty, William 142, 142
Douglas, Mary 34, 179
Drew, Spencer 18
Dubuisson, Daniel 15, 19, 75, 100, 176

Durdin, Andrew 13, 106
Durkheim, Emile 33, 40, 160, 174, 179, 191

east/west 20, 71
Eck, Diana 22, 82
Edmonds, James 13
Eliade, Mircea 13, 33, 37, 39, 40, 41, 64, 82, 87, 98, 174, 191
- new humanism 33, 191
empathy 18
Engler, Steven 35
English Heritage Trust 74
essentialism 37, 48, 77, 86, 98, 172
- strategic 28
Euhemerus of Messene 104f.
examples 4, 138, 148, 186, 189f.
- e.g. 64, 132, 134, 179, 185
- approach 5, 119, 121, 183
experience 2, 36, 41, 43, 66, 67, 76f., 103, 111, 168
- defies explanation 76
- discourse on 55, 83
- experience-past 83-4
- experience-present 83-4, 85
- as facsimile 90
- as internalized residue 84
- pan-human 159
- religious experience 12
- unmediated 77

faith 2, 17, 36, 38, 44, 66, 94, 111, 178
- faith traditions 26
- in transcendence 68
faculty
- collaboration 6, 122, 182
  - with students 162
- collegiality
- contingent 6, 30, 147
- cross-appointments 127, 170
- external funding 136
- job ads 144
- job market 50, 133
  - interview 134
- lines (positions) 181
- research productivity 3, 126, 136, 151, 185
- service 157
- tenure and promotion 18, 144

Finnegan, Eleanor   130, 152
Fish, Stanley   173
Fitzgerald, Tim   34, 46, 68, 101, 167, 169, 174, 175, 176, 178, 187
form vs. content   200
Floyd, George   195
Frazer, James George   54
Freud, Sigmund   174

Gallagher, Eugene   21
gender   44
generalization   50, 52
George, Neil   115
Glaude, Eddie   147
Goldenberg, Naomi   20, 28, 40, 68, 101, 175
governance   14, 28, 45, 66, 69, 70, 72, 111, 170, 186
Graber, Jennifer   45
Granderson, LZ   195 f.
Green, Patrick   142
Griffin, Lauren Horn   164
Grimes, D. Jamil   13

Harvey, John   38
Hecht, Richard   126, 127, 178
Hedges, Paul   112, 115
Hermann, Adrian   106
Hillel Foundation   142
historicization   45, 111, 112, 114
history
– discourse on the past   91–2, 99, 198
– distortion   106
– heritage   74
– historic commissions   73
– past as trope   105
holy the   2
homophobia   18
Hughes, Aaron   11, 15, 20, 143, 147
human nature   64, 85
human rights   71
humanities
– challenges to   6, 120
– defined   119
– digital humanities   123, 139, 145, 148, 149, 185
  – institutional effects   158 f.
– in crisis   168

– intrinsic value   119
– and liberal arts   119
– and the professionalization of the university   120
– public humanities   124, 161, 163
– relevance   119, 147, 162, 191
– Renaissance   119, 131
– and soft skills   120
Hume, David   50

idealism   35, 36, 67
identity   42, 50, 66, 103
– identification (identity-formation)   55, 80, 88, 105, 123, 131, 155, 162, 179, 181, 191, 196
– operationalization   124
– syncretism   73
inference   50
Ingersoll, Julie   XIII, 137
insider/outsider problem   14
intelligent design   34, 41
intentionality   32, 78, 105, 173
– intentional fallacy   37, 104

Jacobs, Steven   141, 143, 184
Jaffee, Martin   138, 143, 146, 147
James, William   87
Jay, Martin   78
John Templeton Foundation   47
Jordan, Louis Henry   180
Josephson-Storm, Jason   20
JSTOR Data for Research (DfR)   163
Jung, Carl   39

Kavka, Martin   18, 19
Kineke, Liz   186
King, Rebekka   13
King, Richard   68, 101, 175
Korzybski, Alfred   92
Krawcowicz, Barbara   96

Latour, Bruno   19
Lease, Gary   149
Lee, Lois   47, 49
Lehrich, Christopher   20
Levine, Amy-Jill   147
Levine, Daniel   143, 184

Levine, Sarah   123
Levitt, Laura   147
Lilly Endowment   35
– primary aim   38
Lincoln, Bruce   1, 54, 89, 101, 109, 147
literary criticism   167, 175, 180
– literature as a category   173
– reader response theory   173
– theory wars   172
Loewen, Nathan   127, 143, 163, 184
looting   201 f.
Lopez, Donald   50
Luce Foundation   34, 143, 164, 165, 182
Luther, Martin   76

Malle, Louis   65
Marcus, Benjamin   72
Marouan, Maha   142
Martin, Craig   11, 20, 21, 48, 101, 154, 168
Martin, Luther   13, 15, 17, 28, 30
Marty, Martin   43
Marx, Karl   94, 174
Masuzawa, Tomoko   25, 26, 68, 101, 147, 175
Material History of American Religion Project   36
material religion   28, 35 f., 43, 52, 64
– embodied religion   35, 37
– lived religion   35, 64
– religion on the ground   35
McDannel, Colleen   28
meaning   38, 103, 173, 174
– alternative approach to   79–80
– contests over   200
– correspondence (referential) theory of   78, 79, 106
metaphor   77
method
– comparison   37, 66, 77, 85, 93, 98, 101, 126, 132, 134, 142, 144, 162, 180, 203
– deconstruction   111 f.
  – exaggerated deconstructionism   167
– description   18, 22, 26, 40, 85, 122, 123, 131, 132, 134, 142, 144, 162, 179, 180
  – not disinterested   201 f.
  – as paraphrase   39, 43
– explanation   40, 88, 114, 131, 144, 162

– interpretation (hermeneutics)   37, 40, 98, 102, 105, 106, 107, 131, 144, 162, 173, 174
– phenomenology   37, 38, 53, 85, 168, 175, 179
  – criticisms of   42
  – re-branded   39, 41
– rectification   40
– redescription   40, 50, 96, 193
– translation   40
Miller, Monica   154
modernity   43, 168
Moore, Diane   21, 22, 25
Morgan, David   50, 51, 52, 97
Murphy, Tim   142
Museum of Tolerance   89

narrativization   100
– omniscient narrator   107
naturalization (normalization)   190, 193–5, 198
Neufeldt, Ronald   178
Newton, Richard   4, 28, 106, 129, 143, 146, 157, 184
Nones   48, 50
Nongbri, Brent   63, 68, 100 f., 105–7, 175
Nonreligion and Secularity Research Network   47
nostalgia   197 f.
North American Association for the Study of Religion (NAASR)   11, 20, 98
Nye, Malory   68, 101, 175

objectivity   7, 63
O'Connell, Joseph   178
Ohnuma, Reiko   143
origins   90, 102, 139
– absent original   104
– rhetoric of   109, 198
Orsi, Robert   2, 36, 87
orthodoxy   199
Otto, Rudolf   87–8
Owen, Suzanne   25, 26, 68, 101, 175
Oxtoby, Willard   53, 178

Paden, William   48
peer review   18

Petersen, Anders Klostergaard   106
Petersen, Kristian   149
Peterson, Jordan   39
piety   33
Plate, Brent   39, 40
Pluralism Project   22
podcasting   3, 34, 156
polling   27, 47, 48, 49
praeparatio evangelica   142
privacy   44
– operational acts of privatization   44
proration   139
Prothero, Stephen   21, 22
Proudfoot, Wayne   26
Public Broadcasting System (PBS)   120

race
– racism   192, 195f., 197
– "whiteness" of antiquity   92
Ramey, Steven   4, 16, 29, 32, 48, 126, 130, 132, 143, 154, 155, 156, 163, 169, 184
realism
– critical   13, 101, 102, 169
– naïve (everyday)   98, 99, 102, 105
reductionism   41, 168
– descriptive   26
– explanatory   26, 40
Reed, Annette Yoshiko   98, 100, 138
reflexivity (self-consciousness)   26, 49, 50, 54, 96, 100, 109
religion
– Abrahamic   2, 24
– and aesthetics   88
– affiliation   49
– of baseball model   48
– civil   43
– definition of   12, 17, 34, 64
– dimensions   25, 28, 172, 180
– discourse on   16, 66
– exemptions   33, 189
– expression   27, 44, 64, 66, 78, 172, 178
– manifestation   25, 26, 27, 33, 36, 37, 39, 44, 64, 86, 168
– as mundane   6, 13, 16, 31, 32, 39, 54, 70, 73, 75, 144, 155, 157, 203
– organizational tool   72
– public   43f.

– scholar of "religion"   111
– singular vs. plural   175
– *sui generis*   64, 176, 177, 191, 203
Religious Freedom Center   72
religious literacy   16, 21f., 33, 35, 66, 186
– defined   25
Religious Literacy Project   22, 25, 26, 27
Religious Studies Project   71, 111, 115
Reynolds, Charlie   140
Richards, I. A.   173
Roach, Catherine   142
Robertson, David   25, 68, 113
Rosenhagen, Ulrich   24
Roubekas, Nickolas   104f.
Rubenstein, Mary-Jane   55

sacred, the   2, 33, 41, 42, 64, 191
– sacred and profane   31f.
– sacred is the profane   31f.
Sacks, Oliver   77
Said, Edward   20, 71
Schaeffer, Kurtis   129, 136, 143, 151
Schilbrack, Kevin   111
Schleiermacher, Fredrich   87
Schmeiser, Peggy   55, 96, 176
Schorey, Shannon Trosper   106
Scientific Study of Non-Religious Belief Project   47
Scott, Joan Wallach   83
secularism   14
– conspicuous religious symbols   74
– insubstantial   47
– secularization thesis   45, 47
– substantial   47
semiotics   187
sexism   197
Sheedy, Matt   106
Shiappa, Edward   48
signification   55, 81, 181, 191
Simmons, K. Merinda   4, 143, 144, 154, 155, 163, 183, 184
Smart, Ninian   14, 48, 63, 172, 178
Smith, Huston   27
Smith, Jonathan Z.   4, 5, 14, 19, 34, 40, 54, 64, 92–3, 96, 97, 99, 100, 105, 109, 121, 125, 147, 148, 156, 174, 179
Smith, Leslie Dorrough   20, 98, 154

Smith, Wilfred Cantwell   45, 67, 68, 86, 101, 174, 178
social constructionism   167
social history   35
social media   50, 123, 125, 129, 130, 151, 189, 193, 202
– Facebook   129, 150, 152, 153, 154, 162
– Instagram   129, 153
– Twitter   125, 129, 152, 154
– Vimeo   125, 156, 162
social theory   5, 67, 121, 124, 129, 134, 135, 145, 163, 165, 168
Society of Biblical Literature (SBL)   104
source
– primary vs. secondary   108
Southern Association of Colleges and Schools Commission on Colleges (SACSCOC)   169
Southern University Group (SUG)   136
specialization   5, 133, 150
– silos   5
spirituality   17, 44
– spiritual but not religious (SBNR)   48, 49, 50
Staal, Frits   182
staff   138
Stausberg, Michael   35
students
– alums   4, 122, 124, 144, 147, 153, 160, 177, 190
– association   130, 144, 152, 153
– double majors   127
– grad tales   129
– graduate   132
   – establishing MA degree   163
   – reinventing   146
– graduation rates   136, 161
– recruiting   3, 128, 129, 135, 150, 176, 185
– retention   3, 135, 159
– scholarships   144
– undergraduate research   128, 161
– workers   160
Stuckrad, Kocku von   14
study of religion
– anthropocentric   142
– comparative religion   11, 63, 85

– critical study of (critical religion)   15, 16, 18, 20, 21, 50, 63. 169, 176, 190
– cross-disciplinary   63, 180
– field vs. discipline   63, 172, 175
– history   11
– history of religions   62
– interreligious dialogue   15, 16, 25, 30, 112
– not about religion   65, 73
– post-critical   13
– post-theoretical   13
– science of religion   11, 13, 16, 63, 85
– stakeholders   124
subjectivity   2
– ghost in the machine   27, 50
Sullivan, Winnifred   45
superstition   17, 66
survival   66
Szanto, Edith   142, 184

Taira, Teemu   68, 101, 111, 114, 115, 168, 175
Taves, Ann   18, 40, 48, 77
teaching
– core curriculum (general education)   126, 127, 145, 171
– coverage   123
– credit hour production   27, 120, 133, 136, 177, 185
   – tuition revenue   185
– curriculum   130, 144, 184
– electives   127
– extra credit   128
– gateway courses   126, 128
   – delayed effect   128
– honors courses   126
– independent study   171
– introductory class   5, 31
– Learning Management Systems (LMS)   152
– one credit hour movie course   129
– online courses   144, 158
– prerequisites   128
– service courses (service departments)   126, 128
– senior seminar   5

– skills   119, 122, 131, 144, 150, 161, 162, 189, 191
　– critical thinking   132
　– digital   163
– teach the controversy   14
theology   14, 22, 63–4, 119
theory
– conspiracy   113
– defining a department   134
– domesticated   19, 31, 35
– "I don't do theory"   123
– as optional   123
– and signification   54
– as snowblower   53
– as snowmaking   53
– wonking   51, 52, 53, 55
Thompson, E. P.   94, 134
Thompson, Thomas   109
tolerance   21, 71, 74–5, 89
– limits of   89
Tong, M Adryael   28, 98, 102
Touna, Vaia   4, 13, 21, 68, 96, 103, 104, 106, 143, 154, 155, 156, 184
tradition   2, 66, 67, 178
trivialization   55
Trost, Theodore   127, 138, 142, 154, 155, 184

truisms   52
Tweed, Thomas   97
Tylor, E. B.   102

Uddin, Asma   70, 72

violence
– never the answer   195 f.

Wach, Joachim   82
Weinberger, Leon   142
Wesley, Charles   76
Wesley, John   76 f.
Whitelam, Keith   96
Wiebe, Donald   13, 15, 17, 29, 30, 63
Wieringa, Jeri   139, 164, 184
Williams, Raymond   83, 85
Wilson, Flip   69
Wittgenstein, Ludwig   79, 81, 84, 88, 93
world-building   48
world religions
– day   27
– paradigm   2, 16, 25, 27, 66–8, 134, 174, 177, 178, 182
– vs. national (ethnic) religion   67
worldview   14, 48

www.ingramcontent.com/pod-product-compliance
Lightning Source LLC
Chambersburg PA
CBHW030650230426
43665CB00011B/1033